Arth
KINNAIRD
FIRST LORD OF FOOTBALL

'He did more to popularise soccer than any man who ever lived.' Sir Frederick Wall

Andy Mitchell

Arthur Kinnaird: First Lord of Football

First published 2011
Copyright © Andy Mitchell

ISBN-13: 978-1463621117
ISBN-10: 1463621116

The author
Andy Mitchell, born 1958 in Edinburgh, is passionate about football and has written extensively on the sport. He has witnessed plenty of football history in the making: as head of communications at the Scottish Football Association, he travelled with the Scotland team from the Faroes to the Far East, and now works as a media officer for UEFA. His only footballing relative scored England's first ever goal - against Scotland.

This book is closely linked to the website www.lordkinnaird.com which is managed by the author. To contact the author, please use the submission form on this website. There is also an Arthur Kinnaird page on Facebook.

Cover illustration from *Routledge's Handbook of Football*, 1867. Cover designed by Maureen Mitchell Design, www.maureenmitchelldesign.com

Back cover image: Detail from *Soccer*, a caricature of Lord Kinnaird published by *Vanity Fair* in 1912.

CONTENTS

INTRODUCTION

ON A windy March day in 1882, a wealthy merchant banker of aristocratic birth finished his lunch, waved goodbye to his wife and jumped into an open carriage outside his home near Grosvenor Square. He drove past Hyde Park Corner, negotiated the busy junctions at Victoria Station, crossed the River Thames at Vauxhall Bridge, and came within view of Kennington Oval.

As he approached, Harleyford Road was thronged with people heading in the same direction. Spirits were high, progress was slow. There were many other cabs but his bright red beard made him instantly recognisable, and soon a shout went up: 'It's Kinnaird!' Some of the livelier spirits grabbed hold of the reins, a crowd gathering round in excitement. There was no threat to the banker inside the cab, quite the opposite. This former public schoolboy was their hero, one of the most famous sportsmen of his era, and they could think of no better tribute than to help him on his way. Releasing the horse from the harness, as one they strained to pull his carriage for the last hundred yards, stopping only at the players' gate. The hero stepped down from the cab, somewhat embarrassed at all the fuss, genially thanked the young men for their trouble, and went inside to meet his team mates. The worshippers dusted themselves down and headed for the pay boxes to hand over a hard-earned shilling.

Three hours later, having witnessed this 35-year-old colossus captain his side to yet another footballing triumph, they cheered again as he performed a celebratory handstand on the pitch. He would not be presented with the small but elaborate silver trophy until the team's annual dinner a few weeks later, but he knew the routine by now: it was his fifth FA Cup victory. His famous handstand – immortalised as a life-size model in the National Football Museum – symbolised the game being turned on its head: the Old Etonians winning the FA Cup in 1882 marked one of the turning points in the history of football, the last hurrah for the southern amateurs against the power of the northern professionals.

Few men bridged the gap as the game changed out of recognition, but Arthur Kinnaird was special, a sporting pioneer

1

who guided football's progress on and off the field for over half a century, from muddy obscurity to national obsession. He would not have admitted it himself, but he was football's first superstar, a figure of such renown that he was presented with the FA Cup to keep. His unique place in sporting history is best summed up in an epitaph from Sir Frederick Wall, the man who ran the Football Association after his death: 'He did more to popularise soccer than any man who ever lived.'

Arthur's record is astonishing: not content with nine FA Cup finals – a total unsurpassed to this day – he played in football's first representative match, organised the first international, was capped for Scotland, and served the Football Association for 55 years, over 30 of them as its President. A consummate athlete, he also won honours in tennis, athletics, swimming and canoeing, and played competitive cricket past his fiftieth birthday.

His life in sport, in itself, provides ample subject matter for a biography, but what makes Arthur so fascinating is the diversity of his achievements, and his unstoppable energy in attaining them. Strongly influenced by evangelical parents, who instilled in him the ethos of philanthropy, he understood from an early age that many of those who did not share his privileged background were condemned to a life of misery, and that poverty brought about evils such as ill health, drunkenness, disease, prostitution and exploitation. He spent his youthful nights teaching homeless orphans to read and write, and throughout his life worked passionately for a vast range of charitable organisations, which were often all that stood between slum dwellers and destitution. An unstinting donor of time, money and energy to causes he believed in, he was described as 'the busiest man in London' and gave away much of the fortune he earned in his career as a banker.

Having inherited an ancient barony, he added his own exuberance to Victorian high society, mixing with royalty, Prime Ministers and Presidents. There was also personal tragedy, with two sons killed in the First World War, losses which contributed to the demise of the house of Kinnaird before the 20th century was out.

As he fought social injustice on numerous fronts, Arthur was enlightened enough to appreciate that not everyone was as devoted as he was: he supported temperance, but was not an abstainer; he attended religious gatherings but did not insist on house guests doing likewise; he was a fervent supporter of Protestantism yet

2

sought an audience with the Pope. The only area where he never compromised was Sunday observance, an issue that would be sure to have him writing letters to *The Times*.

There was such an extraordinary amount packed into Arthur's life that I had often asked myself why no-one had attempted his biography before. The challenges soon became apparent, as he could be infuriatingly elusive: he made few speeches, wrote little, and left no sporting memoirs. Even his cup medals have disappeared; the fact that in the early years they were said to be of 'trifling value' may have something to do with it.

When prevailed upon to speak, it was about his religious philosophy or the workings of his charities, rather than tales of the football field. While some private papers are held in the family archives, including the wonderful scrapbooks he kept of his early sporting career, few of his contemporaries left personal recollections about the early days of football in general, or about Arthur's contribution in particular; even the little volume published to mark his silver wedding does not contain a single mention of the game. Writing the story of his life has been like constructing a jigsaw puzzle whose pieces are scattered to the wind.

Not surprisingly, myths built up around him, which had to be examined. Two anecdotes are raised repeatedly about Arthur, although they vary in the telling. One ends in him declaring enthusiastically 'Let's have hacking!' The other relates to his wife or mother being told 'If he comes home with a broken leg, it won't be his own.' The stories are apocryphal, latter-day concoctions, as while Arthur was robust, energetic and committed, he was never violent or unfair. Thankfully, some who knew him did describe his personality, always with warmth and affection, such as the journalist James Catton: 'Arthur Kinnaird, with his yeoman build and shaggy auburn beard, did not quite look the part of a Scottish laird, until one spoke to him, and heard his rich, resonant voice and his short ejaculatory sentences. Of course, he had the voice and manner of an educated man of distinction. He was a leader, and above all things, a muscular type of Christian.'

Towards the end of his life, when it did come to looking back, Arthur claimed no credit for his own contribution to our national sport, preferring to acknowledge a greater power: 'I believe all right-minded people have good reason to thank God for the great progress of this popular national game.'

3

However, not only do right-minded football fans have reason to thank Arthur Kinnaird for making football great, society as a whole should thank him for his efforts in raising thousands from destitution and oiling the wheels of social change. I sincerely hope this biography, in explaining not just his football triumphs but also his wider contribution, will lead to a new appreciation of one of the great Victorians.

Acknowledgements

I could not have completed this book without the help of a number of people who willingly responded to my queries. Pride of place must go to the Hon Caroline Best, Arthur's great-granddaughter and current owner of Rossie Priory, who trusted me with a pandora's box of Arthur's personal papers and has given every support to the project.

Among many others who gave help and encouragement, I would like to thank Penny Hatfield, archivist at Eton College, who explained some of the quirks of Eton life; John Hutchinson, whose advice on early football was particularly appreciated; David Barber at the Football Association; Kenny Strang at the Scottish Football Museum; Jonathan Smith, archivist at Trinity College, Cambridge; and the staff at the AK Bell Library in Perth and the National Library of Scotland. I received inspiration, help and information from Rob Cavallini, Paul Joannou, Professor David Bebbington, Chris Harte, John Burnett, James Hamilton, Tony Collins, Keith Booth and David Morten. I also have to acknowledge that this book would not have been possible without resources which were inaccessible just ten years ago, but can now be found on the internet, and I must pay a particular tribute to the nameless workers behind the scenes, at the British Library and elsewhere, who have digitised so many newspapers and books. I apologise if I have missed anyone, and I should also emphasise that any errors, omissions and misinterpretations are entirely my own.

Finally, a huge thank-you to my wife Maureen, who has borne with me – often against her better judgement – throughout the long process of research, writing and publication.

CHAPTER 1

A game of kicking the ball; not a game for kicking each other

1847-65

IN THE general scheme of things, it was not a noteworthy birth. The third child of the Hon Arthur Kinnaird and his wife Mary was born in their home at 35 Hyde Park Gardens, London, shortly after noon on Tuesday, 16 February 1847.

Relieved to have a healthy baby brother for Frieda – another daughter had died the year before – the proud parents paid for a two-line announcement in *The Times*, prompting a flurry of congratulations from close family, church ministers and business associates, whose letters were tied neatly with ribbon, put away for posterity and forgotten about. The little bundle did not, perhaps, see the light of day for another 160 years.[1]

Arthur Fitzgerald Kinnaird was born into a life of privilege, philanthropy and evangelical religion. He was destined for a lucrative career in banking and would inherit an ancient barony. Unexpectedly, he also became Britain's first football superstar.

An inexhaustible supply of energy would characterise not just his sporting endeavours but every aspect of his life, and as a young boy he had plenty of opportunities to burn it off: there was open countryside just a short walk away, and the family home was especially handy for the expanse of Hyde Park.

His parents were among the new breed of Victorian social reformers, inspired by William Wilberforce and Lord Shaftesbury: his father, the third son of a peer, was a successful banker and politician, his mother a champion of better treatment for women. They were, above all, determined to improve the lot of the underprivileged and the destitute at home and abroad. Arthur would, in time, put their principles into practice by confronting deprivation head on.

The parental focus combined piety with the practicalities of bringing up a growing family, and Mary Kinnaird put the emphasis on personal development through good example. She stressed the virtue of unselfishness to the extent that her children did not receive birthday presents, but were expected to give them instead. Unusually at that time, she allowed them to have unrestricted access, and they could enter her room without knocking. Mary also insisted that everyone in the household – servants, governesses and children – should learn a verse from the Bible every day, and repeat them on Sunday; Arthur and his sisters adopted this enthusiastically and took on two verses a day, committing huge chunks of the Old Testament to memory. It seems to have been a happy childhood, but in 1856 there were two major changes to the nine-year-old boy's environment: the family moved into central London and he was sent to boarding school soon afterwards.

When Arthur (the father) merged his small private bank to become senior partner of Ransom, Bouverie & Co, he gained access to magnificent apartments above the bank at 2 Pall Mall East. This was not just a smart address in the heart of the city, off Trafalgar Square, it was incredibly convenient: going to work meant walking down a flight of stairs and, as a sitting MP, he was only five minutes away from the Houses of Parliament. It allowed him to spend more time with his family than would normally have been the case for such a busy man. Mary used the large drawing room as a salon, organising soirées to debate major topics of the day, such as India in the 1850s and the American Civil War in the 1860s,'to give an opportunity to visitors from other lands to come and tell London of the many different needs of their countries'.[2] Being within easy reach of Parliament and government offices, politicians and officials would regularly drop in for lunch or to consult her. She hosted weekly Bible readings and provided a base for a range of evangelical bodies, many of which she helped to found, including the British Ladies' Female Emigration Society, the Christian Colportage Association, the Foreign Evangelisation Society, the Union for Prayer, the Zenana Bible and Medical Mission, and the Indian Vernacular Education Society. She described their home as 'the hub of the universe'.

However, the family soon discovered the downside of exchanging the suburban greenery of Hyde Park for the convenience of Pall Mall. London was a city of extremes, and they were now in close proximity to the slums whose residents lived in grinding poverty, right at the other end of the social spectrum. Even wealthy families like the Kinnairds could not avoid being aware of the struggle for existence right outside the privileged confines of their home. To make matters worse, it was decidedly unhealthy. As London's population expanded in the industrial age – it was already three million and would double by the end of the century – the city's infrastructure could not keep up. With fresh running water a luxury for the few, there were cholera epidemics that claimed thousands of lives, a problem which came to a head in 1858 during one of the hottest summers on record. The Thames was little more than an open sewer, and with a reduced flow an appalling smell hung over the city for weeks, commonly called the 'great stink'. It was the final straw for the parliamentarians, including Arthur senior, who had to endure a stifling House of Commons next to the river and they rushed through a bill to fund a massive network of sewers and pumping stations.[3]

The first stage of this development was the completion of Charing Cross Embankment, which facilitated the opening of the great railway terminus in 1864, but the programme of construction, and consequent disruption, carried on for many years. In the meantime, Arthur senior did his bit for sanitation by helping to set up the Metropolitan Free Drinking Fountain Association, 'calculated to minister to the health and welfare of the poorer classes, and to promote habits of temperance among the thousands of working classes thronging the streets of London'. Previously, the only free water supplies came from street pumps, 'the water out of which was in many cases little better than liquid poison'[4].

No sooner had Arthur adapted to his new surroundings than he began his formal education. In the autumn of 1856 he was sent to board at Cheam, a traditional private prep school run by the Rev Robert Tabor, a fearsome autocrat who terrified the small boys in his charge but who had the good sense to lavish hospitality on the parents at Speech Day.[5] Now an affluent commuter suburb, Cheam village was at that time a rural outpost, reached by a slow and uncomfortable 16 mile journey from London Bridge Station on the London, Brighton and South Coast Railway.[6]

Separated from his family for the first time, Arthur was exposed to all sorts of boyish influences which his mother – even with her daily letters – could not reach. No reports survive of his academic record except for his sister Emily's dry comment that he 'did not distinguish himself' in the four years he was at Cheam, but crucially Tabor's regime encouraged him to use up his energy by taking part in organised sport for the first time.

With both cricket and football on the agenda, the school was in the vanguard of the new sports movement, and Arthur was duly elected captain of the school football team. It was an early outlet for his organisational talents, and a remarkable letter survives in the Kinnaird family archive which records the arrangement of an inter-school football match, probably the oldest such document in existence. Sent from Harrow School to 'the captain of the Cheam School Football Eleven' on 12 November 1859, it reads:

Sir,
The following nine will be happy to play a match at football with your club on Tuesday the 6th proximo; we will challenge the whole of your school, the match to be played in the afternoon, and according to the Harrow rules. We have the honour to remain, sir, your most obedient servants,

The letter is signed by nine Harrow schoolboys, each of them countersigned by their housemaster: WA (Wilfrid Arthur) Bevan, CG (Charles Gordon) Browne, WF (William Fairbairn) Bateman, JM (James Morris) Rucker, FW (Frederick William) Verney, MS (Montague Somes) Pilcher, CS (Charles Samuel) Chilver, JR (John Robert) Hollond, and GE (Granville Erskine) Money. At the foot of the letter Arthur added a short note, not the most illuminating of reports but it does at least confirm the game went ahead: 'Match ended in a tie, each side obtaining an equal number of goals.' A draw was not a bad result, given that the Harrow boys were generally two years older, and playing to their own rules. There is no record of the Cheam side, or indeed of them playing other matches, but this was right at the dawn of inter-school football.[7] Playing against another school was fraught with difficulties as there was then no common code of rules, so most games were played within schools, or against teams of old boys.

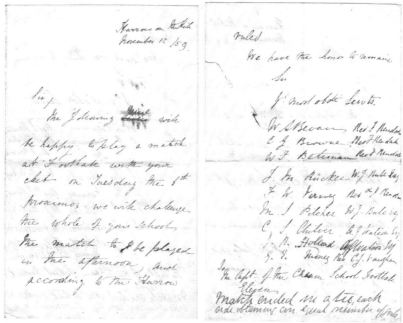

This letter from 1859 arranges a football match between Cheam and Harrow schools. It is probably the oldest such document in existence.

There was, therefore, a real pioneering aspect to a match which involved a group of Harrow youngsters travelling across London to rural Surrey. The genesis of this particular challenge probably lies in the fact that Wilfrid Bevan's name is at the top of the list as his younger brother Roland was then at Cheam and the Bevans were personal friends of the Kinnairds, with close banking and evangelical ties; indeed, Roland went on to marry Arthur's sister Agneta.

Arthur also played cricket for the school and showed promise as a batsman, hitting 50 runs in one match. The cuttings in his scrapbook show that he kept in touch long after leaving, playing for Cheam as late as 1865.

With this solid grounding in sport, and deemed to have been sufficiently 'prepped' academically, Arthur left the school at Christmas 1860 and enrolled at Eton College a few weeks before his fourteenth birthday.

An Eton education

Several generations of Kinnairds had already attended Eton, and Arthur would continue the tradition with his sons, but in the 1860s there were fears that one of the nation's greatest educational establishments was not fit for the purpose of raising men to lead the Empire. There were rumblings in the press about the school's overpaid and inefficient masters, and complaints that a stagnant curriculum was fixated on Greek and Latin with modern sciences virtually ignored. The government was sufficiently alarmed to appoint a Royal Commission[8] to investigate not just Eton, but all nine of the nation's leading public schools. Led by Lord Clarendon, the commissioners were extraordinarily thorough, carrying out interviews over a two year period, and when their report was published in 1864 it sent shockwaves throughout the schools. They recommended reforms to the curriculum, called for an end to outmoded educational practices and abuses, and singled out Eton for strident criticism with no less than 311 pages devoted to the school, containing 64 specific recommendations for change.

Any modernisation arising from the Clarendon Report came too late for Arthur, as it was not formally put into effect until the Public Schools Act of 1868, but it provides a valuable flavour of Eton life. Not least, it was clear that a considerable amount of time was devoted to sport at Eton, with the commissioners complaining that cricket was inordinately time-consuming, and boating took up two hours every day. They also reported that there was plenty of money about, with the average boy said to get between three and four pounds spending money a term: when Edmond Warre, assistant classical master (later headmaster) was asked 'There are several parents who give enormous pocket money?' he gave the acerbic response, 'Yes, they are generally people who are *nouveaux riches.*'[9]

The press had a field day with the findings, and one Old Etonian, Matthew Higgins, launched this provocative broadside: 'Their verdict as respects Eton is simply this: that of all the public schools of England, it is one at which the British parent pays the most for the education of his child, and from which he receives the smallest educational return for his money. The great majority are stated to lead easy pleasant lives spending the majority of their time chiefly in the playing-fields and on the river, and not a little of it in the public houses and taps of the neighbourhood – and if so minded, but not otherwise, acquiring a faint smattering of the classics in the intervals of play.'[10]

These comments from one of their own struck a raw nerve and were met with an indignant response in the *Eton College Chronicle*: 'It seems to me that it were better if this modern Juvenal got the facts of the case correctly before making so foolish and so false an accusation.' The *Chronicle* dismissed the Report, claiming it was 'not of the great importance which has been ascribed to it,' but proceeded to anguish over its findings in a number of succeeding issues.

Just before the commissioners began asking their awkward questions, Arthur arrived at Eton to receive his expensive education, and it has to be said that the lack of academic emphasis suited him down to the ground, while he positively thrived on the sporting opportunities.

Keate House, Arthur's Eton home from 1861-65

At that time, the system at Eton was for pupils to lodge with one of the masters (or tutors) and pay a subscription that included not only board and lodging but also the school fees. It

11

could be a profitable business for the masters, who would move to bigger properties as their finances improved. Arthur found a place in Keate House, run by the Reverend James Leigh Joynes and his wife Elizabeth, a short walk from the school's main entrance; it is still a boarding house to this day. The Eton Census for 1864 revealed that Joynes had 21 upper boys and 14 lower boys in his care, out of 814 pupils at the school. It was an excellent choice for Arthur, as Joynes was keen on sport, having been a renowned athlete himself in his youth, and his boys had just won the House Cup for football. However, the Joynes approach to education (he had a reputation as a strict disciplinarian, ie for flogging[11]) did little to inspire the boy, whose lack of academic achievement persisted. The frustrated tutor wrote to his parents: 'If Arthur does not mend his ways I am afraid we shall have to send him down.' Thankfully, the threat was not carried through, and Arthur struggled on with his studies, although later in life the discovery of this letter delighted his sons when they, too, were at Eton.[12]

Away from the classroom, he adapted quickly to the arcane rules of football as played at Eton. The school boasted (and still has) two different types of football, at the Wall and in the Field, each with a specialist terminology and a strict pecking order of who is allowed to play where, and when.

The Wall Game is played on a narrow strip alongside a high wall of 120 yards length, its only similarities to association football being that it is played with a ball and there are eleven players on each side. The highlight of the season is on St Andrew's Day, 30 November, a match between Collegers (the 70 scholarship holders) and Oppidans (the rest of the school). The goals are a door in the wall at one end, a tree at the other, and neither of them is actually in the field of play; ten yards from each goal is a line to mark an area called calx, and when the ball is pushed into calx there is an opportunity for the attacking side to be awarded a shy, permitting an attempt at goal. Because the defending team can mass in front of the goal, scoring a goal is almost impossible – in two hundred years, only three have been scored in the St Andrew's Day game, the last in 1909 – so the result is generally determined by scoring most shies. 'There never was a more utterly mystifying game for the spectator who sees it for the first time,' according to one commentator, who added: 'The game appears once to have been one of open warfare, whereas today it is essentially trench warfare.'[13]

The Field Game is more popular within the school and more accessible to the outsider, being closer to association football, with no handling and an offside rule. It can be a flowing game but also has regular 'bullies' which resemble a scrum. With no passing allowed, a forward kicks or dribbles the ball while the rest of a four man 'bully' backs him up, trying to negotiate a path through the opposition. The ball is small, and so are the goals, 12 feet wide by 6 feet high. While the aim is to score goals, there is a secondary method of scoring, called a rouge, achieved by a forward grounding the ball over the opposing goal line, but only if it last touched a defender; the ball is then placed in front of the goal, and a struggle ensues as the attacking team strive to force the ball through.

With little possibility of playing external matches[14], Eton teams were effectively restricted to playing against the universities and various military establishments, institutions which were brimming with Etonians. In the outside world, however, change was in the wind. Sir Frederick Wall later asked rhetorically: 'When Kinnaird entered Eton in 1861, what did anyone know about the laws of the game?'[15] The answer was, very little, although by then football's modern revival was already under way, backed by a spirit of compromise which allowed young men from different backgrounds and schools to take part in matches. This led in the autumn of 1863 to the formation of the Football Association in London, and (simultaneously) the drafting of Cambridge Rules by former public school boys at the university.

These movements were not unnoticed at Eton where there was concern that Rugby football was gaining the ascendancy. The *Chronicle* duly argued for a common set of rules that would halt the spread of the handling game: 'It is ridiculous to suppose that Etonians would turn football into what so closely resembles a fight, and wrestling match, as the Rugby game ... by a judicious selection of the good, and a rejection of the bad parts in the existing laws of the various clubs, all might be satisfied, if not pleased.'[16] The writer went on to define what ought to be the distinguishing features of football:

A game of kicking the ball;
Not a game in which the ball should be carried;
Not a game for kicking each other.

As if those principles were not concise enough he added, to qualify the latter point: 'in which case we suppose it would have been called kick-fellow or shin-mate'. He concluded triumphantly: 'Eton is, we believe, about the only place in which the game is what its name indicates – real foot-ball.'

This halcyon view was somewhat divorced from reality, according to one contemporary who lamented the latent brutality of Eton football, especially for younger boys: 'I have been pitched head-long with my face in the mud, and backwards beyond the rouge line, with such force that I almost turned a somersault; I have lain in front of goals, flat as a fried sole, with a score of sprawling fellows above, all squeezing the breath out of me. I have had my shins hacked till they were all blue and bleeding, and caused me the most maddening pain, which of course had to be borne and grinned at.'[17]

The unfortunate author, Reginald Grenville-Murray[18], made it clear that being kicked by an opponent was a genuine hazard: 'I was in the midst of a rouge, and had got the ball between my feet, when an excited boy gave me three kicks on the shin to make me withdraw from the ball. I was jammed so fast in the rouge that I could not so much as move my legs; but when the rouge broke up, I limped towards my aggressor, and asked him what he meant by shinning me? His only answer was to give me another shin, whereupon I kicked him cordially in return. As we were the two smallest fellows on either side, our proceedings were watched with some amusement, and the two elevens actually rested a moment whilst we kicked each other like a pair of young donkeys. Our shinning match was only stopped when it was seen that neither of us was going to give in.

'I never saw any improvement in the public opinion of the school, about shinning. Everybody condemned it as a disgusting, unsportsman-like practice; but, as in the case of duelling of old, it was held that if a fellow shinned you, you were bound to shin him back. This remained the opinion of Eton all the time I was there; and I cannot but think that the keepers of the field were much to blame for never having used their undoubted powers to put a stop to shinning in matches. Any boy who deliberately shinned ought to have been turned out of the School Field.'[19] As other Etonians mention the perils of shinning in their memoirs, there is little doubt that Arthur had to learn his football in the school of hard knocks, laying down the basis for his renowned robust style of play in later years.

Despite his youth, his potential was quickly seized upon and he was chosen for the Joynes' team which reached the final of the 1861 House Football Cup, playing alongside boys up to four years older. He made a strong impression on the team captain, Alfred Lubbock, another future FA Cup finalist: 'At that time he showed every sign of becoming what he afterwards proved to be, an excellent player. He was always an excessively hard worker at the game, and was 'as hard as nails', never tiring, and being capable of running the whole day if necessary.'[20] Lubbock also described Arthur's early style of play: 'At first, instead of keeping the ball close to him in 'running down', he kicked it too hard, and trusted to his running powers to keep possession of it.'

Although Joynes' team lost that final, the following year Arthur won his first football trophy as his house lifted the cup, to general surprise. Lubbock, by now an astute tactician, recalled: 'At the outset there was no particular favourite, and the betting would certainly have been 6 to 4 on the field – Marriott's, Gulliver's or Stevens' perhaps the most likely. My tutor's were not considered to be in it. We first managed to beat Wayte's, then Gulliver's and, to our surprise, had to play Stevens' for the final. I had coached up our eleven beforehand what to do. I gave Tritton strict injunctions, when he saw me running with the ball, to guard behind, and when he had the ball I agreed to do the same. In this way we kept fairly on the safe side, and after a very hard fight we managed to win by 1 rouge to 0. Arthur (now Lord) Kinnaird played for us, but was only a small boy then and in lower division.'[21]

Arthur played both forms of Eton football, and the *Chronicle* gave detailed accounts of sports and school activities. In 1863 'Kinnaird played well' as he captained Joynes' in the Middle Division house matches and later that month he was selected again for the full Joynes' team in the House Cup against Mrs Drury's. Captained by Quintin Hogg, they drew two rouges each but lost the following week's replay in pouring rain.

In 1864, Arthur played at the Wall nine times and in the Field five times in the first two months of the autumn term. The teams were selected under a variety of titles, such as Tutors, Boats, School, Oppidans, Wet Bobs and Those Without O (in their name), but while Arthur was enthusiastic, the Wall game was not his forte.

In the Field, however, he did much better and captained Joynes' for the first time; although his team lost by a goal and two rouges to a rouge, Arthur scored the rouge and 'particularly distinguished' himself.

His first opportunity to try out composite rules came in December, for a select team comprising mainly Old Harrovians[22] against Westminster School in London. Arthur was asked along (probably on the instigation of Quintin Hogg, now playing football regularly in the city), and among his team-mates was Charles Alcock, who may have seen Arthur in action for the first time that afternoon.[23] The two would have a long football future together in years to come.

Football at that time was played only in the Michaelmas half (ie autumn term) at Eton, and as Arthur would leave in the spring of 1865 that effectively brought an end to his football days at the school. However, with sport of all kinds playing such a dominant role in Eton life, there were numerous opportunities for Arthur to show off his athleticism. Although lacking in height he had a muscular physique and a good turn of speed which, allied to sheer determination, meant he excelled in several sports. He was even able to cash in on his talent as the combined entry fees and subscriptions from the houses were distributed among the winners of races, and a good athlete could earn a substantial sum. While this prize money may have raised questions in some circles about the amateur status of the runners, apparently it was not an issue at Eton.

Arthur first appeared in the school's athletic register in November 1863, leading the 350 yards until halfway before being overtaken by Neville Lyttelton and the eventual winner, Charles Legard. Arthur's cash prize of 30 shillings for third place must have been a welcome consolation. In the spring he entered the mile, but 'was out of the race from the cottages,' finishing fifth and last; he had a similar fate in the hurdles.

The following November, out of the blue, came Arthur's greatest success. There was no indication of his impending triumph when, earlier that day, he finished third in his heat in the 100 yards, despite leading till ten yards from the end. There were only five entries for the 350 yards, but the *Chronicle* described it as 'the best race of the day' and reported an exciting close-fought affair: 'About 50 yards from the end Kinnaird spurted, passed Thompson about six yards from home and caught Smith in the last two strides, winning at last by a foot.' Arthur crossed the line in a not particularly fast time of 45 seconds, it being noted that the grass was heavy and the timing was of a 'casual nature', but his prize for winning was £6 and 13 shillings, an extraordinary amount of money given the average wage was around 15 shillings a week; a working man might take months to earn as much. His victory, though, was overshadowed by the sensational sight of Walter Prideaux, star athlete of his year, being the first Etonian to wear shorts as he raced to victory in the 100 yards.[24]

Eton was one of the few schools which took swimming seriously, because of its proximity to the River Thames, and Arthur's powers of endurance stood him in good stead in the swimming competition of July 1864. Over a 300 yard stretch of river, he won his heat in a time of 3 minutes 2 seconds, and came second in the final, just behind his classmate George Edmonstone. The other great Eton aquatic sport was rowing, and in 1864 Arthur was in the crew of the St George, captained by Sir Archibald Lambe, but the craft had an unfortunate accident which has overtones of schoolboys larking about: 'The St George went down below bridge (contrary to orders) and the Victory, coming up, ran into them broadside while they were turning, making a very large hole near the bows; the crew succeeded in getting ashore just before the boat sank. The boat (quite a new one) was of course very much damaged.'[25] The boat was repaired in time for Arthur and the rest of the crew to take part in the annual regatta on 4 June, held traditionally on King George III's birthday amidst festivities and fireworks. The following March he was named in the crew of Monarch, captained by John Mossop, but by the time the boat was raced he had left the school.

Cricket was not a sport he relished greatly, as the game was 'too slow for his energetic nature'[26], but he did win the House Challenge Cup with Joynes' in the summer of 1862[27], largely thanks to Alfred Lubbock's batting. Thereafter he only featured occasionally in reports, his most significant contribution coming in his final year, when he took nine wickets and scored 13 runs against Marriott's. Arthur also played fives, and entered the Fives Challenge Cup in his final month at school in March 1865. Paired with Charles Alexander, they reached the fourth round before losing to Neville Lyttelton and Edgar Lubbock.

17

Confirmation that Arthur was highly regarded among his fellow pupils came in his election as a member of the Eton Society. This elite debating group, generally known as 'Pop' and still in existence, had a ceiling of 28 members and there was fierce competition to be voted in, so it was a mark of Arthur's esteem when, at its meeting on 5 December 1864, he was chosen from 24 nominees, having been proposed by the departing Thomas Sargent. One of the great joys of the 'Pop' records is that contributions to the debates were all written down by the boys themselves and Arthur's scratchy handwritten contributions to three debates can still be seen in the debating record. He agreed with the premise 'That the crusades did benefit Europe'[28], and supported 'The system of promotion at Eton'[29]. His view on 'Ought England to back with Canada?'[30] was 'we ought to keep Canada as we could lose all our influence in those parts'. In his last meeting he remained silent, and his final act at Eton was to propose two new members.

An interesting sideline to Arthur's membership of 'Pop' is that he was photographed with the other members, and the image recorded that he had already grown the bushy red beard which so distinguished him for the rest of his life.[31] It was not forbidden for a boy at Eton to grow facial hair, but although quite a few sprouted a moustache or sideburns, a full beard was rare. Unfortunately, Arthur never revealed whether his beard was to add an aura of gravitas, as a tribute to some religious leader, or simply that he was too busy to shave.

Religious beginnings

If there was one man who influenced Arthur more than any other at Eton, it was the charismatic Quintin Hogg. They would go on to play football together for Scotland in the unofficial internationals, and for Old Etonians in the FA Cup, but most of all Hogg gave him a clear sense of religious direction.

Two years older, also in Joynes' House, Hogg had many outward similarities: the son of a wealthy MP and from an ancient Scottish family, he did not greatly distinguish himself at Eton in the academic sense, and had a passion for sport. Arthur was his fag, a duty imposed on all the younger boys in the house to act as a kind of unpaid servant for the older boys (the system was less severe at

Eton than the common conception of a public school fag, shaped by the story of the violent bully Flashman at Rugby).

At that time, a religious revival was sweeping the British Isles, whipping up a stir that was tantamount to mass hysteria at times. The established church did not appreciate the methods of the revivalists, who were denounced as 'fanatics'[32] and even 'pestilential interlopers'[33]. (These views held little sway with the Kinnaird family, as Arthur's father was a mainstay of the Evangelical Alliance, while a leader of the movement was the Rev Baptist Noel, mentor to his mother.) Arthur was newly converted to evangelicalism, his moment of truth coming during his first trip abroad, when his father took him to the Evangelical Alliance conference in Geneva in September 1861. Inspired by a sermon from Rev Joseph Denham Smith, he made the decision to become an evangelical Christian, 'a role from which he never swerved'[34], and when he returned the following month to Eton, he found spiritual guidance with Hogg. Arthur was spellbound by the older boy's calm authority and leadership, becoming his devoted acolyte.

Hogg's masterstroke was in starting Bible study classes, gatherings which had their origins in his annoyance at being disturbed on a Sunday by rowdy games in the passage outside his room. To keep the younger boys quiet he invited them to tea, and read stories to them. After a time, he proposed that the meetings should conclude with a chapter of scripture and a prayer, although he later said it was a 'sore struggle' to get the boys to agree. Hogg's talent as a story teller won them over, and in time it became a regular class, although just taking part required strength of character, according to Arthur's sister: 'It needed courage for a schoolboy to carry a Bible up the staircase of his house and be known as going to a Bible reading. Quintin knew this and wished them to practise bearing the scorn or laughter of the boys who would not join them.'[35] One is reminded of the experience of a different Arthur, in *Tom Brown's Schooldays*, who was ridiculed for saying bedside prayers on his first day at Rugby, and only saved from the bullies by Tom's swift defensive action.[36] Another who joined the class was Thomas Pelham – who scored the winner for Wanderers in their first ever FA Cup tie in 1871 – and a close bond grew between the three which lasted for the rest of their lives. When Hogg left Eton late in 1863, Arthur took over the leadership of the

19

classes, and he in turn was succeeded by Pelham, who remained at school until the summer of 1866.

In time, the trio would make a decisive impact in the deprived streets of central London, where they were able to put their charitable instincts into practice. The instigator, again, was Hogg, who had gone into business with a firm of tea merchants and as he travelled about the city he felt an overwhelming sense of pity for the poverty-stricken street urchins, resolving to do what he could to bring them out of their misery. While social improvers like Lord Shaftesbury (who was actively supported by Arthur's father) had led movements to replace child exploitation with child education, the process of change was slow, and virtually the only access to education for orphans and slum children were missions and ragged schools. Hogg decided to take unilateral action by teaching a couple of boys to read, his eagerness matched only by his naivety as he selected a likely pair, and sat down with them one night in the spring of 1864 at the Adelphi Arches, near Charing Cross Embankment. 'With an empty beer bottle for a candlestick and a tallow candle for illumination, two crossing sweepers as pupils, your humble servant as teacher, and a couple of Bibles as reading books, what grew into the Polytechnic was practically started. We had not been engaged in our reading very long when at the far end of the arch I noticed a twinkling light. 'Kool ecilop!'[37] shouted one of the boys, at the same time 'doucing the glim' and bolting with his companion, leaving me in the dark, forming a spectacle which seemed to arouse suspicion on the part of our friend the policeman. However, after scrutinizing me for some time by the light of his bull's-eye, he moved on.'[38]

The incident brought home to him that, as an Eton boy, he was utterly clueless about the way of life in the slums. So, to get closer to his targets, he bought second-hand shoeblack clothes, and set to work at nights doing whatever came up, holding horses or blacking boots, to experience something of the hardships, albeit with a home and a job to return to each morning. After a few months he was joined by Arthur, on his summer holidays from Eton (although not before his father took him back to Geneva for the celebrations to mark the 300th anniversary of Calvin). Needing a base for their activities, they clubbed together to hire a room in a rundown street called Of Alley, at a cost of £12 a year, and there they started their own ragged school in June 1864. Of Alley, close to Charing Cross railway station, owes its curious name to being on the site of the old palace of George Villiers, Duke of Buckingham, providing the names of George Court, Villiers Street, Duke Street, Of Alley, and Buckingham Street. It is now called York Place – although the street sign still alludes to its former identity – but it remains a decrepit passageway to nowhere, smelling of stale urine.

Proud of their venture, they invited a few friends to the opening of their room including the Rev Richard Killick (minister of the Kinnaird family's parish church, St Clement Danes), the evangelical Lord Radstock, and Tom Pelham. After the slum boys departed, the little band of workers held an all-night prayer meeting. The school was at first used mainly to teach boys to read, with a female teacher in charge, and was such a success that they soon introduced classes for girls. When the summer came to an end, Hogg continued on his own and Arthur returned to Eton for the new term, but would visit at weekends and resumed operations in earnest when he left school the following Easter.

By the time the summer of 1865 was out, demand for their services had grown so much that they added a second room. The venture provided Arthur with a cause to which his energy and single-minded commitment was ideally suited, and his work with the slum kids would consume his free time (or what was left of it after university, football and work in the bank) for years to come.

---

[1] The 15 letters are held in the AK Bell Library, Perth: MS100, Baron Kinnaird of Rossie muniments.

[2] Emily Kinnaird, *My Adopted Country*, p8

[3] See Stephen Halliday, *The Great Stink of London*, for further details.

[4] *The Times*, 22 June 1865.

[5] See *Recollections of Cheam School*, *The Times*, 17 October 1927.

[6] In 1934, Cheam School moved to its present site in Newbury, Berkshire.

[7] The earliest recorded football match between schools was Merchiston Castle School against the Royal High School in Edinburgh on 13 February 1858.

[8] Generally known as the Clarendon Report, its full title was *Report of Her Majesty's Commissioners appointed to inquire in the Revenues and Managements of certain college and schools, and the studies pursued and instruction given therein.*

[9] *Clarendon Report*, p185

[10] Paterfamilias, *Cornhill Magazine*, 6 July 1864

[11] Joynes was later caricatured in *Vanity Fair* magazine in academic gown and holding a fierce-looking birch. Cartoon by 'Spy', 11 July 1887.

[12] Emily Kinnaird, *My Adopted Country*, p112

[13] *Fifty Years of Sport*, Vol 3, p51

[14] Eton did play a tentative match at Winchester in December 1862.

[15] Frederick Wall, *Fifty Years of Football*, p27

[16] *Eton College Chronicle*, 15 October 1863

[17] James Brinsley-Richards, *Seven Years at Eton 1857-1864*, p151

[18] By the time the book was published in 1883 he had changed his name to James Brinsley-Richards.

[19] James Brinsley-Richards, *Seven Years at Eton 1857-1864*, p154

[20] Alfred Lubbock, *Memories of Eton*, p109

[21] Alfred Lubbock, *Memories of Eton*, p154

[22] Described as Thompson's Eleven, the team was put together by Old Harrovian Arthur Thompson.

[23] *Bell's Life*, 10 December 1864

[24] *Fifty Years of Sport*, Vol 3, p100

[25] *Eton College Chronicle*, 10 March 1864

[26] Emily Kinnaird, *My Adopted Country*, p112

[27] *Bell's Life*, 24 August 1862

[28] Eton Society Book, 30 January 1865, p14

[29] Eton Society Book, 27 February 1865, p82

[30] Eton Society Book, 6 March 1865, p102

[31] Gilbert Coleridge, *Eton in the Seventies*, p170

[32] *The Times*, 23 September 1859

[33] George E Morgan, *A Veteran in Revival*, p19

[34] Emily Kinnaird, *My Adopted Country*, p113

[35] Emily Kinnaird, *My Adopted Country*, p112

[36] *Tom Brown's Schooldays*, p248-250

[37] Backwards slang for 'look police'.

[38] Ethel Hogg, *Quintin Hogg a biography*, p50

CHAPTER 2

The student who became the master
1865-69

THE THOUGHT of a bushy-bearded student being invited to join the Football Association would send a shiver down the spine of any self-respecting 'blazer' today. But football in the 1860s was a young man's game and Arthur Kinnaird was welcomed with open arms by the sport's governing body in 1868, just two years after his introduction to the Association game.

His sporting destiny as an undergraduate would also include championships at tennis, swimming and canoeing, but all this was a blank canvas when Arthur matriculated at Trinity College, Cambridge, in October 1865.[1] He went to university fresh from accompanying his father to America on a trade mission of merchants and financiers, who were aiming to invest in the railways now that the Civil War was over.[2] Described in the American press as 'the English capitalists', the group was led by the entrepreneur Sir Morton Peto, who brought his nephew, Morton Peto Betts, fresh out of Harrow and later to find fame by scoring the winning goal in the first FA Cup Final. No doubt he and Arthur, both aged 18, had plenty of time on the voyage to debate the respective merits of Harrow and Eton rules. Travelling in their own first class railway carriage, the investors were feted by local business leaders with banquets and receptions wherever they went: they had their photo taken at Niagara Falls near the site for a new bridge that would link the USA and Canada; then it was Chicago, Cincinnati and (in a 17 hour journey) as far west as St Louis.

The Kinnairds broke off from the main party to visit the White House[3] as they had a personal invitation to meet the President, and were greeted enthusiastically by Andrew Johnson, not long in office after the assassination of Lincoln. The reason for this special treatment was that Arthur senior had been an outspoken supporter of the Union, as the *New York Times* reported: 'During the whole period of the rebellion, Mr Kinnaird was an earnest, ardent and most efficient friend of the Union and the government. In all the high circles – official, social and religious – his advocacy of our cause was fearlessly outspoken and persistent. Indeed, Hon Arthur Kinnaird was second to no-one in England in zeal for our cause, and in the influence exerted on our behalf; and it is to be regretted that his too brief visit will prevent any suitable expression of our sense of his personal worth, and of the great services he rendered our country.'[4] The following week, at a banquet in St Louis, they also met General Ulysses Grant, who had visited the Kinnaird household before the war and would succeed Johnson as President in 1869.[5]

As a postscript to the visit, Arthur senior and Sir Morton Peto each sent an unsolicited gift of a £50 banknote to the State Department, with the wish that it be used for the relief of freedmen of the southern states. This prompted an effusive letter of thanks from the astonished commissioner of the Bureau of Refugees, Freedmen and Abandoned Lands.[6] However, such largesse on Sir Morton Peto's part was short-lived, as within a year he was bankrupted by the failure of the London, Chatham and Dover Railway.

By then, young Arthur had embarked on student life, secure in the knowledge that he would go to work in his father's bank when he finished at university, regardless of academic performance. He started a Bachelor of Arts (BA) degree and although there was no great expectation that he would apply himself to his studies, he did rather well. For the first two years, he studied the components of the general exam – Acts of the Apostles in Greek, a Greek set book, a Latin set book, elementary algebra and elementary mechanics – gaining a second class placing (of four).[7] In his third year he sat the special exam, and faced with a choice of subjects he chose law[8], a subject he took to with relish. When the results were announced, he astonished his family by finishing in the first class, getting the second highest mark of all the candidates.[9]

Despite this academic success, there is evidence to suggest that Arthur was not the most diligent of students. He enjoyed a busy social calendar and could be found amusing himself at the Cambridge Caledonian Club or with the Magpie and Stump, an

24

exclusive but none-too-serious gentleman's debating society which he joined shortly after it was founded.[10] Most of his leisure time, however, was devoted to sport, which had the incidental benefit of allowing him to mix with some great intellects, such as his tennis-playing contemporaries at Trinity, Arthur Balfour (a future Prime Minister) and George Darwin (son of Charles, and himself a brilliant scientist). Many Sunday evenings were spent at Balfour's rooms in New Court, drinking claret and discussing current affairs, and perhaps the claret had something to do with one student prank that went wrong. It was the fashion to ring the doorbell of an unpopular tutor and run away, but Trinity student Hugh Elliot recalled: 'One night I was walking down Jesus Lane with Kinnaird and AJB (Arthur Balfour). It was suggested that we should pull Dr Ransome's bell. AJB put out his hand as if to pull the bell, though he did not touch it, nor as a matter of fact intended to ring it. As he stretched out his arm, a policeman who was concealed behind a doorway sprang out and charged him with ringing the bell.'[11] Balfour was fined £1 in the police court the next morning, despite Arthur giving evidence on his behalf that the bell had not actually been pulled.

More pertinently, Arthur was in the right place at the right time to experience the blossoming of football, and his stocky build, strength and stamina made him the ideal player. Having arrived at university a novice in all but the convoluted Eton games, he was introduced to Association rules halfway through his first year and simply exploded onto the scene: within months he was selected to play for London and by the time he graduated, he had a place on the national governing body.

Football in the 1860s was energetic but primitive. Dribbling and charging were the key components of the game, teamwork was defined by backing up the dribbler, and there were almighty scrimmages to gain possession: contemporary illustrations show whole teams blocking the goal to prevent opponents scoring.[12] There were limited changing and washing facilities, and almost any surface was deemed acceptable: reports referred regularly to glutinous mud and once 'a heavy downpouring of rain falling from the commencement of the match until the termination, pools of water covered almost the entire surface of the green'.[13] On one occasion, a gravel path ran across the pitch. Even seeking refuge in the outfield of cricket pitches was no guarantee of a pristine surface, according to this description of West Kent, one of Arthur's clubs: 'Instead of injuring the turf, as some feared, football has undoubtedly improved it, by destroying the short heather which was always trying to establish itself.'[14] One wonders how the participants could take enjoyment from the game but, quite simply, they found football an invigorating release from day-to-day life, and would willingly turn out in all weathers.

Arthur himself never missed an opportunity for a match, and it is possible to follow his progress in detail as he carefully cut out reports of the matches he played, from *Bell's Life*, *The Sportsman* and any other paper that covered sport, and glued them into a scrapbook.[15] Three little books of clippings, covering a decade from 1865, have survived intact and give an insight into the early development of the game. What is more, his annotations and corrections in the margins are invaluable, as with football reporting in its infancy, spellings of player names and their initials could vary from match to match; he even turns up on occasion as KF Arthur.

He had hardly settled into his spacious rooms in Market Place, a short walk from Trinity College, than he was back at his old school to play football. He had developed such a reputation that Francis Pelham, older brother of his friend Tom, selected Arthur to play for Cambridge University in the prestigious St Andrew's Day Field Game. He helped his side to victory over Oxford by a goal and a rouge to nil, and what is more, as the railway journey from Cambridge to Eton was via London, he could also visit his parents and spend a couple of evenings with Quintin Hogg in the ragged school at Of Alley.

When Arthur was in London for the winter break he played for the first time under the rules of the Football Association and, as so often in his life, the introduction came thanks to his mentor. Hogg had founded an Old Etonian[16] side in London, and initially lined him up for a match against Westminster School, probably played under an amalgam of school rules. It finished 4-0 for the Etonians, for whom 'Kinnaird and Hogg played remarkably well'.

Hogg then took Arthur into exciting new territory with his first Association match, against a Wanderers side captained by Charles Alcock. The match report for the 0-0 draw on 3 January 1866 was brief, and although it gave details of who won the toss (Wanderers) and the weather (windy), not even the venue was reported[17] and there was precious little about the play: 'The

26

Wanderers were far heavier than their opponents, but the Etonians seemed to have the advantage in speed. Mackenzie and Martin played well for the former, Kinnaird, Langley, Sargent and Hogg kept the ball going for Eton.' Two days later Hogg asked him to captain the Etonians against Civil Service, who had Alcock as a guest player, and once again Arthur's contribution was highlighted in the brief report: 'In spite of the immense agility of Mr Kinnaird and the long kicking of Mr Hogg, no goal was obtained on either side.'

A couple of Old Etonian matches against Charterhouse School followed, then in March they came up against Harrow Chequers, the first time the old boys of Eton and Harrow had met under Association rules. It ended goal-less, although the Etonians dominated the match, and the weather was blamed: 'Interest was very much lessened by the perfect hurricane of wind which swept across the field and quite prevented any good play on either side.'

Harrow captain Alcock was sufficiently impressed by the young terrier in the opposition ranks to invite him to join Wanderers, the pre-eminent club, although Arthur would not actually play for them until the following year.

Alcock also asked him to play for London against Sheffield in football's first ever representative match, which concluded

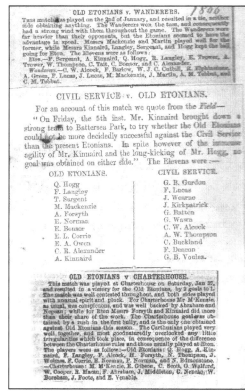

These cuttings from Arthur Kinnaird's scrapbook report his first association football matches in January 1866 against Wanderers and Civil Service

the season. Captained by Arthur Pember, President of the FA, London won with ease by two goals and four touchdowns to nil, while the visitors had to adapt to the local style of play: 'The laws of the Association, as amended a short time ago, were in force, and worked very well indeed, showing that the changes then made were most judicious.' According to *Bell's Life*, 'although Sheffield were overmatched, many of the Londoners were badly knocked about' but there were no hard feelings and the teams dined together after the match in Covent Garden.

The football season over, Arthur's attention turned to swimming and in the Cambridge University Aquatic Sports he won his heat in the 50 yards race, but in the 200 yards 'Kinnaird was too much exhausted by his previous efforts to show well'[18]. The following day he was third in the 50 yards final, well behind another Etonian, Robert McKerrell.

His summer holiday meant hard work in the slums with Hogg and Pelham. As the mission had reached capacity in the original rooms in Of Alley, the young philanthropists rented the house next door for £30, and Hogg, the oldest and by all accounts the most dedicated of the three, even retained a room in the attic to sleep in. They faced a further challenge as that summer saw the last great London cholera epidemic, leading to over five thousand deaths. Hogg dodged out of a holiday in Scotland to assist with the dying, but while he recalled his own close encounters with death and disease in his memoirs, he did not mention Arthur, whose role is less clear. Most likely Arthur did carry on working, despite the threat of infection, but his commitment can be weighed against his name appearing in cricket match reports, playing for Hayes in August[19], and again in October for Rossie Priory against Perthshire[20], while visiting his uncle.

On his return to Cambridge for the autumn term, Arthur threw himself into his football, playing 16 matches of various codes before Christmas. His growing influence was reflected in the number of teams he captained, a role which was particularly important in those days as the captain would not only select the team, he would make the arrangements for venue, kick-off time, length of match, and agree with his opposite number which set of rules would be in force. With no referees, there were regular disputes, with games often interrupted to argue an interpretation of the rules, and a glance through contemporary match reports reveals how challenging this could be, with variations on handling, offside, touchdowns, bases, rouges, scrimmages, charging, size of goals and number of players.

However, there was no need to discuss the rules when his season began on familiar territory at Eton, with matches at the Wall and in the Field on consecutive days. Arthur was now sufficiently established to choose his own team and five of his players stayed overnight to take part in both. As if to emphasise his leadership qualities, he and Lord Edmond Fitzmaurice formed the Eton Football Club at Cambridge, and what made their team unusual was its availability to meet opponents under differing sets of rules, agreed on a match by match basis, a pragmatic approach which was an excellent means of ensuring a regular fixture calendar. Eton FC's first recorded match was a 3-0 victory over St John's College, in which 'Kinnaird, who has wonderfully improved this season, and Lord Fitzmaurice got the goals for Eton, and both played very well indeed throughout.' Then a one-sided challenge against the rest of Cambridge University was declared drawn, even though Eton FC got 15 touchdowns to nil 'but owing to the wet and not being accustomed to the large ball, they were unable to get a goal'. A match against Harrovians at Cambridge, also goal-less, was played on a frosty Parker's Piece 'by the University rules enacted in 1863 by representatives of Harrow, Eton, Rugby, Marlborough, Shrewsbury and Westminster'. The sides met again two weeks later, and this time victory went to Eton thanks to a late strike from Charles Cuthell 'at ten past four'.

It was not all plain sailing, which was made clear in December 1866 when Arthur and Lord Fitzmaurice had a letter published in *The Times*. Describing themselves as 'Captains of the Eton Football Club at Cambridge', they refuted an allegation that the Cambridge team had failed to appear for the St Andrew's Day match: 'Sir, - In *The Times* of Saturday, in speaking of the football match, which is usually played at Eton between the old Etonians at Oxford and Cambridge, it was stated that owing to some 'unexplained circumstances' the Cambridge Eleven did not appear. The unexplained circumstances were the following – that the College tutors at Trinity put their unconditional veto on the match taking place at Eton, and therefore the Cambridge Eleven, who are chiefly drawn from Trinity, were unable to come.'[21]

In fact, the match went ahead a day late but had to be moved to Cambridge to accommodate the irksome tutor, the Rev William Collings Mathison, whose reasoning 'is at present a mystery to all save the reverend gentleman himself'. Cambridge won by Francis Pelham's goal to a rouge, although Oxford were a man short. After the match 'the two elevens and some others partook of a dinner in Kinnaird's rooms in the Market Place and drank health to old Eton, and ill-luck to the enemies of Football.' Clearly Arthur's position was sufficiently elevated that he was deemed a worthy host for such a gathering.

To kick off his winter break in London, Arthur took a mixed team of Etonians and Harrovians to play Forest School, with Charles Alcock snatching an equaliser two minutes from the end. Three days later, Etonians defeated Wanderers 1-0, with Arthur scoring the only goal which was reported as 'a rather lucky chance' or 'very cleverly obtained' depending on which paper you read, and he was praised for his 'untiring perseverance' and 'indefatigable exertions'. He was promptly invited to play for the opposition, finally making his debut for Wanderers in a 1-1 draw against Old Harrovians at Battersea Park. Played 12-a-side in a thick fog, the rules that day were loosely based on those of Westminster School but with the use of hands forbidden. Football teams at that time often played with differing numbers of players, eleven being an optimum rather than a requirement, and in Arthur's second outing for Wanderers they only had eight men, but still managed to beat Westminster. The holidays concluded with a couple of exhibition matches for Eton and Harrow against 'The World'.

To celebrate his 20th birthday he was made captain of Wanderers for his first fixture in Oxford; playing under Westminster rules but with an Eton ball, his team secured victory with the only goal of the game. Players had to adapt to the vagaries of local rules — Arthur was disappointed that a goal he scored for Eton FC at Charterhouse was disallowed as it was not 'kicked' — and also to different team colours, so he was able to conclude his helter-skelter season by guesting for Old Harrovians at Hitchin.

He had managed 27 games for ten different teams over the course of the season, but his sporting endeavour was far from over: in 1867 he also won a Cambridge University swimming title, the fives championship, a couple of athletics prizes, and topped it off with victory in an international canoe race.

He showed he had learned from the previous year's swimming experience by pacing himself to win the University half mile title[22], and further afield, he won a gold medal in the Amateur Athletic Club aquatic sports for finishing second to Robert McKerrell over the same distance, swum in the River Thames at Teddington[23]. In the fives championship, he partnered Spencer Lyttelton to win the inaugural Challenge Cup[24], and in the University Boat Club Athletic Sports, Arthur sped to victory in the 150 yard hurdle race, having already won the hurdles title at his college boat club sports[25].

Canoe adventures

What really marked out Arthur that summer was his most unlikely sporting accomplishment, winning a canoe race at the Universal Exhibition in Paris. His enthusiasm for paddling, however, nearly ended in disaster off the west coast of Scotland with his life – and that of a future Prime Minister – at risk. The story began the previous year when John MacGregor, a Scottish devotee of canoeing, published a volume of his exploits, *A thousand miles in the Rob Roy canoe on the rivers and lakes of Europe*, which brought the sport to a vast audience. He capitalised on its success by forming the Canoe Club in London, which proved immensely fashionable and attracted young aristocratic types, among them the Prince of Wales (whose patronage led to it becoming the Royal Canoe Club in 1873, the title it still has today).

Arthur, being a fan of water sports, was soon hooked and spent £15 commissioning a carpenter, probably Searle of Lambeth, to build an oak Rob Roy canoe which he named *Rossie* in honour of the family estate. It was delivered in time for the Canoe Club's first regatta, or grand muster, held at Thames Ditton in April 1867, which was such a success that the *Illustrated London News* published an engraving of the large crowd of spectators, and described how Arthur won the captain's challenge cup: 'The great event of the day was the canoe chase over land and water. Four flags were arranged at the angles of a square, and the starting-point was fixed midway between them. The course was diagonally across, round all the flags, and back to the starting-point. The excitement was very great when Mr Kinnaird and the purser (Col. Wright) went for the same flag, and finally emerged from behind a tree, 'heads and tails' to the

31

water side. The purser was in first with the head of his boat in the right direction, so away he went to the next flag. Kinnaird's boat, however, had its nose the wrong way, so he bucketed across, jumped on land, and tore away to the next flag; here the purser rounded the flag together with the owner of the *Rossie*. In the end Mr Kinnaird won, the purser being 2nd, and the chevy 3rd.'[26] Arthur's technique was unorthodox but effective: 'He succeeded not so much from the speed of his paddling, as from the *élan* with which he landed and embarked, and handled his canoe on the banks.'[27]

The *Illustrated London News* depicted the excited crowd at the Canoe Club regatta in 1867

MacGregor was invited by Emperor Napoleon III to demonstrate his canoes at the Paris Exhibition that summer, in the hope that it would inspire French youth to take up the sport, and Arthur signed up to join the delegation of English canoeists, travelling to Paris the day after his half-mile swim in the Thames. MacGregor, ever the opportunist, paddled all the way there from London, and in his subsequent memoir[28] related the excitement of the canoe chase, which was again won by Arthur ('the Englishman'):

'Five French canoes entered, but there was only one English canoeist ready in his Rob Roy to meet all comers. All dashed off together on being started, and ran with their boats to the water. The

32

Frenchmen soon got entangled together by trying to get into their boats dry; but the Englishman had made up his mind for a wetting, and it might as well come now at once as in a few minutes after, so he rushed straight into the river up to his waist, and therefore, being free from the crowding of others, he got into his boat all dripping wet, but foremost of all, and then paddled swiftly away.

'The rest soon followed; and all of them were making to the flag boat anchored a little way off, round which the canoes must first make a turn. Here the Englishman, misled by the various voices on shore telling him the (wrong) side he was to take, lost all the advantage of his start; so that all the six boats arrived at the flag-boat together, each struggling to get round it but locked with some other opponent in a general scramble. Next, their course was back to the shore, where they jumped out and ran along, each one dragging his boat round another flag on dry land, amid the cheers and laughter of the dense group of spectators, who had evidently not anticipated a contest so new in its kind, and so completely visible from beginning to end. Again, dashing into the water, the little struggling fleet paddled away to another flag-boat, but not now in such close array. Some stuck in the willows or rushes, or were overturned and had to swim; and the chance of who might win was still open to the man of strength and spirit, with reasonably good luck. Once more the competing canoes came swiftly back to shore, and were dragged round the flag, and another time paddled round the flag-boat; and now he was to be winner who could first reach the shore and bring his canoe to the Tribune: a well-earned victory, won by the Englishman, far ahead of the rest.'

MacGregor admitted 'the strain was severe upon pluck and muscle', but barely with time to recover there was another challenge for Arthur: 'Among the visitors to the regatta was M. Forcat, and he brought up for exhibition, and for the practical trial by the winner of the canoe chase, a very narrow and crank boat, rowed by oars jointed to a short mast in front of the sitter, and thus obtaining one of the advantages possessed by canoeists, that their faces are turned to the bow, and so they see where they are going. We tried to dissuade our young canoeist from entering hastily a new sort of boat very easily capsized. He had his own wit, and his own way, however, because he was a Scot, and only 'English' in the sense we use that word for 'British' – and too frequently used it is, to the dire offence of the blue lion of the North. 'He's upset,' they cried in a minute or so. But we might well let so good a swimmer take his chance; so he merely pushed the boat ashore, and then took a pleasant and gratuitous swim, until he was finally captured and put into the Rob Roy's cabin, and changed his wet clothes as rapidly as a modest man dare to do behind a plaid screen and before the curious world.'

Arthur's appetite for adventure was whetted and on returning from Paris, he was invited with Arthur Balfour to Dunvegan Castle on the Isle of Skye, ancestral home of their Cambridge tennis partner Reginald MacLeod, later to be clan chief. The trio had decided to circumnavigate Skye in their canoes, a trip which nearly ended in disaster as the craft were plainly not intended for travel in the open sea: 'The Rob Roy canoes were thirteen feet long, built of oak, decked with cedar, propelled by a double-bladed paddle, carrying a small mast and single sail. They were just broad enough in the beam to accommodate a single person, who was at once passenger, captain, crew, motor and ballast. He was seated very near the bottom of the well, where his weight gave stability to the boat, and though his position was comfortable, it was also unchangeable. Except in the smoothest water he could not stand up, or even kneel, without risking an upset.'[29]

Journeying down the west coast of Skye they were given hospitality in a shooting lodge and a farm, but by the third night the spirit of adventure started to wane as they found only a deserted cottage where they went hungry and were bitten by bedbugs. Things took a turn for the better as they headed across 16 miles of open water to the island of Rum, where they stayed as guests of Captain William MacLeod of Orbost, who rented the island from Balfour's grandfather. Arthur and MacLeod then crossed to Eigg, camping in a cave with a grisly history: in 1515, MacLeod's ancestors had trapped the local clan inside and killed all 395 men, women and children. A storm blew up on their way back to Rum, tossing the little boats around, and it was only with great difficulty that the exhausted pair navigated their way to safety. Reunited with Balfour, they rested until the weather abated, and struck out for the Skye coast; but a few days later they gave up at Portree and returned overland by cart to Dunvegan.

Balfour later admitted that it was 'a very hare-brained adventure' and remarked candidly that the trip could easily have proved fatal. He posed the rhetorical question, 'It may be asked why our legal guardians (I was under twenty) permitted us to run risk so obviously useless? At the time I never heard the question raised.'[30] It is interesting to speculate how the course of world history could have changed if the future prime minister had been dashed on the rocks. The trio did at least achieve the accolade of having their exploits commended at the first annual meeting of the Canoe Club, where it was announced that upwards of 200 canoes had been built since the formation of the club. Arthur eased off canoeing after the Skye adventure, but did continue his club membership for a while and won another chase on the Thames in June 1869.

Between sporting events, there was much work to be done at the ragged school. While Arthur's involvement was restricted to the occasional weekend in term-time, the summer provided an opportunity for much greater commitment – six evenings a week, according to his sister Emily. The building in Of Alley had again run out of space and Arthur and Pelham embarked on a more ambitious venture, renting premises about half a mile to the north in a court off Hanover Street (now Endell Street), where they started the Castle Street Working Boys' Home with accommodation for 40 boys, supervised by paid staff. They quickly became well-known figures in the community, nicknamed after local streets: 'The little urchins used to run after these two young Cambridge men calling out 'There go Long Acre and Shorts Gardens', alluding to their respective heights. Tom Pelham was very tall, Arthur Kinnaird very short.'[31] Hogg allocated some of the vacated space at Of Alley as a home for young women, under the guidance of his older sister Annie, and 'here on Sundays he would gather the unsatisfactory boys and girls of the neighbourhood and give one of his never-to-be-forgotten racy religious talks. Then together these three would seek out the young boys who at that time slept under railway arches or under carts; many were practically homeless.'

Joining the football establishment

When Arthur returned to Cambridge in October 1867 for his third year, the term opened with football's first ever club tour. Charles Alcock brought Wanderers to Cambridge to play five matches on consecutive days, and Arthur showed his stamina by playing enthusiastically in all of them. In the opening game, Eton FC had the upper hand over Wanderers by scoring three touchdowns to nil, but it ended goal-less. Arthur then changed sides and turned out for Wanderers in three matches against the Cambridge Harrovians (Tuesday), St John's College (Wednesday) and King's College (Thursday). The tour culminated on Friday afternoon at Parker's Piece with Arthur inspiring Cambridge University to a 3-0 win (more precisely three goals and three touchdowns to nil), although it was spoiled as a contest as Wanderers had expected reinforcements from Oxford but only two turned up, so they played with nine men.

The week was deemed a great success, even though playing under Cambridge rules did not please this reporter[32], who wrote what sounds like an early criticism of the 'long ball' game: 'After a careful examination of the University rules, and a practical experience of their working, we can express anything but a favourable opinion of the game they encourage: the long kicking, which is such a prominent feature of the style, is at times oppressively tedious, and literally reduced the various portions of the game to a trial of strength between the goalkeepers of the rival sides.'

As if that were not enough for Arthur, on Saturday he travelled to Eton for his sixth match in six days, the school winning 'in spite of the desperate resistance offered by the Strangers, for whom KF Arthur worked with all his wonted energies'. That same day there was a county match, Middlesex v Surrey & Kent, for which Arthur was not selected; maybe they thought he would be exhausted (although Alcock did take part).

From then until the Christmas holidays Arthur played in matches which were mainly of local interest in Cambridge. At home for the winter break, he captained an Old Etonian side to a goal-less draw against Wanderers and arranged two matches against schools, although it was a problem to find sufficient recruits: three schoolboy substitutes made up the numbers against Forest School, and a few days later there were only eight Etonians against ten Westminsters. The holidays concluded with a double-header repeat of the previous year's challenges, Eton and Harrow against The World. In the first, despite playing with nine men to The World's thirteen, Arthur's team kept the score down to a single goal; two weeks later, with ten-a-side, the game ended goal-less.

These were insignificant contests compared to an important match which did much to establish the credibility of the Football

Association, which was finally starting to blossom, largely thanks to the efforts of Robert Graham, the secretary. The FA had been struggling to make an impact after the initial enthusiasm of its founding in 1863, and adoption of the Association game was far from universal, not helped by the failure of the major public schools and the universities to take up membership. Graham realised the FA could only survive if it expanded its sphere of influence, and in 1867 had written to every known football club in the United Kingdom, his circular letter promoting 'a code of rules at once simple and easy of adoption ... free from unnecessary danger, yet retaining all that is most scientific and interesting.'[33] In doing so, he effectively saved the FA from extinction, as his efforts trebled the number of members to 30 clubs, including its first public school adherents, Charterhouse and Westminster.

To mark this rapid expansion, and to demonstrate the FA's newly redrafted rules, a Kent v Surrey county match was organised on 25 January at the West London Running Grounds in Brompton, albeit with 12-a-side. Arthur was appointed captain of Kent, which was quite an accolade as the players were among the most prominent of the day:

Kent: AF Kinnaird (Trinity College, Cambridge), E Lubbock (West Kent), JB Martin (Wanderers), FG Paulson (Charterhouse School), EO Berens (Crusaders), AJ Baker (No Names), WJC Cutbill (Crystal Palace), D Allport (Crystal Palace), AC Chamberlain (Crystal Palace), P Norman (Old Etonian), EA Hoare (St John's College, Cambridge), JT Goldney (Old Harrovian).

Surrey: RG Graham (Barnes), J Cockerell (Crystal Palace), CC Dacre (Clapham Grammar School), P Rhodes (Wanderers), H Richardson (Reigate Hill), FB Soden (CCC, Clapham), JE Tayloe (CCC, Clapham), A Thompson (Wanderers), RW Willis (Barnes), J Turner (Crystal Palace), EC Morley (Barnes), W Collins (Barnes).

There were no goals, but it was 'a contest as exciting and full of interest as any witnessed during the present season,' and 'great satisfaction was expressed by the whole body of players at the working of the rules lately published by the Football Association, and their simplicity and efficacy met with universal approval.' It was a clear sign that football was emerging from its teething

37

troubles with a format that was widely acceptable and easily understood.

There was further recognition for Arthur the following month, when he was elected to the committee of the FA at its annual meeting on 26 February 1868, held in the Freemasons' Tavern. It is worth examining why they were keen to have this 21-year-old student on board. He was not even the youngest of six newcomers[34], all aged under 30, who brought an injection of vigour and ideas. Arthur was already well known his fellow committee members, having played with or against every one of them, and had the right credentials despite his relative inexperience. He was proven as a talented leader on and off the field and, crucially, had grown out of his Etonian upbringing to be an enthusiastic advocate of the Association game. Arthur's influence would be a key factor in the development and promotion of association football, and Charles Alcock said later that for a while the FA was known as 'Kinnaird, Alcock and Fitzmaurice's Association'.[35] As Lord Edmond Fitzmaurice was only on the FA committee for two years, it seems reasonable to infer that Arthur held considerable sway from the start. No-one, however, could have foreseen that he would remain in office at the FA for the rest of his life and this meeting marked the start of an incredible 55 years at the heart of the national game.

His season concluded in various guises: in an ad-hoc team called the Flying Dutchmen he was described as 'the greatest flyer of all the Flying Dutchmen' after scoring all four of his side's goals; a Field Game at Eton was played in the Masters' Field as the usual pitch was being prepared for cricket; he turned out for Wanderers in a comfortable win at Hitchin; and on the last day of February he captained Cambridge University to a 2-1 victory over Charterhouse.

Spring and summer brought new sporting challenges and successes, with Arthur securing University championships in swimming and tennis. First, he raced well in the Boat Club Athletic Sports, where he won the quarter mile in 57 seconds, came second in the hundred yards sprint and the mile, and even entered the long jump and putting the weight. He was not so successful in the annual University Sports, failing to get past the first heat in 100 yards sprint. In March, Arthur retained his University fives challenge cup[36], partnered by his cousin William Hoare, beating Charles Alexander and Charles Knight; this all-Etonian decider was held on the same day as a Canoe Club meeting in Cambridge, which he had to miss.

His preferred court sport, however, was tennis. Not to be confused with lawn tennis (invented in 1873), this was the traditional sport of real tennis which has medieval origins and is played in an enclosed court, requiring particular dexterity and skill. Real tennis courts were scarce in England at that time (and are even more so today) but Cambridge was equipped with three venues: the 'old' court, said to date from the reign of Charles II; the East Road Court built in 1853 for the Duke of Wellington, with a slate floor; and the most popular, in Burrell's Walk, which opened in 1866 and is still the home of the Cambridge University Real Tennis Club.

By winning a University play-off in June 1868, Arthur was selected to represent Cambridge in the annual match against Oxford, held at the MCC court in London[37], thereby winning his 'blue'. He won his singles contest convincingly, three sets to love, against Walter James of Christ Church, Oxford, but in the doubles, which were lost 1-3 to the pairing of Walter James and William Goschen, there is an element of intrigue about his playing partner. The official records gave his name as RD (Robert Drummond) Balfour[38], but in Arthur's cuttings book he crossed out RD and wrote in AJ – the future prime minister Arthur James Balfour. This has been confirmed by new research[39] even though AJ, a self-confessed tennis addict, made no mention of winning a blue in his memoirs.[40] It is an accolade which has so far escaped his biographers.

Cambridge University 100 yards swimming championship medal, 1868

By then, Arthur had also captured another two swimming titles, and his family still holds the medals he won in the Cambridge University 50 and 100 yards races; he also came third in the 200 yards. His time in the 50 yards was 39 seconds, in the 100 yards it was 1 minute 27 seconds.[41]

To conclude a successful summer, he did well in his exams and his BA degree was conferred at a Congregation in the Senate House on 20 June 1868.[42] Despite finishing his studies and having work waiting for him in his father's bank, Arthur seemed reluctant to leave university life behind and returned to Cambridge in the autumn for no obvious reason other than his sport and his social life, and there is nothing to suggest he did any serious studying.

Dividing his time between London and Cambridge, Arthur played only five football matches that autumn, including an appearance for Cambridge in the St Andrew's Day game at Eton. Oxford won by a goal to a rouge, even though 'Rigden, Kinnaird and Hoare did all they knew to avert defeat'. The only match of significance was Eton Football Club's comfortable 3-0 win over Wanderers.

During the Christmas holidays, Arthur scored an early goal in the newly-created Gitanos' win over Bedouins at Blackheath – 'wandering' names were a popular choice for teams with no fixed ground. While he would play again for Gitanos against CCC[43], in the meantime he captained Old Etonians in a 1-1 draw with Wanderers at Middlesex County Cricket Ground, enlivened by the reporter's wonderfully acerbic comment that the ground 'was by no means improved by the intersection of a gravel path'. Shortly afterwards, Arthur faced Wanderers again, this time for West Kent, a club for whom he qualified thanks to his father's country home in Hayes.[44]

Football's major representative match of the season was on 27 February 1869, and for a second time Arthur was appointed captain of Kent, leading them to a 2-0 win over Surrey at Barnes. Next, he enjoyed his first games for Wanderers for a year, scoring seven goals in three matches: two against Westminster, a treble as Upton Park were routed 8-0 and 'AF Kinnaird, by his brilliant runs, well merited the frequent applause he elicited from a large concourse of spectators,' then two more at Charterhouse; all of which made him the club's top scorer for the season. He also experienced Charterhouse School's arcane cloisters football, which was played in a brick-covered passage, using the northern and southern doors (which were at right-angles) as goals[45]; Arthur's team owed their 4-0 defeat 'to their ignorance of the specialities of the Cloisters game than to any inferiority in play'.

Always eager to take up any opportunity for sport, he enjoyed a weekend in Hayes by entering nearby Beckenham Cricket Club's annual sports and won the 100 yards sprint, also coming second in events as diverse as the high jump, hurdles and quarter

40

mile.[46] Beckenham was to become a summer ritual for many years to come.

Despite having graduated the previous year, Arthur was still eligible to represent Cambridge at tennis and in June 1869 he won a second blue against Oxford. He repeated his singles victory with a straight sets whitewash of Cecil Clay, an old Harrovian who was described as 'completely overmatched'[47], while in the doubles, partnered again by AJ Balfour, they went down to Clay and Goschen. This brought down the final curtain on his student days.

---

[1] Arthur had actually secured his place at Trinity the previous summer, being admitted on 11 June 1864 as a pensioner, ie a fee-paying student. However, being only 17 he chose to stay on at Eton for another two terms. Cambridge University at that time had only around two thousand students, about a quarter of them at Trinity, which was the preferred destination for many Etonians.

[2] Their principal target was the Atlantic and Great Western Railway.

[3] They spent the morning sightseeing at the war crimes trial of Captain Henry Wirz, who was charged with mistreating Union soldiers in a prisoner-of-war camp.

[4] *New York Times*, 8 September 1865

[5] *New York Herald*, 12 September 1865; and subsequent reports.

[6] *New York Times*, 28 April 1866

[7] *Morning Post*, 14 June 1867

[8] The other choices were theology, moral science, natural science or mechanism and applied science.

[9] *The Standard*, 18 June 1868

[10] Its first meeting was at Trinity College in the spring of 1866.

[11] Blanche Dugdale, *Arthur James Balfour*, p26

[12] See CW Alcock, *Football, The Association Game*, p76, for a description of playing styles.

[13] Charterhouse v Civil Service, 30 January 1867

[14] *Scores and Annals of the West Kent Cricket Club*, p211

[15] Match reports quoted here, unless stated, come from these cuttings books.

[16] Arthur played for various Eton-based football teams at Cambridge: Eton Football Club refers to the Old Etonian team at Cambridge University; Old Etonians refers to teams of former pupils from a wider source; Eton College refers to the school team, with current pupils sometimes bolstered by members of staff; scratch teams, such as Mr Kinnaird's XI or Lord Fitzmaurice's XI, were mainly Etonian but might also include guests.

[17] Battersea Park in London is a likely candidate.

[18] *Eton College Chronicle*, 4 June 1866

[19] *Bell's Life*, 18 August 1866

[20] The match, on 6 October 1866, ended in an innings defeat but Arthur was his side's top scorer with 19 and 14, and took three wickets.

[21] *The Times*, 3 December 1866

[22] *Bell's Life*, 15 June 1867

[23] *Penny Illustrated Paper,* 13 July 1867

[24] *Bell's Life*, 25 May 1867

[25] On 23 February 1867, as well as winning the hurdles, he came second in a 2 mile walking race, third in the 440 yards handicap, and ran in the mile and 100 yards sprint.

[26] *Illustrated London News*, 4 May 1867

[27] *Morning Post*, 30 April 1867

[28] John MacGregor, *The Voyage Alone in the Yawl 'Rob Roy'*

[29] AJ Balfour, *Chapters of Autobiography*, p42

[30] AJ Balfour, *Chapters of Autobiography*, p49

[31] Emily Kinnaird, *My Adopted Country*, p110

[32] Probably Charles Alcock himself.

[33] RG Graham, *The Early History of the Football Association*, Badminton Magazine, January 1899, p75-87

[34] The youngest recruit was WJ Dixon, only 19. The others were Lord Edmond Fitzmaurice (21), GG Kennedy (23), KA Muir Mackenzie (22) and James Kirkpatrick (26).

[35] Alcock was speaking at an MCC dinner; quoted in Keith Booth, *The Father of Modern Sport*, p118

[36] *Morning Post*, 30 March 1868

[37] Arthur was elected a member of the MCC in May 1868 (as was AJ Balfour).

[38] RD Balfour, a cricket blue, had in fact left Cambridge in 1866.

[39] See *Bell's Life*, 6 June 1868, which reports on the qualification matches; there is further confirmation by Lady Monkswell in ECF Collier, *A Victorian Diarist*, p114

[40] AJ Balfour, *Chapters of Autobiography*, p36-7

[41] *The Standard,* 2 June 1868

[42] *Bury and Norwich Post*, 23 June 1868. This corrects the mistaken date of 1869 which is given in the *Alumni Cantabrigienses*.

[43] Clapham Cricket Club's football eleven.

[44] West Kent FC was an offshoot of the cricket club of the same name, and their home games were played in the outfield of their Chislehurst ground.

[45] The cloisters game at Charterhouse came to a natural end when the school moved to Godalming in 1872.

[46] *The Field*, 12 June 1869

[47] *The Field*, 26 June 1869

CHAPTER 3

The birth of international football
1869-71

WHEN A 17-YEAR-OLD schoolboy called Robert Crawford gave Scotland the lead against England in March 1870, he was cheered by just a few hundred people at Kennington Oval. It was the start of something big: a century and a half later, Andrés Iniesta's goal for Spain that won the biggest prize in international football, the World Cup, was seen by a worldwide audience of almost a billion.

The first England v Scotland match, which Arthur played a lead role in organising, was an event of fundamental importance to the growth of football even though, at the time, it was considered little more than a novelty. The concept quickly captured the public imagination and provided the spark that would take the game far beyond its London heartland.

The international was just one of 27 matches Arthur played in the 1869-70 season. He had taken advantage of living in the centre of London to devote considerably more time to his unbridled enthusiasm for the game, and was helped by the prevailing attitude that it was possible to be a member of several clubs, and indeed to play for clubs of which one was not a member. Arthur was never short of invitations so, while around half his games were for Wanderers, he also played against them on a regular basis and featured for many different clubs. In fact, his first five matches under association rules that autumn were for Old Etonians, Wanderers (twice), West Kent and Gitanos.

His opening game of the season, on 23 October, was significant as he played at the Oval for the first time. The outfield of the Surrey cricket headquarters had only recently been made available for football, and with such luxuries as changing rooms for the players it quickly became established as the principal football venue in the capital. Arthur graced the Oval on many occasions in the years to come, and his debut was a successful one as he captained a nine-man Old Etonian team to a 2-0 victory over Wanderers, scoring the opening goal after an hour's play. At the same place three weeks later, the weather – so often a feature of match reports – was a decisive factor as Arthur's West Kent team benefitted from perhaps the first recorded own goal: 'one of the Civil Service backs, in attempting to save his lines, had his kick so frustrated by the wind that the ball was driven back into the goal, West Kent consequently scoring a goal by this accident.' The elements also dominated as Wanderers defeated the schoolboys of Westminster in a fog 'sufficiently dense to render the ball invisible at a distance of twenty paces'; it didn't stop Arthur scoring the only goal of the game.

Although he settled, more or less, on Wanderers as his club of choice, among the other outfits he appeared for was Crusaders, who defeated Civil Service despite having only seven men; curiously he was described as a Crusaders player in the first international, even though this was the only game he ever played for them. He captained Wanderers against Harrow Pilgrims, securing victory thanks to another own goal: 'the first rush carried it [the ball] up to the Harrow goal, into which after a short scrimmage it was driven by an unfortunate kick on the part of one of the defending side.' However, having beaten the Harrow old boys, Wanderers lost against the present schoolboys thanks to a rule which the match reporter attributed to 'a free indulgence in the objectionable system of catching, to which we have frequently called attention as the chief blot of the Harrow game.' Clearly, the Association rules still had some way to go before being universally accepted.

Early in the new year, the football talk in London had turned excitedly to just one subject, the international. Previously, the highlight of each season had been county matches involving Kent, Surrey and Middlesex, but the idea of an England v Scotland contest was mooted to broaden the FA's horizons. No-one has ever claimed personal credit for coming up with the idea, but there were already internationals in cricket[1] and shooting[2], and the football version was likely to have been prompted by the Scottish background of almost half the FA committee: alongside Arthur were James Kirkpatrick, Kenneth Muir Mackenzie and Gilbert Kennedy, all of whom would go on to represent Scotland in the unofficial

44

internationals, while Robert Willis, who had served as FA secretary, had a Scottish father. As the committee members had been recruited specifically to come up with ideas to expand the game's horizons, what better than an appeal to national pride? The contests would generate a greater nationalistic fervour than the Victorians could ever have imagined, although initial opinions were mixed: while the *Sporting Gazette* called it 'by far the most important match of the season'[3], *Bell's Life* dismissed it as 'merely a meeting of certain members of the clubs who play Association rules'[4].

The build-up began when newly-elected FA secretary Alcock published a letter in *The Sportsman*, which gave prominent coverage to football and, conveniently, counted him among its staff: 'A match between the leading representatives of the Scotch and English sections will be played at The Oval on Saturday 19 February, under the auspices of the Football Association. Players duly qualified and desirous of assisting either party must communicate with Mr AF Kinnaird of 2 Pall Mall East, SW or Mr J Kirkpatrick, Admiralty, Somerset House, WC on behalf of the Scotch, or with Mr Charles W Alcock, Boy Court, Ludgate Hill, EC or Mr RG Graham, 7 Finch Lane, EC on the part of the English.'[5]

Although the invitation was hidden in the middle of a page, there was a flurry of responses from potential 'Scotch' players for Arthur and Kirkpatrick to consider. Footballers were drawn from a small circle of public schools, military officers, civil servants and city professionals, so most were already well known to them, but it would not have been easy to find eleven Scots in London who were up to the task. Indeed, almost immediately there were claims that some players' Scottish links were tenuous, selected because they had a 'Mac' in their name, been shooting in the Highlands, or a fondness for whisky. Even Alcock, who should have known better, later called it a 'counterfeit' and added: 'At the outset it was a poor imitation of the genuine article, as the Scotchmen were in some cases merely Scotch residents in London, while a few had no better qualification than Scotch extraction – some even hardly had this claim.'[6] However, close inspection of the first Scotland team, most of whose origins have never before been published, challenges these impressions. Although only Kenneth Muir Mackenzie was of Scots birth, four had parents born in Scotland, and five had Scottish grandparents: therefore they would all – with the possible exception of Alexander Morten, a last minute replacement – have qualified for

45

Scotland under modern regulations, which allow for eligibility based on birth back to grandparent level.

The Scotland players who faced England, and their Scottish roots

James Kirkpatrick. Born 22 March 1841 in Toronto, Canada, died 10 November 1899 in Forest Hill, Kent. Both his parents were born in Dumfriesshire.

Arthur Fitzgerald Kinnaird. Born 16 February 1847 in London, died 30 January 1923 in London. His father was born in Perthshire.

William Henry Gladstone. Born 3 June 1840 in Hawarden Castle, Wales, died 4 July 1891 in London. His father's parents were born in Leith and Dingwall.

Robert Erskine Wade Crawford[7]. Born 5 September 1852 in Elizabeth Castle, Jersey, died 23 May 1894 in Hendon, Middlesex. His mother's parents were born in Fife.

William Alexander Baillie-Hamilton. Born 6 September 1844 in Brighton, died 6 July 1920 in London. Brother of Charles, below.

Charles Robert Baillie-Hamilton. Born 24 September 1848 in Greenwich, Kent, died 28 July 1927 in Eton. Their grandfather was born at Mellerstain, Berwickshire.

William Lindsay. Born 3 August 1847 at Benares, India, died 15 February 1923 in Rochester, Kent. His father was born in Dundee.

John Wingfield Malcolm. Born 16 April 1833 in London, died 6 March 1902 in Hyères, France. His father was born in Argyllshire.

Kenneth Augustus Muir Mackenzie. Born 26 June 1845 at Delvine, Perthshire, died 22 May 1930 in London.

George Croughly Gordon. Born 21 June 1850 in London, died 20 August 1899 in Cue, Western Australia. His grandfather was born in Banffshire.

Alexander Morten. Born 1831[8] in London, died 24 February 1900 in London. His heritage is unknown.

The match plans were upset as a severe frost in London made the Oval surface unplayable – even the Thames froze over – and the contest was put back two weeks to Saturday 5 March 1870. Although this represents the starting point of international football, the five England v Scotland matches over the succeeding two years have no official status and are generally regarded as 'pseudo-internationals' as they were restricted to London-based players. These games and the players who took part are ignored by the record books, with the first officially-recognised international taking place in Glasgow in November 1872.

Because of the postponement, the original Scotland selection had to be amended: Lord Kilmarnock was required for army duties, and his place was taken by George Gordon; then, when Robert Ferguson called off at the eleventh hour, Alexander Morten was asked to play in goal. The English drew their players from a solidly public school background, with four Harrovians, three Etonians and two from Westminster (including 16-year-old Walpole Vidal); they were joined by two young businessmen, Alexander Nash and Alfred Baker.

England: CW Alcock (Old Harrovians, captain), EE Bowen (Wanderers), AJ Baker (No Names), WC Butler (Barnes), WP Crake (Harrow School), E Freeth (Civil Service), E Lubbock (Old Etonians), A Nash (Clapham Rovers), JC Smith (Crusaders), AH Thornton (Old Harrovians), RWS Vidal (Westminster School).

Scotland: J Kirkpatrick (Civil Service, captain), AF Kinnaird (Crusaders), WH Gladstone MP (Old Etonians), REW Crawford (Harrow School), CRB Hamilton (Civil Service), WAB Hamilton (Old Harrovians), W Lindsay (Old Wykehamists), JW Malcolm MP (London Scottish Rifles), K Muir Mackenzie (Old Carthusians), GC Gordon (No Names), A Morten (Crystal Palace).

The footballing public was intrigued, 'the entire limit of the ground being lined by an enthusiastic array of the supporters of both sides,' and the unexpectedly large crowd was entertained by an exciting match whose outcome remained in doubt right up to the final minute. On ground that was slippery because of overnight rain, England had a breeze at their backs, but the teams were finely balanced and after 45 minutes there was no score. The elevens then changed ends, half-time in a scoreless match being an innovation to the rules which had only been introduced the previous month.

As England became more adventurous in search of a goal, Alcock made a disastrous tactical mistake by moving his goalkeeper

47

upfield to support the forwards. The ball broke to Scotland's youngest player, Robert Crawford, a Harrow schoolboy, who spotted the gaping hole in the English defence and his clever shot from distance (also described as 'a lucky long kick'[9]) found the empty goal, inducing wild celebrations: 'the partisans of the Scots being apparently almost overpowered with joy'[10]. There were just 15 minutes left for the England players to get back on level terms, and the Scots held firm against their desperate onslaught until the final minute when Baker, 'by one of the finest runs that have ever been witnessed,' dribbled his way through the Scots defence to shoot home the equaliser. Thus the world's first football international ended in a 1-1 draw. With honours even, and satisfaction that it had proved such a popular event, there was soon talk of a rematch and the FA announced in the summer that two more internationals would be organised in the succeeding season.

Arthur managed to fit in five more games before the end of the season, notably on 19 March, when his boundless enthusiasm saw him play twice for Wanderers on the same day. He started off against Charterhouse in a 1-1 draw, then hurried across town to the Oval, accompanied by Alfred Baker – no slouch himself, being the winner of the 100 yard sprint at the Amateur Athletic Championships that summer. By the time the pair arrived, Wanderers were already two goals up against Hampstead Heathens, but Arthur joined in for Wanderers and Baker for the Heathens.

There was a lengthy summer break without football and, with his commitments in the ragged school and at the bank, little opportunity for Arthur to indulge in sport. He did fit in one visit to the Oval, but it was more of a social outing as he scored a couple of runs for the Private Banks cricket side in their annual match against the Joint-Stock Banks.[11]

With much to look forward to in the new football campaign, particularly with two internationals scheduled, Arthur started the season with gusto, and by the time of the England v Scotland clash in November he had five games for Wanderers under his belt. Like any football player in those days, he had to contend with dreadful conditions, such as at Charterhouse, where the ground was 'in a condition utterly unfit for play, the centre of the ground being occupied by a circular patch of soft mud of no mean width, through which it was almost impossible to wade'; and against Brixton, where the match kicked off in a fog 'so intense that the goals were entirely invisible'.

Meanwhile, in response to criticisms that the first international had featured only Scots living in London, Alcock had written to newspapers north of the border: 'It is the object of the committee to select the best elevens at their disposal in the two countries, and I cannot but think that the appearance of some of the more prominent celebrities of football on the northern side of the Tweed would do much to disseminate a healthy feeling of good fellowship among the contestants.'[12] Most football in Scotland at that time was played under Rugby rules, but his appeal roused the interest of Queen's Park, virtually the only active association football club in the country. Daunted by the cost of sending players to London, they nominated club member Robert Smith, who had lately departed Glasgow and was now playing for South Norwood. He was joined in the side by Galfrid Congreve and Henry Primrose, also born in Scotland, but others had more tenuous connections. Quintin Hogg could claim to come from an ancient (although long departed) Scottish family, and Gilbert Kennedy was great grandson of the Earl of Cassillis, but Charles Nepean's closest link was a cousin who married a Scot (it did not stop him playing four times for Scotland). A last-minute replacement, William Bailey, had no Scottish credentials at all.

England's selectors, chaired by Alcock, retained five players and had a strong accent on youth among their new recruits, with four still at school: Thomas Carter (captain of the Eton field eleven), Walter Paton (captain of the Harrow eleven), Henry Preston (Eton) and Walpole Vidal (Westminster). The others were Robert Walker, who would later introduce football to Malaya, and John Cockerell, an athlete who once defeated WG Grace in a quarter mile race.[13] For the first time, umpires were appointed: Morton Peto Betts and Alexander Morten took on the role, and as each team supplied one umpire there is perhaps a clue that Morten did indeed have a Scottish heritage.

England: CW Alcock (Harrow Pilgrims, captain), AJ Baker (Wanderers), TN Carter (Eton College), J Cockerell (Brixton), WP Crake (Barnes), TC Hooman (Wanderers), E Lubbock (West Kent), WB Paton (Harrow), HE Preston (Eton College), RWS Vidal (Westminster), RSF Walker (Clapham Rovers).

49

Scotland: J Kirkpatrick (Civil Service, captain), AF Kinnaird (Old Etonians), REW Crawford (Harrow), HW Primrose (Civil Service), CEB Nepean (Oxford University), Q Hogg (Wanderers), W Lindsay (Old Wykehamists), GF Congreve (Old Rugbeian), R Smith (Queen's Park), W Bailey (Civil Service), GG Kennedy (Wanderers).

It was a fine day at the Oval on 19 November, with a crowd estimated at between six and seven hundred, and Nepean kicked off punctually at three o'clock. Fifteen minutes later, England scored what turned out to be the only goal of the game when Alcock dribbled towards the Scotland lines, and passed to Walker who had a simple task to kick the ball into the goal. After ends were changed, Scotland had more of the play: 'the Scotchmen, mainly by reason of some well-concerted play by AF Kinnaird and J Kirkpatrick, appeared likely to recover the goal they had lost although, owing to the remarkable strength of their adversaries in point of defence, each of their assaults met with a repulse.' Handicapped by an injury to Hogg, who was 'so lame as to render the least exertion painful', their attempts to equalise eventually ran out of steam, and in the closing minutes it was England who came closest to scoring, a shot from Alcock going just past the post.

In the Scottish press, the game was denounced as a sham, although Alcock was quick to respond: 'I assert that of whatever the Scotch eleven may have been composed the right to play was *open to every Scotchman* whether his lines were cast North or South of the Tweed and that if in the face of the invitations publicly given through the columns of leading journals of Scotland the representative eleven consisted chiefly of Anglo-Scotians ... the fault lies on the heads of the players of the north, not on the management who sought the services of all alike impartially. To call the team London Scotchmen contributes nothing. The match was, as announced, to all intents and purposes between England and Scotland.'[14] Later he wrote again, inviting candidates to contact Arthur or Quintin Hogg; interestingly, he points out that anyone wishing a souvenir of the November international could write in and purchase a photograph of the England eleven, taken by the London Stereoscopic Company, but regrettably no copies are known to have survived.[15]

With Rugby rules considerably more popular north of the border, one unintended consequence of this debate was that the code's Scottish followers were galvanised into challenging their English counterparts to stage a 'proper' international. Thus the first fully representative Scotland v England football match took place in Edinburgh under Rugby rules, in March 1871.

Arthur carried on with his energetic schedule and managed two games in a day at Eton, turned out for West Kent and Gitanos, and in December, the day after playing for nine-man Wanderers against Etonian Rovers in continuous rain, joined Alcock and Hogg in the first South v North match at the Oval. This game showed off football's growth by featuring a number of provincial players, with the teams based on 'place of origin'. A severe frost prevented him from playing over the next month, but once it lifted he continued to demonstrate his versatility: 'as usual conspicuous for his energy' for West Kent (against Wanderers), he helped Eton Club to win at Charterhouse, 'rendered efficient aid from first to last' as AJ Baker's Eleven beat Westminster, was 'untiring both forwards and back' with Gitanos, then victorious with Wanderers against Hampstead Heathens and Westminster. In the last of these Arthur had to retire halfway through, but was not badly injured and two days later, on 25 February 1871, he was fit enough to play for Scotland against England.

Exactly who played for Scotland in the third international is open to question, as team lines vary from newspaper to newspaper, and the match reports only agree on nine of them. Kirkpatrick, Gladstone, Hogg, Kinnaird, Smith, Lindsay and Nepean all returned, while newcomers included John Inglis, a Charterhouse schoolboy who came from a Scots-Canadian family which had left these shores many generations previously, and Arnold Kirke Smith, a future England international *against* Scotland, who had a Scottish grandfather.

Of the other two, most newspapers list CE Primrose (Civil Service) as a late replacement for William Baillie-Hamilton; allowing for a misprint of his first initial, it was Scots-born Gilbert Edward Primrose, whose brother Henry had already played for Scotland. The identity of the final player was shrouded in mystery: Robert Crawford dropped out and was reportedly replaced by F McLean of University College, Oxford. However, there was no McLean at Oxford at that time, and his name is in inverted commas in *The Sportsman*, indicating an alias. *The Times* and Alcock's *Football Annual* list F Chappell in the line-up, a strong hint that McLean was a pseudonym for Frederick Chappell[16], another future England international (indeed, F McLean later crops up in a possible England team in November 1872, a match for which Chappell was selected).

England, for their part, made three changes, with William Butler returning to the side, and two newcomers, 17-year-old Charles Stephenson and Arthur's Harrovian friend Morton Betts.

England: E Lubbock (West Kent), CW Stephenson (Westminster), J Cockerell (Brixton), MP Betts (West Kent), CW Alcock (Harrow Pilgrims), AJ Baker (Wanderers), WC Butler (Civil Service), WP Crake (Barnes), TC Hooman (Wanderers), RWS Vidal (Westminster), RSF Walker (Clapham Rovers).

Scotland: J Kirkpatrick (Civil Service), WH Gladstone MP (Old Etonians), Q Hogg (Wanderers), AF Kinnaird (Wanderers), JF Inglis (Charterhouse), W Lindsay (Old Wykehamist), AK Smith (University College, Oxford), CEB Nepean (University College, Oxford), R Smith (Queen's Park), GE Primrose (Civil Service), 'F McLean' (University College, Oxford).

The match was, as usual, played at the Oval, in front of around 600 spectators whose 'partisanship ran high'[17]. On a breezy day, Scotland made the early running and Nepean gave them the lead after quarter of an hour, having already had a good shot saved by Cockerell. The change of ends which followed the goal gave England the wind at their backs, but 'the faultless back play of Hogg and Gladstone prevented any direct triumph of the attacking party'. At length, England did equalise when Walker's shot crept just inside the post, but although they tried to build on their success it was to no avail, the game ending in a 1-1 draw.

Arthur's season wound up with a couple of games for Wanderers, who beat Forest Club 2-0 then drew with The World select. The football over, Arthur showed he was still a sporting all-rounder, winning two trophies at Wanderers' inaugural sports meeting at the Lillie Bridge ground, in the 120 yards hurdles and the 300 yards.[18] Then in June he played his annual match of cricket for the Private Banks[19], and although he appeared in the equivalent fixture the following summer, it was the last time he played cricket seriously until the late 1880s.

Always running: the busiest man in London

Not many international footballers hold down a high powered job in the city, and still find time to spend their nights teaching in the slums.

A place in the family bank, Ransom, Bouverie & Co, was waiting for Arthur when he left Cambridge, and within a few months he was appointed a partner.[20] His home in Pall Mall East was directly above the bank, helping him to maintain a tight schedule: 'Every morning at nine o'clock would see him running downstairs – he always ran – to the partners' room, where, with other members of the firm, he would interview and advise investors who came for guidance on how to get the most out of their money. His cheerful manner and pleasant address to strangers as well as friends made him a useful member of the firm. He learned from talking and delighted in the conversation of interesting people. They also found him an intelligent listener, but it was always with a practical purpose that he liked to gather information, as all his spare time was spent in what were called evangelistic meetings, or Sunday Boys' Classes.'[21]

It was a career path which would lead ultimately to a directorship of Barclays Bank, but in the meantime he had more pressing concerns. Each night he would head to the little ragged school, and his sister Emily wrote of Arthur's double life: 'His heart and soul interest was in social work and in 'his boys' who were working for their living under very different conditions. Every evening he was off with Quintin Hogg to hunt out slum boys, teach them in night schools, or visit similarly-minded young men in the East End. Only once a week would they return to the house to dine with the family.'[22] Constantly juggling his working life with his charity work, not to mention one or two football matches each week, indicates a kind of hyperactivity. As his sister said, 'he always ran'.

Inspired by evangelical mottos such as 'Saved to serve' and 'Ye are not your own', the trio of Arthur, Hogg and Pelham tried to make the boys' education as attractive as possible, their generosity extending to day trips to Southend, as an escape from the foul city air. They were proud of their work, which had already been a demonstrable success: 'In 1864 the boys were ragged, unkempt, ignorant, without even the desire to rise; in four years' time those same boys had become orderly, decent in dress and behaviour; had, in fact, climbed several rungs up the ladder of civilisation and were anxious to continue climbing.'[23]

The emphasis of their mission moved away from basic schooling towards life skills for older boys and girls after the introduction of the Elementary Education Act in 1870, which guaranteed that the state would provide a formal education for children under 12 (although Victorian priorities were such that this came two years after the Public Schools Act). There was, in any case, a natural hiatus when Hogg, who worked for a sugar importer, was called away on business to the West Indies in the autumn of 1869 and, on his return, founded the Youths' Christian Institute, devoted to the 'better class boys'.

Arthur, who worked with Pelham through that winter at their Castle Street Home, could never focus on a single cause like Hogg. He did not yet have the confidence to be a leader, in stark contrast to his usual role on the football field, and was much happier using his professional skills as a treasurer for anyone who needed him. As a steadfast believer in committee work he went on to serve a staggering variety of philanthropic interests, with one of the earliest of his many appointments as treasurer of the St Giles's Mission, which 'has raised very many from degradation and vice'[24]; that was to be a consistent theme.

This attraction to behind-the-scenes roles was much to the frustration of his mother, who wanted Arthur to go into politics and 'fit himself for the position into which he was born'[25] by taking an interest in affairs of state. Attempts were made by his Liberal MP father, flush with success after Gladstone's landslide election victory of 1868, to get Arthur involved. He encouraged him to write to the Prime Minister with suggestions for Irish church reform[26], and took him on a visit to his Perth constituency, but although Arthur sat dutifully on the stage while his father regaled a crowded City Hall with details of the work he was doing for his constituents[27], it was not a role he had any intention of fulfilling. He was so seldom home, his mother had few opportunities to take him to task. Nevertheless, domestic life could be exciting, with high profile guests including General Gordon, of Chinese and African military repute, and the

54

explorer Henry Stanley, feted in London for his discovery of Dr Livingstone.[28]

His parents were sufficiently enlightened to allow Arthur's elder sister Frieda to marry a doctor, Alfred Jones[29], rather than someone of aristocratic birth, which caused a minor scandal and meant there was no society wedding, and no marriage notice in *The Times*. Arthur's only other sister to marry, Agneta, took the more conventional route with a union to Roland Bevan, of another prominent evangelical banking family. A ceremony that probably meant more to Arthur was Hogg's wedding to Alice Graham, daughter of a Glasgow MP, on 16 May 1871. Arthur was best man, and the service was conducted by James Joynes, their former housemaster at Eton. While the Hoggs went off on a lengthy honeymoon in America, Arthur also had a complete change of scene.

Having established himself as one of the top players in association football, Arthur set sail for India that autumn to tour the Christian missions and hospitals which were supported by his mother. With the sea voyage alone taking eight weeks each way, he missed the entire 1871-72 football season, including the first FA Cup competition, which was won by his club, Wanderers. There were also two more unofficial internationals, both won by England.[30] When Arthur returned to action, he had lost none of his vigour and it would be a year of triumph as he not only captained his side to FA Cup success, he also finally pulled on the dark blue of Scotland in a full international.

---

[1] An annual cricket match between All England and 22 of Scotland was first played in Edinburgh in 1849.

[2] The Elcho Shield, between the best shots in the Volunteer movement, was first contested in 1862 between England and Scotland.

[3] *The Sporting Gazette*, 12 March 1870

[4] *Bell's Life*, 9 March 1870

[5] *The Sportsman*, 5 February 1870

[6] CW Alcock, *Association Football*, The English Illustrated Magazine, 1891, p285

[7] The family surname changed to Copland-Crawford in 1872.

[8] Morten's precise date of birth and the identity of his parents have yet to be ascertained.

[9] *Glasgow Herald*, 7 March 1870

[10] *The Sporting Gazette*, 12 March 1870

[11] *Morning Post*, 9 June 1870

[12] *Glasgow Herald*, 3 November 1870

[13] In the Blackheath Sports in 1866

[14] *The Scotsman*, 28 November 1870

[15] *The Herald*, 7 January 1871

[16] Frederick Chappell changed his name to Frederick Brunning Maddison in 1873.

[17] *The Sportsman*, 27 February 1871

[18] *Morning Post*, 10 April 1871

[19] *Morning Post*, 14 June 1871

[20] *London Gazette*, February 1870; his father was senior partner.

[21] Emily Kinnaird, *My Adopted Country*, p114

[22] Emily Kinnaird, *My Adopted Country*, p114

[23] Ethel Hogg, *Quintin Hogg a biography*, p56

[24] *The Times*, 31 December 1872

[25] Emily Kinnaird, *My Adopted Country*, p114

[26] Gladstone replied that there was 'considerable force' in Arthur's arguments; letter dated 15 January 1869, Kinnaird family archive.

[27] *Dundee Courier*, 3 September 1869

[28] Years later, Arthur helped to raise funds for Stanley on his 1887-89 mission to Africa to save Emin Bey, and was a member of the Emin Bey Relief Expedition committee.

[29] Jones was an early champion of homeopathy and included among his clients George, 9th Lord Kinnaird, who was a Vice-President of the London Homeopathic Hospital and president of the Dundee Homeopathic Dispensary.

[30] England won 2-1 on 18 November 1871 and 1-0 on 24 February 1872.

CHAPTER 4

'Without exception, the best player of the day'

1872-74

THE FIRST time Arthur Kinnaird played in an FA Cup tie it was the final, he was captain, he scored, and his side won. The same month, he was capped for Scotland. It was March 1873, the climax to a momentous season in which he was judged 'without exception, the best player of the day'.

Football was starting to gain a national following, especially after the feasibility of travelling four hundred miles to play football was established by the participation of Queen's Park in the first FA Cup competition.[1] This realisation also heralded the end of the unofficial internationals between England and Scotland, as the prospect of genuine international competition was now on the horizon.

After his winter in India, Arthur's reputation was undiminished, and having played a couple of games for Gitanos and Wanderers he was selected to represent London in Sheffield in the first major contest of the season. A regular series of inter-city matches had started in earnest while he was away, and had quickly grown sufficiently in stature to attract an 'immense assemblage' of 5,000 spectators to Bramall Lane. They saw the Londoners comprehensively beaten 4-1 after struggling to adapt to the Sheffield rules, in particular the interpretation of offside, which was said to be 'so diametrically opposed to the usages of the south as to be unpalatable to the southerners generally'[2].

Nonetheless, it was seen as a useful prelude to the first 'true' international, scheduled for the end of November. There was still no national organisation in Scotland – the Scottish FA was not established until the following spring – but the Queen's Park committee felt sufficiently confident, in their position as the pre-eminent club, to take up Charles Alcock's challenge on behalf of the nation and host the international in Glasgow. They also appointed themselves as selectors of the Scotland team, and in mid-October Archibald Rae, club secretary, issued this appeal: 'Will you allow me, through your columns, to invite Scotch players who may wish to take part in the match to send their names and addresses to me, either direct, or through their captain or secretary, no later than Monday the 21st inst, so as to afford time for co-operation and practice?'[3]

So many applicants put their names forward that Queen's Park tested them out at practice matches. In the first, particular praise was given to the rugby international Thomas Chalmers who was 'a capital goalkeeper, albeit the rules were new to him'. The game was spoiled by heavy rain, the ground being 'chiefly marsh and pond' while 'the quantity of mud carried off by the players at the end of the game was tremendous'.[4] A second trial was played but again, wet weather conspired against good football.

Even though Arthur did not participate in the trials, it is clear that he was under consideration to play for Scotland, as a list of 17 possible players was published: Thomas Chalmers (Glasgow Academicals), Robert Gardner (Queen's Park), William Cross (Merchistonians), Joseph Taylor (Queen's Park), Rev James Barclay (Dumfries), Robert Smith (South Norwood), Arthur Kinnaird (Old Etonians, and captain of London-Scotch international team), Lieutenant Henry Renny-Tailyour (Royal Engineers), James J Thomson (Queen's Park), James Weir (Queen's Park), David Wotherspoon (Queen's Park), William Ker (Granville), James Smith (South Norwood), William McKinnon (Queen's Park), Alex Rhind (Queen's Park), Robert Leckie (Queen's Park) and Archibald Rae (Queen's Park).[5]

However, voices within Queen's Park argued that, as the club was organising the match, the honour of representing Scotland should be restricted to club members. These dissenters won, and when the team was announced on 25 November there was no place for any of the outsiders who had featured in the 'possible' selection: Scotland's eleven players, reserves, referee and umpire were all Queen's Park members. As if to emphasise the point, the team would play in blue jerseys, white knickerbockers, and blue and white striped stockings, which just happened to be the Queen's Park colours of the time. The strip was adopted for the national team and has remained ever since.

The FA had chosen the England team at a committee meeting on 14 November, with Alcock as captain, deciding that they would wear 'white jerseys and the England arms embroidered on left breast, dark blue caps, and white flannel trousers or knickerbockers'. However, their plans were thrown into disarray two days later, when a friendly at the Oval between the old boys of Eton and Harrow got out of hand. Described in *The Graphic* as 'a friendly, but most vicious game of football'[6], it ended with Alcock so severely injured that he missed not just the international, but only played once more that season. For the record, the Etonians won 2-1.

This unfortunate clash may also have led to Arthur's notorious reputation of being fond of hacking, although the story did not appear until many years later in *Pastime*, a weekly sports journal edited by Nicholas Lane 'Pa' Jackson, founder of the Corinthians Football Club. In a biographical sketch of Arthur, by then President of the FA, Jackson wrote: 'The keen rivalry which at one time existed between the Old Etonians and Old Harrovians lent an additional zest to the matches between them, and in one of these Lord Kinnaird's energy was expended as much on the shins of his opponents as on the ball. This at length caused a protest from the captain of the Harrovians, who asked, 'Are we going to play the game, or are we going to have hacking?' 'Oh, let us have hacking!' was the noble reply.'[7] Jackson repeated the anecdote in his 1900 book *Association Football*[8], adding the detail that the opposing captain was Alcock; and embellished it further in his autobiography[9], in which Arthur's response was 'Well, Charlie, if you leave it to me, we will have hacking.'

The question is: was it a true story? As this was the only time Arthur led the Old Etonians against Old Harrovians with Alcock as opposing captain, it is reasonable to surmise that the tale is based on this game. However, it cannot have been all-out warfare as, despite the 'vicious' comment in *The Graphic*, other reports[10] talk of the high standard of football and do not mention injuries or foul play at all.

Hacking was, in fact, anathema to early exponents of the association game, and its outlawing was one of the principal factors which caused the Rugby men to withdraw from the Football Association in 1863, when Francis Campbell of Blackheath claimed that hacking was 'the true football game' and that doing away with it would remove all the courage and pluck of the game. Eton condemned hacking in its rules (as did Harrow) and after seven years of playing under association rules, it seems inconceivable that Arthur would have gone around kicking his opponents. Certainly, the game was robust and physical, and Arthur commented later in life that he and Alcock would not have lasted five minutes in the modern game, but that would have applied to most players of that era.

Arthur was determined, energetic and enthusiastic, but there is nothing in contemporary reports to indicate that he was thought of as an unfair or dirty player. On the contrary, James Catton, one of the great football reporters, wrote: 'He was fair, above board, and was prepared to receive all the knocks that came his way without a trace of resentment.'[11] One can only conclude that the 'hacking' remarks, if made, were spoken in jest, or that Jackson's story was apocryphal. Unfortunately, as soon as his little story was published in 1892, Arthur's reputation was sealed.

Significantly, Alcock himself never accused Arthur of hacking in his many books about football. The *Football Annual* for 1873, which he edited, simply reported: 'We regret to have to add that a severe injury, sustained in this match, has incapacitated the Harrow Captain from any further active service in the football field.' It was certainly painful, as a year later he wrote that he was 'still smarting under the sore of a wound that has perforce kept me from active football'.[12] If Alcock felt any annoyance with his friend, it must quickly have evaporated, as Arthur was appointed Wanderers captain in his place for the FA Cup Final.

Undaunted by his injury, Alcock did make the trip to Glasgow to act as England's umpire, for what is now recognised as the world's first international match. It was a great success, attracting almost 4,000 spectators to the West of Scotland Cricket Ground, generating a profit of £33 and 8 shillings, which Queen's Park set aside as an international fund for the return later in the season. Arthur was not even invited to travel north; instead, he spent the day with a depleted Wanderers side which went down 2-0 to the Royal Engineers at the Oval.

Despite appalling winter weather, many more matches followed: twice he was picked for Middlesex against Surrey at the Oval, scoring in 'a perfect quagmire' in December's 4-2 defeat, and claimed the opening goal in February's 3-1 win. He also featured for London in January's return against Sheffield, which finished 1-0 thanks to Charles Chenery's late goal, a victory for stamina as it rained with a vengeance and the field was 'one vast expanse of adhesive mud'. It raises the question as to what condition a pitch had to reach before it was finally judged unplayable.

Arthur captained Old Etonians when they met Old Harrovians again at the Oval, showing there were no hard feelings from the 'hacking' match in November, but rubbed salt in the wound with another victory. Alcock was back on the sidelines, having broken down in his attempted comeback for Surrey; in his place, Betts was the Harrovian captain, his last game before he left for South America to work for the next three years.

And so to the greatest month in Arthur's football career, in which he won his only full cap for Scotland, captained Wanderers to FA Cup success and, for good measure, went on tour with the London select.

The England v Scotland return was fixed for Kennington Oval on 8 March, and although this was still a week short of the formation of the Scottish FA, it is considered number two in the official series. This time the English took the opportunity to hold a couple of trials to assess the available talent; these also gave Arthur an opportunity to size up the opposition, as he played in one of them, his Wanderers side defeating a 'Candidates' selection 3-1. The outcome of the trials was a complete overhaul of the England side, as only three survivors from Glasgow took the field against the Scots.

Queen's Park again organised the Scotland team, with power of selection granted to the club captain, Robert Gardner, but there was only enough money in their international kitty to pay for seven players and an umpire to travel to London at £4 a head; Robert Smith of South Norwood (still a Queen's Park member) also retained his place. They were supplemented by Arthur and two other London-based players, Henry Renny-Tailyour and John Blackburn of Royal Engineers. Both sides were photographed, but only the grainy image of the Scotland team survives, showing Arthur in the front row with beard, cap and knee-length trousers (contrary to the common conception that he always wore long white flannels). Having lined up in Glasgow with eight forwards, one half-back, one back and a goalkeeper, the English adopted the more

61

pragmatic Scottish formation of six forwards, two half-backs and two backs.

FOOTBALL ASSOCIATION.

ENGLAND *v.* SCOTLAND.

PLAYED AT KENNINGTON OVAL,
ON SATURDAY, MARCH 8, 1873.

ENGLAND WON BY FOUR GOALS TO TWO.

THE ENGLISH ELEVEN WEAR WHITE JERSEYS WITH ENGLISH ARMS IN BLACK
ON THE LEFT BREAST.

ENGLAND.

A. MORTEN (*Crystal Palace*), CAPT.	Black cap and brown stockings.
*A. G. BONSOR (*Wanderers*)	Light blue and red cap.
*C. J. CHENERY (*Crystal Palace*) ...	Blue & bk. cap, blue knickerbockers, blue stockings
W. E. CLEGG (*Sheffield*)	Blue cap.
A. G. GOODWYN (*Royal Engineers*)	Yellow blue and black stockings and cap.
E. H. GREENHALGH (*Nottingham*)	Red white and blue cap.
HUBERT HERON (*Uxbridge*)	Blue stockings, blue cap with yellow cross.
L. S. HOWELL (*Old Wykehamists*)...	Cerise cap.
**W. S. KENYON SLANEY (*House-hold Brigade*)	Red gold and black cap.
R. W. S. VIDAL (*Oxford University*)	White knickerbockers, dark stockings.
P. G. VON DONOP (*Royal Engineers*)	Red and blue stockings and cap.

UMPIRE—C. W. ALCOCK (*Wanderers*), Hon. Sec. of Football Association.

SCOTLAND.

THE SCOTTISH ELEVEN WEAR BLUE JERSEYS WITH SCOTTISH LION IN WHITE
ON THE LEFT BREAST.

R. GARDNER (*Queen's Park, Glasgow*) CAPT.	Light blue cap.
G. BLACKBURN (*Royal Engineers*) ...	Scarlet and blue fez.
W. GIBB (*Clydesdale Club*)	Black cap with magenta stripes.
*W. KER (*Queen's Park, Glasgow*) ...	No cap.
A. F. KINNAIRD (*Wanderers*) ...	Blue and white cap.
W. McKINNON (*Queen's Park, Glasgow*)	Blue and scarlet cowl.
*H. W. RENNY TAILYOUR (*Royal Engineers*)	Blue and black cap, yellow tassel
R. SMITH (*South Norwood Club*) ...	Black cap.
J. TAYLOR (*Queen's Park, Glasgow*)	White cap blue stars.
J. J. THOMSON „ „ ...	Blue with white stars.
D. WOTHERSPOON „ „ ...	Scarlet cowl.

UMPIRE—A. RAE, Hon. Sec. of the Scottish Association.
REFEREE—T. LLOYD, Crystal Palace Club.)
* Those marked thus got goals.

MERSER & GARDNER, Machine Printers, 270, Kennington Road, S.E.

One of the oldest match cards in existence, for England v Scotland in 1873. Overprinted with the scorers, it belongs to a descendant of Alexander Morten

Upwards of 3,000 spectators were attracted to the Oval, producing receipts of £106 and one shilling.[13] Ground hire was £10, over £15 was spent on lunch and dinner for the Scots and after other expenditure was taken into account the FA was left with a handsome profit of £73 8s 6d.[14] A marquee was provided for ladies, who were admitted free, and a match card helped the spectators to identify the players by their headgear and stockings.

England

Alexander Morten (Crystal Palace, captain), black cap and brown stockings

Alexander George Bonsor (Wanderers), light blue and red cap

Charles John Chenery (Crystal Palace), blue and black cap, blue knickerbockers, blue stockings

William Clegg (Sheffield), blue cap

Alfred Goodwyn (Royal Engineers), yellow blue and black stockings and cap

Ernest Harwood Greenhalgh (Nottingham), red white and blue cap

Hubert Heron (Uxbridge), blue stockings, blue cap with yellow crest

Leonard Sidgwick Howell (Old Wykehamists), cerise cap

Captain William Slaney Kenyon-Slaney (Household Brigade), red gold and black cap

Robert Walpole Vidal (Oxford University), white knickerbockers, dark stockings

Pelham George von Donop (Royal Engineers), red and blue stockings and cap.

Scotland

Robert Gardner (Queen's Park, captain), light blue cap

John Edward Blackburn (Royal Engineers), scarlet and blue fez

William Gibb (Clydesdale), black cap with magenta stripes

William Ker (Queen's Park), no cap

Arthur Fitzgerald Kinnaird (Wanderers), blue and white cap

William McKinnon (Queen's Park), blue and scarlet cowl

Henry Waugh Renny-Tailyour (Royal Engineers), blue and black cap, yellow tassel

Robert Smith (South Norwood), black cap

Joseph Taylor (Queen's Park), white cap blue stars

James John Thomson (Queen's Park), blue with white stars

David Wotherspoon (Queen's Park), scarlet cowl.

Referee: Theodore Lloyd (Crystal Palace)
Umpires: Charles Alcock (England) and Archibald Rae (Scotland)

The Scotland team which faced England in 1873: (back) Gibb, Smith, Renny-Tailyour, Thomson, Ker, McKinnon; (front) Wotherspoon, Blackburn, Gardner (captain), Kinnaird and Taylor.

Scotland won the toss, Howell kicked off into a stiff breeze, and the game roared into action with four goals in the opening twenty minutes, the sides changing ends each time. First, the English took the initiative by racing to a two goal lead, thanks to Captain Kenyon-Slaney's shot in the second minute, then Bonsor's free kick which was deflected past the visiting goalkeeper. It raised fears that Scotland were going to be outclassed but they rallied and had drawn level by the time twenty minutes were on the clock. Renny-Tailyour scored to finish off a brilliant dribble by Arthur, then Gibb got the equaliser by shooting home from behind a scrimmage.

Having regained the momentum, Scotland faltered and England were able to dominate play for much of the rest of the match. There was no half-time break – that only applied if no goals were scored – and the home side deservedly went ahead after about an hour as Kenyon-Slaney again scored with a left-foot shot. Gardner kept the English at bay with a succession of fine saves but could do nothing to prevent Chenery from making it four. Defeat was a blow for Scots morale at the time, but if the English felt that this victory proved the superiority of the southern game, their confidence was misplaced: England would win only once against their oldest rivals in the next 15 years.[15]

As for Arthur, he would not have realised it at the time, but this proved to be his only international. The Scottish FA adopted a policy of selecting only players with Scottish clubs, and not until his career was over, in 1896, did they next pick another 'Anglo'. In the meantime, he did win many other representative honours and just the following weekend, captained the London team on a short Easter tour to Sheffield and Nottingham, travelling north on the Friday evening to be fully prepared.

The game at Bramall Lane was played one half each under Sheffield and London rules, in front of double the crowd for the international the previous Saturday, who each paid sixpence admission (ladies free). London went down to a narrow defeat, as Clegg put the home side ahead after 20 minutes, Chenery equalised midway through the second half, then Albert Thompson had the misfortune of slicing a kick into his own goal for the winner; Arthur nearly equalised but his shot hit the bar just before the end. On Easter Monday the Londoners met the Notts Club[16] at Trent Bridge and drew 0-0. London were a man short for the first half, and as Notts had the better of the few chances it was a busy time in defence for Arthur, who 'especially distinguished himself by some truly fine play'.

That left Wanderers less than two weeks to prepare for the FA Cup Final, which was played at Lillie Bridge. It was their first and only competitive match of the season as the FA Cup was originally deemed to be a challenge competition, so they had received a bye into the final to meet the 'best of the rest', while their opponents, Oxford University, had negotiated four ties but no semi-final because Queen's Park withdrew rather than travel south.[17] With Alcock still injured, Arthur was asked to captain the eleven, but there was no special preparation, not even a warm-up match: when Wanderers team faced Upton Park on the Saturday before the final, just nine players turned up and, of those, only Charles Wollaston was in the cup final team. There were actually three Wanderers – Arthur, Charles Thompson and Alex Bonsor – in a Gitanos side that lost 1-0 to Royal Engineers at Chatham on the Thursday afternoon, just two days before the final.

Wanderers
Goal: Reginald Welch
Back: Leonard Howell

65

Half-backs: Edward Bowen, Charles Thompson[18]
Forwards: Arthur Kinnaird (captain), Charles Wollaston, Robert Kingsford, Alexander Bonsor, William Kenyon-Slaney, Julian Sturgis, Rev Henry Stewart.

Oxford University
Goal: Andrew Leach
Back: Charles Mackarness
Half-back: Francis Birley
Forwards: Arnold Kirke Smith (captain), Charles Longman, Walpole Vidal, Frederick Maddison[19], Harold Dixon, Walter Paton, John Sumner, Cuthbert Ottaway.

Referee: Alfred Stair (FA honorary secretary)
Umpires: John Dasent (Gitanos) and John Clark (Maidenhead)

The cup final had a morning start, to avoid a clash with the afternoon's Boat Race between Oxford and Cambridge. It was no surprise that the student footballers wanted to witness the action on the Thames, but it turned out to be a depressing day for the dark blues as Wanderers retained the cup, and Cambridge won the Boat Race by three lengths. Arthur, playing in his first FA Cup tie at the age of 26, confidently led the Wanderers to victory, and even scored the opening goal. He was at the peak of his game, with his skill and speed turning the match in his team's favour.

Oxford actually made the stronger start, pressing their opponents hard in the early stages, but were caught by a breakaway, as Arthur surged out of defence with the ball at his feet: 'Gradually the Wanderers aroused and almost half an hour had passed when AF Kinnaird took advantage of a favourable opportunity, and by a splendid run outpacing the opposite backs, he placed a very well obtained goal to the credit of the Wanderers, to the intense delight of their eleven. Ends were changed.'[20] He was soon on the move again: 'Kinnaird made another fine run but Maddison just caught him in time, sending him a regular purler.'[21]

Wanderers could not add to their narrow advantage and the game remained in the balance until the last ten minutes, with both sides having goals disallowed. Then Oxford's star man Ottaway had to leave the field injured and as his colleagues tried desperately to get back on level terms they moved Leach, their goalkeeper, into attack. The plan backfired as Wollaston broke away to score Wanderers' second 'entirely owing to the absence of the man between the posts'[22]. Although Ottaway limped on for the final stages, there was no way back for Oxford, who were criticised for being determined to walk the ball into the net rather than shooting from distance.

Among Arthur's admirers in the 2-0 victory was the reporter from *Sporting Life*, who wrote 'the success of the Wanderers was in a great measure due to the extremely brilliant play of their captain forward'. That summer, his abilities were further praised by Alcock's *Football Annual* in the highest possible terms: 'Without exception the best player of the day; capable of taking any place in the field; is very fast and never loses sight of the ball. An excellent captain.'[23]

Football in 1874, from Charles Alcock's *Football: the Winter Game*

It is worth considering, at this point, why Arthur was so highly rated, as he did not have a natural athlete's physique: he was stocky and muscular, at around 5 feet 6 inches[24] and weighed 11 stones 9 pounds.[25] However, he was blessed with a boundless energy which suited him to the physical demands of football, and once said: 'I can never understand players who complain of playing an extra match in midweek. Why, I think nothing of playing three hard games within one week, and even then expect to take a little exercise – to keep myself fit.'

Arthur's versatility stood him in good stead, playing with equal facility in goal or in attack – sometimes both in the same match – although he seems to have developed a preference for a half-back role. He could also run at great speed, first demonstrated by his athletic successes at school and university, and NL Jackson referred to his 'extraordinary quickness', adding that 'Kinnaird's feet always moved twice as fast as any other man's in a scrimmage'.[26]

Having such an engine and a powerful physique were essential at a time when charging was an integral part of the game, and Arthur certainly held nothing back. This was confirmed by William Pickford, a later FA President who knew Arthur well: 'The honest heavy charging of the early days – the harder the better – in which such old players as Kinnaird and others rejoiced, gradually lost favour.'[27] Or, as CB Fry, another great sporting all-rounder, put it: 'The cheerful ruthlessness of football as played by Lord Kinnaird and Charlie Alcock and their contemporaries was soon legislated out of the game when professionalism swept over the world of Association football. Accidents and injuries became too expensive.'[28]

Like all great personalities, Arthur certainly stood out, instantly recognisable by his bushy red beard. According to James Catton: 'There was a time when the white ducks of Kinnaird, for he always wore trousers in a match, and his blue and white quartered cap were as familiar on the field as the giant figure of WG Grace with his yellow and red cricket cap.'[29]

Unfortunately, Arthur was unable to don his blue and white cap again until January 1874, having been laid low by serious illness.[30] In his absence, Old Etonians had entered the FA Cup for the first time, but scratched from the competition without kicking a ball. He was still recuperating when he played in goal for Wanderers against Harrow Chequers at the Oval; the match report commented: 'We were pleased to see AF Kinnaird, though not yet able to reach beyond the light duties of goalkeeper, once more in the football field, after a severe illness.' At the end of the month, he travelled with Wanderers to Oxford for a cup replay[31], again in goal, and was unable to prevent his club's first ever competitive defeat. The students went on to win the trophy, beating Royal Engineers in the final, while Arthur played no more games that season.

He had recovered fully by the autumn of 1874, and was back to full fitness with a revitalised Etonian eleven that would go all the way to the FA Cup final.

---

[1] Queen's Park had played Wanderers in the FA Cup semi-final, drawing 0-0; however, they could not afford to return to London for a replay, and scratched from the competition.

[2] *Penny Illustrated Paper*, 9 November 1872

[3] *Glasgow Herald*, 15 October 1872

[4] *Glasgow Herald*, 11 November 1872

[5] *Glasgow Herald*, 19 November 1872

[6] *The Graphic*, 23 November 1872

[7] *Pastime*, October 1892

[8] NL Jackson, *Association Football*, p147

[9] NL Jackson, *Sporting Days and Sporting Ways*, p54

[10] eg *Morning Post*, 18 November 1872; *Bell's Life* 23 November 1872

[11] JAH Catton, *Wickets and Goals*, p246

[12] CW Alcock, *Football: Our Winter Game*, p94. Alcock must have rued the Eton-Harrow rivalry, as he ricked his back in the 1874 old boys match, keeping him out of the following week's England v Scotland match.

[13] The exact attendance was 2,934, according to William Pickford, *A Few Recollections of Sport*, p160; the gate receipts equate to 2,121 paid admissions at a shilling each.

[14] Sir Frederick Wall, *Fifty Years of Football*, p78

[15] In 1879, England beat Scotland 5-4; their next victory was in 1888 in Glasgow.

[16] Now known as Notts County

[17] Queen's Park had suggested an arrangement whereby they would play Oxford on the Monday after the international, and (if they won) remain in London for the final against Wanderers on the Saturday. It was turned down by the other clubs.

[18] Charles Thompson and his brother Albert changed their surname to Meysey-Thompson in 1874.

[19] Frederick Brunning Maddison was previously known as Frederick Chappell, having changed his name the previous month, February 1873

[20] *The Sportsman*, 1 April 1873

[21] *Daily News*, 31 March 1873

[22] *The Sportsman*, 1 April 1873

[23] *Football Annual*, 1873

[24] According to Lady Monkswell in ECF Collier, *A Victorian Diarist*, p114

[25] Match card, Wanderers v Vale of Leven, 13 April 1878

[26] NL Jackson, *Association Football*, p147

[27] William Pickford, *A Few Recollections of Sport*, p88

[28] CB Fry, *Life Worth Living*, p265

[29] JAH Catton, *Wickets and Goals*, p245; however, in two known football photographs of Arthur, he appears in shorts in one of them, long trousers in the other.

[30] The nature of his illness has not been recorded.

[31] They had drawn 1-1 in December.

CHAPTER 5

'Truly ye've got a most tremendous licking!'

1874-78

CUP FINAL day was just not the same without Arthur. He was the FA Cup specialist *par excellence* and won it five times, playing in nine of the first twelve finals. Even after 140 years of the competition, he still holds the outright record for the most cup final appearances, two ahead his nearest challengers.[1]

Even his tally of five victories stood for well over a hundred years. Although equalled by two near-contemporary players, Charles Wollaston of Wanderers (1872-78) and James Forrest of Blackburn Rovers (1884-91), it was not broken until Ashley Cole lifted his sixth FA Cup in 2010, having won three each with Arsenal and Chelsea.

Captivated from the start by the spirit of the competition, Arthur appreciated the potential of entering an Old Etonian eleven, and put together a team of Eton's finest for the first time in 1874. Among the recruits were several who had also previously won the cup with Wanderers, such as Alexander Bonsor, Albert Meysey-Thompson, and William Kenyon-Slaney. Strictly speaking, this was not a bona fide entry, as the Old Etonian Football Club was yet to become a member of the FA and was not formally established until 1878, but under the looser rules of the day there was nothing to prevent them entering.

Arthur played in all seven matches of their inaugural cup campaign, although it took some time to get going: Old Etonians needed three attempts to dispose of Swifts, a team from Slough, but at least the FA recognised their efforts by granting a bye into the third round. In the breathing space between cup rounds, despite an enforced winter break due to heavy frost, Arthur also turned out for the Gitanos and made his sole appearance this season for Wanderers, scoring the final goal as Harrow Chequers were crushed 9-1.

He was also in demand from select teams, playing for Middlesex in a continuation of the series with Surrey, drawn 1-1, then travelling with the London side to Sheffield, where the extraordinary interest in football in the city generated a crowd of 8,000. They cheered the home eleven to a 2-0 victory although London were two men short and had to recruit local substitutes. When Sheffield came to the Oval for the return, the match contrasted starkly as it was played in a subdued atmosphere in front of less than a thousand spectators. Although London celebrated a 3-1 win, all the goals coming in the second half, it was clear that association football in the capital still had some way to go in capturing the public imagination.

The FA Cup campaign resumed against Maidenhead, a match won by a disputed goal and although Maidenhead were reported to be considering a protest it came to nothing. A month later the Etonians met Shropshire Wanderers in the semi-final, with Quintin Hogg making a rare appearance in midfield, and a goal by Bonsor took them into the final. Just two weeks later they faced Royal Engineers, who had been beaten finalists in two of the first three FA Cup competitions.

Old Etonians
Goal: Charles Farmer
Back: Francis Wilson
Half backs: Albert Meysey-Thompson, Edgar Lubbock
Forwards: Robert Benson, William Kenyon-Slaney, Frederick Patton, Alexander Bonsor, Cuthbert Ottaway, Arthur Kinnaird (captain), James Stronge.

Royal Engineers
Goal: William Merriman (captain)
Back: George Sim
Half backs: Gerald Onslow, Richard Ruck
Forwards: Pelham von Donop, Charles Wood, Herbert Rawson, William Stafford, Henry Renny-Tailyour, Alexander Mein, Cecil Wingfield-Stratford.

Referee: Charles Alcock (FA honorary secretary)
Umpires: James Dasent (Gitanos) and John Giffard (Civil Service)

The thousand or so spectators who rolled up to the Oval on 13 March 1875 were not to see a winner that day. Old Etonians had the best of the early exchanges and Bonsor scored a wind-assisted goal direct from a corner kick after about half an hour, but that meant changing ends and losing the advantage of the strong wind at their backs. Ten minutes later the Engineers were back on level terms when von Donop's cross bounced in off Renny-Tailyour's knee. The unfortunate Ottaway, who had limped out of the 1873 final, sprained his ankle and had to be carried off, leaving the Etonians with ten against eleven for the remainder of the match, but even with half an hour extra time, neither side could break the deadlock, and it ended 1-1.

The replay was scheduled just three days later, on Tuesday afternoon, and several Etonian players could not arrange time off work at short notice. Meysey-Thompson, Benson, Kenyon-Slaney and the injured Ottaway all had to withdraw, while Farmer moved into attack, making way for Henry Drummond Moray in goal; the other newcomers were Matthew Farrer, Thomas Hamond and Alfred Lubbock.

Old Etonians
Goal: Henry Drummond Moray
Back: Francis Wilson
Half backs: Matthew Farrer, Edgar Lubbock
Forwards: Thomas Hamond, Alfred Lubbock, Frederick Patton, Charles Farmer, Alexander Bonsor, Arthur Kinnaird (captain), James Stronge.

Royal Engineers fielded an unchanged eleven and soon used their strength to gain an advantage. A free kick for handball right in front of the Eton posts resulted in a goal which was disallowed for offside, but Engineers continued to press and 'from a sharp bully, forced it through the posts again'. This time the goal stood, later credited to Renny-Tailyour, although it would have been hard to tell who got the final touch in a crowded goalmouth. Etonians were further handicapped by a knee injury to Bonsor, who played through the pain but was little more than a passenger. There were chances at either end but the army side made sure of victory about ten minutes from time with another robust goal: 'the Engineers completely penned their opponents, and after several spirited bullies in front of goal, forced it through'[2]. Again Renny-Tailyour claimed the final touch, as the Royal Engineers recorded their first and only FA Cup triumph.

Arthur wound up his season with an Easter weekend trip to Sheffield, the game being played one half under each set of rules, and for the first time the London eleven (including eight Wanderers players) returned home with a victory, thanks to a double from Jarvis Kenrick.

A mission and a marriage

Arthur had made his third visit to Geneva in September 1872, accompanying his parents to the Evangelical Alliance conference, where the main topics were rationalism and superstition. However, he would soon find a new focus for his religious fervour through a charismatic American evangelist who was touring Britain. His name was Dwight Leman Moody, who not only opened Arthur's eyes to new evangelical opportunities, but also led indirectly to his marriage.

Moody was a crowd-pulling preacher from Chicago, and Quintin Hogg was sufficiently intrigued to go and hear him there while on honeymoon. He promptly invited the American to London in the summer of 1872, took some of his boys to hear him preach and Moody's magnetic power apparently converted them to Christianity en masse.

This was just a taste of what was to come: in one of the great events of the mid-Victorian era, Moody embarked on a religious revival tour of Britain which lasted two years. He brought a musical partner, Ira Sankey, who played the organ and led the singing with a 'tenor voice of extraordinary range and capacity'[3]. Their hymns and tunes were considered new and uplifting, and the public flocked to see them wherever they went. They had already conquered the north of England, Scotland and Ireland by the time they arrived in London on 9 March 1875, and the anticipation was sufficient to attract two thousand churchmen to a planning meeting at Freemasons' Hall.

Moody and his family stayed with the Hoggs, while Sankey was a guest of the Kinnairds, who allocated a room in their house – which was directly opposite the mission base at the Opera House in Haymarket – as a campaign office. Although Arthur had the distraction of playing in an FA Cup Final (and replay) that month, he threw himself into the mission's organisation, and Moody's son later recalled his contribution to its success: 'Arthur Kinnaird, a keen athlete, diligent in business and thoroughly democratic in spirit, found in the mission the same religious service in which he heartily believed and to which he could devote himself.'[4]

Arthur and Hogg were appointed joint secretaries to the mission and they placed advertisements in the main daily papers, inviting people to write in for tickets. The response was so great that they had to employ three secretaries, William Paton (a preacher who subsequently became Arthur's private secretary), Rupert Paul and a Miss Rimington, as thousands of applications poured in for up to four events each day. Soon the city was in their thrall, and it was not just the common people who were excited: the Prince and Princess of Wales came to one meeting, while the Prime Minister, William Gladstone, wrote in his diary after being introduced to Moody and Sankey: 'The sight was wonderful, & touching in a high degree.'[5] It was all funded by Moody and Sankey's *Sacred Songs and Solos*, which sold in vast quantities at sixpence a copy to generate royalties of £7,000.[6]

It would be wrong, however, to assume that everyone was as enthusiastic, and sections of the press accused Moody of 'ignorance, sensationalism and vulgarity'[7], while his audiences were said to be composed of 'the most ignorant, the most superstitious, the weakest and the most credulous; the hysterical and the unthinking'[8]. The strength of this opposition became clear in June, when Arthur's enthusiasm got the better of him in trying to arrange for Moody to speak to the boys at his old school. This provoked a furious correspondence in *The Times*, including one condemnatory letter signed by 74 Etonian Members of Parliament, which forced the relocation of the meeting to Windsor. The affair did not show up Arthur in a good light, as he was accused of spreading misinformation to allow the meeting to take place.[9]

Despite these misgivings, by the time the London mission closed on 11 July, it claimed to have attracted an astonishing two and a half million people, over half the then population of London.

In a punishing schedule of 285 meetings over four months, the audience numbers are worth quoting in detail: in Camberwell, sixty meetings attended by 480,000 people; in Victoria, forty-five meetings, attended by 400,000; in the Opera House, sixty meetings attended by 330,000; in Bow, sixty meetings, attended by 600,000; and in the Agricultural Hall at Islington, sixty meetings, attended by 720,000. Arthur travelled to Liverpool in early August to wave Moody and Sankey off on their return crossing to America. He was not alone – thousands came to the quayside to see them embark.[10]

By then, his life had taken an unexpected turn, as he got more than just a glow of religious satisfaction out of the mission: he met a young woman called Alma Agnew, who played the harmonium to lead the singing when Sankey could not attend. Their daily involvement in the revival meetings was possibly the first time that Arthur had the opportunity to speak to a single woman without family supervision. Despite having five sisters, it is likely that he would have been ill-at-ease in female company as his life had been largely spent in the all-male environments of school, university and bank.

His courtship with 20-year-old Alma was probably engineered, or at the very least strongly encouraged, by their mothers, who were cousins – Arthur's grandmother Louisa Noel was the sister of Alma's grandfather Charles Noel. What is more, both fathers were active in the Evangelical Alliance, and Sir Andrew Agnew was actually present at Arthur's christening many years before. Alma could also claim a long Scottish ancestry, as the Agnews had been hereditary sheriffs of Wigtown since 1451. With religion, family, social background and Scottish roots in common, everything was in place for a match and it was quickly settled.

If Arthur had any lingering doubts, he had an ideal opportunity to secure his father's backing, as at the end of May they travelled to Edinburgh to attend the Reformatory and Refuge Union conference. Within a few days of his return to London the young couple announced their engagement.

The wedding was arranged just ten weeks later, on 19 August 1875, a sumptuous affair at Lochnaw Castle, the Agnew ancestral home, in the south west corner of Scotland. None of Arthur's football chums appear to have been invited, and with Quintin Hogg unavailable, Arthur's best man was an old Harrovian, John Hew North Gustave Henry Hamilton Dalrymple – Lord

Dalrymple for short – the future Earl of Stair. They had been at Trinity College, Cambridge, together but given the short notice the choice of best man may have been based as much on convenience as close friendship, as Dalrymple's home was in nearby Stranraer. There is a nice football connection too, as in 1905 he donated Stair Park, home of Stranraer FC, to the people of the town.

FASHIONABLE MARRIAGE AT LOCHNAW CASTLE

The marriage of Mr Arthur Fitzgerald Kinnaird, only son of the Hon. Arthur Kinnaird MP, and heir presumptive to Lord Kinnaird of Rossie Priory, to May Alma Victoria, daughter of Sir Andrew Agnew, Bart., and Lady Louisa Agnew, was celebrated at Lochnaw Castle, by Stranraer.

The popularity of Sir Andrew Agnew and his family in Stranraer and neighbourhood was shown by the lively interest taken in the marriage by the public. Flags floated from various houses in the burgh, and all the way to Lochnaw the farm-houses were similarly decorated.

Miss Agnew was led into the room by her father, and attended by the following 10 bridesmaids: Misses Louisa, Constance and Marguerite Agnew (sisters of the bride); Misses Emily, Gertrude and Louisa Kinnaird (sisters of the bridegroom); Lady Constance Carnegie, Miss Clifton, Miss Noel and Miss Constance Henry. The bride and bridesmaids were dressed in white. The bridegroom was attended by Lord Dalrymple as best man. After the ceremony the company, numbering nearly 100, were entertained to a sumptuous luncheon.

By this time, a large party of the tenantry, merchants in Stranraer, and others had assembled to drink the bride's health and see the happy pair off. They started in a carriage and four for Girvan amid a perfect shower of flowers and old slippers and great cheering. On passing through Stranraer they were loudly cheered by large crowds which had collected along the streets. The tenantry and others were afterwards entertained to cake and wine. [11]

The honeymoon couple travelled north to stay at Rossie Priory, and as part of Alma's introduction to Arthur's way of life he took her to the Perth Conference, an evangelical gathering which would become part of their annual routine. On their return to London, the newly-weds moved into a new home at 50 South

77

Audley Street, just off Grosvenor Square, and there the following summer they had the first of eight children, Catherine.

'Very fast, with great pluck'

As well as FA Cup campaigns with Old Etonians, Arthur continued to be invited to play for Wanderers, and made a memorable trip with them to Glasgow. It was the first time an English club had travelled north of the border, while their hosts, Queen's Park, were protecting a record of having never been beaten. They had been itching for a rematch ever since the undecided FA Cup semi-final of 1872, and this was to prove a decisive triumph for the Scots.

Hampden Park, the earliest dedicated football ground in Scotland[12], was packed with ten thousand fans, who witnessed a stunning display of the superiority of Scottish football at that time. The match card reveals the tactical formation of the teams: Wanderers with seven forwards while Arthur, in his usual blue and white cap, was at right back. Although he and some colleagues were praised for their individual play, Queen's Park were 'brilliant in the extreme' and their goalkeeper did not even touch the ball in the first half. They were three up at the break and the final score was 5-0.[13] The teams were entertained that evening at the Crown Hotel in George Square, after which Arthur took advantage of being in Scotland to visit his new parents-in-law at Lochnaw Castle. While there, he was subject to some serious ribbing from Scottish friends who sent him a card with a drawing of a lion rampant, and the verse:

Move on! Ye Wanderers nor try to wrest
The golden crown from off my tawny crest
Five goals ye've lost in sixty minutes kicking
Truly ye've got a most tremendous licking! [14]

Arthur's next match also ended in heavy defeat, as Middlesex went down 5-1 to Surrey at the Oval. Although he did turn out again for Wanderers in a friendly, for the serious business of the FA Cup he was in the blue and white of the Old Etonians. Arthur was injured in the defeat of Pilgrims, keeping him out of football for a month, but returned for the second round tie against

This verse was sent to Arthur Kinnaird after Wanderers were crushed 5-0 by Queen's Park in 1875

Maidenhead, who were a shadow of the previous season and went down 8-0. On New Year's Day, in the first of only two Sheffield fixtures this season, the northerners were thrashed 4-0 in London, with Arthur getting the third goal. Then it was back to FA Cup action, as Clapham Rovers were dispatched thanks to Bonsor's goal, to put the Old Etonians into the semi-final against Oxford University, and again a single goal, this time from Sturgis, saw them through.

A week later they learned that their opponents in the final would be none other than Wanderers, who had knocked out Swifts. Rather bizarrely, as players then could still be members of more than one club, Arthur's last match before the final was *for* Wanderers at Westminster School, alongside several of the players who would be in opposition just a couple of weeks later. With a foot in both camps, he must have felt a twinge of mixed loyalties as he approached his third FA Cup Final on 11 March 1876. It was undoubtedly a clash between the two strongest English teams of the day and around 3,000 came to the Oval to see the sides do battle.

Wanderers
Goal: William Greig
Backs: Alfred Stratford, William Lindsay
Half backs: Frederick Maddison, Francis Birley (captain)
Forwards: Charles Wollaston, Hubert Heron, Frank Heron, John Hawley Edwards, Jarvis Kenrick, Thomas Hughes.

Old Etonians
Goal: Quintin Hogg
Backs: James Welldon, Albert Meysey-Thompson
Half backs: Edward Lyttelton, Alfred Lyttelton
Forwards: Arthur Kinnaird (captain), William Kenyon-Slaney, Charles Meysey-Thompson, Alexander Bonsor, Julian Sturgis, Herbert Alleyne.

Referee: Walter Buchanan (Clapham Rovers)
Umpires: William White (South Norwood) and Robert Ogilvie (Clapham Rovers)

Arthur started the match in attack but was injured in the early stages, and after about half an hour dropped back into goal.

80

With limited mobility, he was unable to prevent Edwards converting Wollaston's cross to give Wanderers the lead shortly before half-time. Early in the second half the Etonians used their combined strength to equalise in robust fashion: 'owing to the wind and its defenders being forced back upon the posts, they were knocked down, and ball, Wanderers and Etonians in a body went through the space between them.' The actual scorer could not be identified, hardly surprising given the mass of bodies and the broken goalposts.

With honours even at 1-1, the teams had to replay a week later, when bitterly cold weather restricted the crowd to about half the size. While Wanderers were able to select the same eleven, the Etonians were weakened by four enforced changes as Hogg, Welldon and the Meysey-Thompson brothers dropped out; but perhaps the biggest Etonian handicap was Arthur himself, who had not recovered from the previous Saturday's exertions, and 'was only half a man for the occasion, being palpably lame and unfit to play'[15]. Lubbock, too, was not match fit, just recovering from an illness.

Old Etonians
Goal: Francis Wilson
Backs: Edgar Lubbock, Matthew Farrer
Half backs: Edward Lyttelton, Alfred Lyttelton
Forwards: Arthur Kinnaird (captain), William Kenyon-Slaney, Alexander Bonsor, Julian Sturgis, Herbert Alleyne, James Stronge.

Old Etonians did start well and made the early running, forcing goalkeeper Greig into several saves, but Wanderers found their form and after about half an hour's play scored twice in quick succession: Wollaston got the first, and they went straight back up the field for Hughes to score another. Early in the second half Hughes made it 3-0, the final score. This second successive final defeat concluded the Old Etonians' early attempts at winning the FA Cup, and they would not even take part in the competition for another couple of years.

Arthur still had one more game to go and his season ended in disappointment with London in Sheffield. Starting out in defence, he moved into goal in the second half, but to no avail as the northerners scored six without reply. This marked the high point of

Sheffield's short period of dominance, as while the steel city was the earliest hotbed of football, it lost its impetus by holding on too long to a set of rules that was not followed elsewhere. By now, the association game was taking root in neighbouring Lancashire, initially at mill-towns like Turton and Darwen, and it was from here that football would spread like wildfire across the north.

Arthur was described that summer in the *Football Annual* as 'still among the first players of the day; very fast, with great pluck'[16], and when Old Etonians withdrew from the 1876-77 FA Cup without playing a match, his services were quickly snapped up by Wanderers. Still struggling from the leg injury he had picked up in the cup final, he played most of the season in goal, and although this may have gone against his attacking instincts, it worked a treat as Wanderers reached the final without losing a goal. Then, when the moment came for decisive action in the final, his team trailing, the ever versatile Arthur moved into attack to save the game.

The season had not promised as much in its early weeks. Arthur was fortunate to miss out on a rematch against Queen's Park, which ended in a 6-0 humiliation for Wanderers. It was the first time two national cup winners had met, so it was a hugely prestigious victory for the Scots, although in those innocent days there was no proclamation of the 'champions of the world'.[17] He returned to action on 11 November, having been selected to play in attack for London for their regular trek north to Sheffield, but following hard on the heels of the Queen's Park defeat, there was something amiss with football in the metropolis, as the Londoners were downed 5-1.

Arthur and Wanderers continued with their missionary work at the public schools, and not until mid-December did they face strenuous opposition, the students of Oxford University, who showed they still had considerable strength by winning at the Oval. In the serious business of the FA Cup, Wanderers strolled through the early stages: a bye over Saffron Walden Town, a 6-0 win away to Southall, Pilgrim were dispatched 3-0, and conveniently Wanderers were given a bye into the semi-final. They filled in time in February with a series of friendlies, winning well against Clapham Rovers but losing to Upton Park and Royal Engineers, before Arthur played a rare game up front and scored the only goal at Westminster.

The FA Cup was hardly a paragon of forward planning, as there were just three teams in the semi-finals: Wanderers, Cambridge University and Oxford University. As Oxford were beneficiaries of a bye it meant that, to win the cup, Wanderers had to beat both of the Varsity teams, a feat they accomplished within the space of five days. First up was Cambridge, who came to the Oval on a Tuesday afternoon and were duly sent down by a first half goal from Hubert Heron. Wanderers had the minimum of time to prepare for the challenge of Oxford on 24 March 1877, but kept their momentum going to lift the trophy once more.

Wanderers
Goal: Arthur Kinnaird
Backs: Alfred Stratford, William Lindsay
Half backs: Francis Birley (captain), Frederick Green
Forwards: Thomas Hughes, Charles Wollaston, Hubert Heron, Henry Wace, Jarvis Kenrick, Charles Denton.

Oxford University
Goal: Edward Allington
Backs: Owen Dunell, William Rawson
Half backs: Edward Waddington, James Savory
Forwards: Henry Otter, Edward Parry (captain), John Bain, Alexander Tod, Philip Fernandez, Arnold Hills.

Referee: Sidney Wright (Great Marlow)
Umpires: Beaumont Jarrett (Cambridge University) and Conrad Warner (Upton Park)

In capturing another winner's medal, Arthur wrote himself into the record books but not in a way he would have liked. Playing in goal, he had to face into the wind and rain as Oxford had the better of the early exchanges, then from a corner kick 'Waddington drove the ball smartly into the centre of the posts and Kinnaird inadvertently stepped back between the posts with the ball in his hands.'[18] Oxford appealed to the umpires who, after some deliberation, agreed the ball had gone over the line. Arthur had earned the unwanted distinction of the first cup final own goal.

After the break, Wanderers made an astute tactical change, moving the limping Wollaston into goal, unleashing Arthur to play up front. With his support the cup holders came back strongly, but there were only a few minutes left when Heron crossed for Kenrick to shoot home the equaliser. This put the game into extra time, and early in the first period Lindsay scored what turned out to be the winner: after his corner kick was headed out by an Oxford player, 'he had a second kick again directing it into the centre of the Oxford posts, this time so cleverly that the goal keeper could not save his charge.'[19]

There is a strange postscript to Arthur's own goal, as for over a hundred years the score was recorded as 2-0 rather than 2-1. As there is nothing about the incident in the FA minutes, it has been surmised that Arthur protested after the match that he had not crossed over the line and the ruling body duly amended the score to 2-0, ignoring the fact that extra time would not have been necessary if it had not been a goal. This false score remained in the official records until quite recently when, following a review of contemporary reports, the goal was 'reinstated' by the FA.

Quite possibly the goal was debated after the season's end, when Arthur attended a special meeting of the FA[20], held primarily to resolve its differences with the Sheffield FA, which centred on the method of throw-in. There were two proposals on the table, one submitted by Arthur, the other by the Clydesdale Club of Glasgow (one of several Scottish members of the FA); Arthur's motion that the ball must be thrown in at right angles got ten votes, while there were 33 in favour of allowing the ball to be thrown in any direction. This small step was the final element in bringing the Sheffield FA into line with the rules of the national body.

Away from football, in June 1877 Arthur showed he was still capable of athletic feats as a member of the Private Banks Sports Club, which had a ground in Catford. He took part in the long jump, coming second with a creditable 17 feet 2 inches, and was third in the 100 yard sprint, but failed to finish either the hurdles or the mile. The following year he took the more passive role of judge, and in later years he and his wife presented the prizes.

After a season mainly in goal, Arthur was fit for a return to outfield play in 1877-78, which was to be his last full campaign for Wanderers, and he celebrated by securing his third cup winner's medal. In sparkling form, his first match was a convincing 4-0 win over Royal Engineers in a friendly, and four days later Wanderers opened their FA Cup campaign by scoring nine against Panthers, a military officers' team, at Sandhurst. He was again captain of London at Sheffield, playing as a back, and in front of 'at least 10,000' on 17 November, his side scored three times in each half to win 6-0, their best result in the series. Arthur was not selected for the next London game, at home to Birmingham, but was hardly missed in an 11-0 drubbing.

Back in FA Cup action, Wanderers repeated their first round goal-feast at High Wycombe and this time Arthur did score one of the nine. He missed the third round tie against Barnes as he was in mourning for his uncle George, Lord Kinnaird; from this point on, Arthur became 'the Honourable' – being the son of a Lord – and took the traditional title Master of Kinnaird, given to the Kinnaird heir presumptive.[21]

The Barnes match was drawn and Arthur returned to score in the replay, a convincing 4-1 win, then he celebrated his 31st birthday with a 3-0 quarter-final victory over Sheffield at the Oval. With only three teams in the semi-final, Wanderers had the good fortune to be the recipients of a bye, while Royal Engineers edged out Old Harrovians to set up a repeat of the very first FA Cup final. Arthur kept in trim as a guest player for Civil Service in a match at Westminster, then two days later took part in Wanderers' third nine-goal performance of the season, against the Surrey Rifles.

The final at the Oval, on 23 March 1878, was another personal triumph for Arthur, who captained the side to victory and was responsible for one of the goals.

Wanderers
Goal: James Kirkpatrick
Backs: Alfred Stratford, William Lindsay
Half backs: Arthur Kinnaird (captain), Frederick Green
Forwards: Charles Wollaston, Hubert Heron, John Wylie, Henry Wace, Charles Denton, Jarvis Kenrick.

Royal Engineers
Goal: Lovick Friend
Backs: James Cowan, William Morris
Half backs: Frederick Heath, Charles Mayne
Forwards: Morgan Lindsay, Horace Barnet, Robert Hedley (captain), Charles Haynes, Francis Bond, Oliver Ruck.

Referee: Segar Bastard (Upton Park)
Umpires: Conrad Warner (Upton Park) and Beaumont Jarrett (Old Harrovians)

Wanderers made an early breakthrough, thanks to Kenrick, after just five minutes, but the Engineers fought back strongly and were on level terms with 'a determined rush'; the scorer has never been identified. Undaunted, Wanderers regained the upper hand before half time, and the goal could be credited to Arthur although reports are not clear who got the final touch: 'after a free kick by Kinnaird the ball was a second time driven between the Engineers' posts.'[22] The Engineers thought they had equalised early in the second half, only for Hedley's effort to be ruled offside, and Wanderers made sure of victory with another strike by Kenrick, who converted Heron's through ball to make the final score 3-1.

A major talking point was the bravery shown by Wanderers' veteran goalkeeper James Kirkpatrick, erstwhile captain and selector of the Scotland unofficial eleven in 1870, who fractured his arm early in the game, but played on through the pain without realising the extent of his injury. He retired from playing after winning his medal, a fitting end to his long career. Amidst the post-match celebrations, however, few could have guessed that this was the last time the famous Wanderers would lift the cup; indeed, events moved so quickly that within three years the club had effectively ceased to exist.

Arthur's season ended with something of a novelty as he captained Wanderers against Vale of Leven, who had supplanted Queen's Park as top team in Scotland, retaining the Scottish Cup two weeks earlier, with this trip to London as their reward. In heavy rain the visitors confirmed the superiority of Scottish football by running out 3-1 winners, despite being 'fatigued by travel and sight-seeing, strange ground, the superior weight of their antagonists, and last but not least, the whole of the game being played under the English throw-in to which the Vale were almost entire strangers.' It was heralded as a victory for teamwork: 'the result of the match plainly shows that individual dribbling, though it be of the highest order, cannot stand against the passing game, and to this style of play the Vale are indebted for their victory.' Arthur presided over the post-match supper in the Freemasons' Tavern, and in his congratulations to the visiting players he promised to go to Glasgow for a return and demonstrate what they had learned from the Scots' excellent display of passing.[23]

He did indeed fulfil his promise, taking a team north in December 1879, but it was not the Wanderers. Instead, he travelled with the resurgent Old Etonians, who were about to occupy his full attention. With Arthur at the helm, the public school game was on the verge of dizzy heights of success.

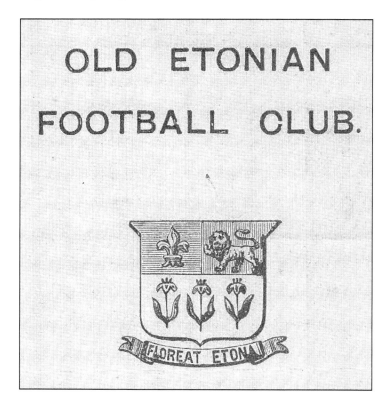

[1] Ryan Giggs, Roy Keane and Ashley Cole are all on seven cup finals at the time of publication.

[2] *Sporting Life*, 17 March 1875

[3] George Morgan, *A Veteran in Revival*, p172

[4] William R Moody, *The Life of DL Moody*, p231

[5] Matthew (ed), *Gladstone Diaries*, Vol IX, p32

[6] Later, in the USA, the book made $357,000 in ten years, leading to (apparently unfounded) suspicions that the preachers were lining their pockets.

[7] *The Saturday Review*, 26 June 1875, p809

[8] *The National Reformer*, 18 April 1875, p241

[9] *The Times*, 21-26 June 1875

[10] *Liverpool Mercury*, 5 August 1875

[11] *Glasgow Herald*, 20 August 1875

[12] The first Hampden was home to Queen's Park FC until 1883; the current national stadium is the third Hampden Park, and opened in 1903.

[13] Arthur missed Wanderers' return against Queen's Park in February, when their 2-0 victory not only gave a measure of revenge but was also the first time the Glasgow side had ever lost a match.

[14] Card in the Kinnaird family archive; it was sent anonymously from Ochtertyre, near Crieff, the home of Sir Patrick Murray.

[15] *The Graphic*, 25 March 1876

[16] *Football Annual* 1876; he was given the same assessment until 1881.

[17] In 1887, when Scottish Cup holders Hibernian defeated their English counterparts Preston North End, the match was proclaimed as the Championship of the World.

[18] *The Sportsman*, 26 March 1877

[19] *Oxford University Herald*, 31 March 1877

[20] On 17 April 1877

[21] The earliest surviving colour image of Arthur is a portrait of him as Master of Kinnaird, painted by W Teesdale in 1880.

[22] *The Sportsman*, 25 March 1878

[23] There is an extended report in Ferguson and Temple, *The Old Vale and Its Memories*, p40-50.

CHAPTER 6

Glory days with the Old Etonians
1878-83

ARTHUR WAS showing no signs of easing up. Now into his thirties, he had three FA Cup wins under his belt, and had served for ten years on the FA committee. That experience, combined with his career as a banker, had made him an obvious choice to be elected honorary treasurer of the FA in February 1878.

Since 1872, Charles Alcock had been joint secretary and treasurer, but in the intervening years the game's finances had grown out of recognition, largely due to the proceeds of the internationals and the FA Cup, and there was now a pressing need for a dedicated treasurer: the FA's total income in 1868-69, when Arthur first came onto the committee, was £4 and 2 shillings, whereas by the end of the following decade it had grown to over £329. Arthur not only accepted the role, he also turned the position into a business opportunity, as under his direction the FA placed £200 on deposit at Ransom's Bank[1], where he could no doubt make sure it was well looked after!

He was listed in the FA minutes at the time of his appointment as a representative of Wanderers, who were about to win the FA Cup for the fifth time and had few challengers for the position of top club in the country. However, Wanderers were to have the rug pulled from under their feet as, led by FA President Francis Marindin, the Old Etonians Football Club was properly constituted in October 1878.[2] A committee was appointed and, with this added emphasis on organisation, it acted as a clarion call for all Etonian footballers who had, until then, appeared in a variety of colours. It was an inspired move that paid immediate dividends: previously the Etonians had been essentially a scratch club, largely dependent on the efforts of Arthur to persuade friends to turn out on a Saturday, with no comeback if they should decide they had better things to do.

The new team was widely tipped to make an impact, and the opportunity to do so arose sooner than expected as the FA Cup first round draw threw up a titanic contest: Wanderers v Old Etonians. Arthur had actually opened his season by playing for the Wanderers, scoring a goal as they lost 3-2 to Old Harrovians, but by the day of the cup-tie, 9 November, his focus was entirely on the challenge of putting together an Etonian eleven to tackle his erstwhile colleagues. Wanderers still had eight of their cup final team but could find no answer to the might of Eton's finest, who knocked out the holders by the astonishing score of 7-2. Only when six goals down did Wanderers get any consolation, quickly scoring twice, before the Etonians put the seal on a fine victory with the seventh.

The victory heralded a short spell of domination by the public school old boys' clubs, as Old Etonians and Old Carthusians won three of the next four competitions, while Wanderers, who had done so much to popularise the game and had dominated the early FA Cups, were never the same again. In the meantime, just to show there were no hard feelings, Arthur turned out for Wanderers in a friendly at Westminster later that month.

Some commentators imagined that an Etonian FA Cup triumph would be little more than a formality, and with Arthur in fine form that seemed to be the case as they continued on their way with a 1-0 win at Reading, on a skating rink of a pitch, and a 5-2 defeat of Minerva. There was a shock in store, however, when Darwen, a little known team from a mill town in Lancashire, travelled to London for a fourth round tie. Darwen had already been to the Oval in the previous round, where they surprised the Remnants, a team of public school old boys, winning 3-2 after extra time.

The Old Etonians were a different prospect, however, and on a miserable Thursday afternoon in February the Darwen eleven, wearing makeshift kit, did not give the appearance of likely challengers. As the Etonians strolled to a 5-1 half time lead, helped by a Harry Goodhart treble, it looked all over, but the mill-hands had a secret weapon, or rather two: they were among the earliest exponents of veiled professionalism, and lined up with the 'Scots professors' James Love and Fergus Suter, both signed the previous summer. Under pressure, James Welldon headed into his own goal and Darwen astonished their opponents by scoring three more in the last 20 minutes, bringing the match to the unlikely conclusion of a 5-5 draw.

With no provision in the rules to change venue for the replay, Darwen had to return to London and again thwarted Arthur's side, twice coming from behind to level at 2-2. This was not in the script. A third match was hastily arranged for the following Saturday, and impoverished Darwen had to depend on a public subscription to find the money at short notice for yet another trip to London; the Etonians themselves chipped in £5 towards their fares. This time the northerners were out of luck, as well as stamina, and although there was a glimmer of hope when Suter brought it back to 2-1, Old Etonians won comfortably, 6-2.

The unexpected delay in disposing of Darwen meant time was running out for the competition to be completed, and led to the Etonians playing cup ties on four consecutive Saturdays. The next week, they faced Nottingham Forest in the semi-final and in the absence of Major Marindin, who was ill, Arthur captained the side. In front of only a few hundred spectators, the sides played a goal-less first half, then both scored soon after the break, with Whitfield's opener for Etonians almost immediately cancelled out by Bishop. The winner, five minutes from the end, came with a bit of good fortune as Luntley conceded an own goal after a 'loose scrimmage' in front of the Forest posts.

It was straight into the final against Clapham Rovers a week later, on 29 March 1879. The match was expected to be a close contest, and so it proved for around 3,000 spectators who packed round the ropes at the Oval. Arthur retained the captaincy as Major Marindin had not recovered, his customary place in goal taken by John Hawtrey. The old 1-1-8 formation had been superseded and both teams lined up in a more pragmatic 2-2-6: not exactly *catenaccio*, but a recognition that forwards had to be countered by a more robust defence.

Old Etonians
Goal: John Hawtrey
Backs: Lindsay Bury, Edward Christian
Half backs: Arthur Kinnaird (captain), Edgar Lubbock

Forwards: Charles Clerke, Norman Pares, Harry Goodhart, Herbert Whitfield, John Chevalier, Mark Beaufoy.

Clapham Rovers
Goal: Reginald Birkett
Backs: Robert Ogilvie (captain), Edgar Field
Half backs: Norman Bailey, James Prinsep
Forwards: Frederick Rawson, Arthur Stanley, Stanley Scott, Herbert Bevington, Edward Growse, Cecil Keith-Falconer.

Referee: Charles Alcock (FA honorary secretary)
Umpires: Segar Bastard (Upton Park), Charles Leeds (South Norwood)

HON. A. F. KINNAIRD.
(CAPT.)

The first half saw play swing from end to end, with both sides missing chances to go ahead: Clapham goalkeeper Birkett tipped a corner kick from Arthur onto the crossbar and over, while at the other end 'it required all the well-known powers of Bury and Kinnaird to keep the enemy out of their quarters'[3] and Bevington missed a simple chance when he 'muffed his final kick unaccountably'[4].

The only goal came in 65 minutes, when Goodhart ran down the left wing and his cross fell at the feet of Clerke, who shot home just inside the post, 'the signal for enthusiastic applause from the partisans of Eton'[5]. Clapham had nothing left in reserve to mount an effective comeback, and the Etonians safely saw out the match to win the cup for the first time, providing Arthur with his fourth winner's medal.

The 'new' Old Etonians could reflect on an outstanding debut season and had quickly built up a considerable strength, as the old school magazine commented: 'The venture was warmly taken up by Old Etonians in London and at the two Universities. There are now about 70 members, and there is every reason to hope that the club will each year be recruited with the best football talent which Eton can produce.'[6]

Arthur concluded his season in the unaccustomed role of umpire in the England v Scotland match, which had been put back to 5 April (Boat Race Day) because of snow on the original date, 1 March. England marked up an unlikely 5-4 victory, turning round a 4-1 half-time deficit, to record their only success over Scotland between 1873 and 1888. Reports indicate that Arthur's national loyalties had weakened as he was seen after the match vigorously congratulating Billy Mosforth, England's winger, for his brilliant play.

In 1879-80, the Etonians found the path to success was a rocky one, brought down to earth with a bump as they attempted to defend the trophy. The holders had sailed through the early stages thanks to a walkover against Barnes and a second round bye, so they contented themselves with friendlies. As many of the line-ups for these games were not reported in the press it is not possible to be sure that Arthur played in all of them, but he did captain the team in a 1-0 victory over Cambridge University.

He then undertook an eventful Etonian tour to Scotland, starting at Hampden Park, Glasgow. Arthur had not been back to the ground since Wanderers' drubbing from Queen's Park in 1875, and while it was not such a crushing defeat this time, again his team conceded five. The opposition was Vale of Leven[7], who chose to play at Hampden because of the status of a match which brought together the winners of the Scottish Cup and the FA Cup, but driving wind and rain kept the crowd down to just 800. While the Etonians did make some early attacking forays, the Vale team had the advantage of the strong wind at their backs to pile on the pressure, and built a 4-0 half-time lead. After the break, as the pitch turned into a quagmire, the Etonians exploited the conditions for their own benefit, scoring two quick goals – the second from Arthur, playing at half-back – but a defensive blunder let in the Vale for a fifth, and it ended 5-2. The visitors still drew praise in the press: 'The Etonian players are the best exponents of the game seen in Scotland, and under different weather circumstances would prove a good match for their Scotch opponents.'[8]

The storm was gathering so much momentum that the following day, at its peak, it caused one of Britain's worst railway accidents, the Tay Bridge Disaster. Over 70 train passengers were killed as the bridge collapsed, which brought an unexpected summons for Major Marindin, who had played in goal as Etonian captain at Hampden. On retiring from the army he had become an investigating officer of railways with the Board of Trade, and was a regular visitor to Scotland on railway business (he had actually inspected the Tay Bridge before its opening in the summer of 1878). He could hardly have been closer to the scene of the disaster as Arthur had invited him to stay for a couple of nights at Rossie Priory, which is just ten miles west of the bridge's northern landfall. Marindin set off immediately for Dundee to launch the investigation, ducking out of the rest of the tour.

Arthur took over as captain and travelled with the rest of the team to Edinburgh where, with a local man as substitute goalkeeper, they faced a city select and won 4-3. The climax of their short tour was on New Year's Day in Lancashire, where they were given a rapturous reception in the mill town of Darwen. Their plucky opponents from the spring were determined to get revenge for their FA Cup defeat and achieved their aim in front of 8,000 spectators, 'the largest field ever seen in Lancashire'[9], winning 3-1. Arthur in goal 'was several times compelled to handle the leather freely'; he was deemed culpable for two of the goals, being charged out of the way for one and caught too far off his line for another. Darwen was then in the vanguard of northern football and continued to progress, reaching an FA Cup semi-final in 1881, before being overtaken by teams from bigger towns, whose owners had deeper pockets to seduce players.

Back in London, the Etonians returned to FA Cup action, again coming up against Wanderers in the third round. The game was originally scheduled for the previous week at Vincent Square, but the Westminster school authorities would not sanction the use of the ground, so the Oval was the venue. While a repeat of the previous season's seven goal performance was not on the cards, it ended in a comfortable 3-1 victory for the Etonians, who had Major Marindin back in goal, with Arthur at half back. The match turned out to be the Wanderers' last ever cup-tie, with one of the major contributory factors in their demise being the formation of the Old Etonians and other 'old boy' teams, who had taken their best players.

The campaign continued with a straightforward 5-1 victory over West End, Goodhart claiming a hat trick in the first ten minutes and Arthur scoring twice, but hit the buffers in the quarter final: Clapham Rovers grasped the opportunity to avenge their defeat in the previous season's final, scoring the only goal of the game through Clopton Lloyd-Jones. The wind which had backed Clapham in the first half dropped after the break, and a downpour further hampered any attempt at a comeback, so the equaliser never came, even though the press judged the Etonians the better team. Clapham went on to win the cup for the only time, overcoming Oxford University in the final, while Arthur, uniquely in a nine year spell, had to watch the final from the sidelines.

His season ended with a return against Vale of Leven at the Oval, which turned out to be another lesson from the Scots. Although the Etonians held the lead at half-time thanks to Alfred Lyttelton's goal, the visitors adapted well to association rules (the first half was played under Scottish rules) and scored three times to win convincingly. Vale's reputation had made the game a major attraction in the city, with about two thousand spectators present.

Approaching the veteran stage, another memorable FA Cup campaign for Arthur began in the autumn of 1880 with a 10-0 whitewash of Brentwood, and the only reason he did not score was that he was in goal. The following month, a match at Hendon resulted in a comfortable 2-0 win, and that was succeeded by further victories over Hertfordshire Rangers and Greyfriars. At new year, Arthur played at Sheffield in the opening match of another Etonian tour, winning comfortably at Bramall Lane, but opted out of continuing to Scotland where, without him, the team lost to Queen's Park and Vale of Leven before edging past Edinburgh University.

The cup quarter-final brought a trip to Wolverhampton, where their opponents were Stafford Road, a Great Western Railway works team which included Charles Crump, later to work with Arthur at the FA. On a sloping pitch, the Etonians scored once in each half and held on for a 2-1 win. The match gave NL Jackson,

95

one of the umpires, a typical anecdote for his memoirs: 'An incident occurred which afforded one of the many proofs of the active and vigorous methods adopted by Kinnaird for assisting his side. During the game Ray, the Stafford Road goalkeeper, fell on the ball after saving a shot. Macaulay had promptly fallen on top of him, and soon a regular Rugby scrimmage was formed, with all the players assisting. After this had been in progress for some minutes, Kinnaird, who was buried in the thick of it, was observed to be wriggling out backwards, and when free he rushed to the referee saying 'I claim hands! Somebody must have handled the ball.' Receiving a negative reply, he immediately buried himself in the melee.'[10]

The semi-final stage was something of an anti-climax as, once again, there were only three teams left in the competition. It was the last time this anomaly was allowed in the competition, but it suited the Old Etonians who received a bye, while Old Carthusians defeated Darwen. Having had this free passage into the FA Cup Final on 9 April 1881, Arthur led his team into battle as the scions of Charterhouse and Eton played for the glory of being the judged the best side in England.

Old Carthusians
Goal: Leonard Gillett
Backs: Elliot Colvin, Walter Norris
Half backs: James Prinsep, Joseph Vintcent
Forwards: William Page, Edward Wynyard, Alexander Tod, Edward Parry (captain), Lewis Richards, Walter Hansell.

Old Etonians
Goal: John Rawlinson
Backs: Thomas French, Charles Foley
Half backs: Arthur Kinnaird (captain), Bryan Farrer
Forwards: John Chevalier, William Anderson, Harry Goodhart, Reginald Macaulay, Herbert Whitfield, Philip Novelli.

Referee: William Peirce Dix (Sheffield)
Umpires: Charles Wollaston (Wanderers), Ernest Bambridge (Swifts)

The honours went convincingly to Old Carthusians, who could have won by more than three unanswered goals in their first and only success in the competition. Their captain, Parry, missed a simple chance before Wynyard opened the scoring after half an hour from Prinsep's corner kick. The Etonians did have some opportunities, but were pressed hard and the game was mainly played in their own half. Early in the second half, Wynyard had another goal disallowed for offside before Parry finally got on the scoresheet fifteen minutes from the end to double the advantage. Victory was secured by an own goal, 'the ball going between the posts off the body of one of the Etonians'[11], although it was also reported that 'the ball glanced between the posts off Tod's chest'[12].

The match marked the summit of the public school era, as change was lurking just around the corner, or more accurately in the mill towns of Lancashire. Semi-finalists Darwen had already given notice that things were stirring in the north, and although they would never reach the final themselves, their rise heralded a decade that would turn the old order on its head, as professionalism forced its way into football.

Economics had everything to do with it. Around 4,000 Londoners had come along to the Oval to cheer the two teams of ex-public school men, a crowd that was hardly greater than that for the first final almost a decade earlier. It demonstrated the limited appeal of football when confined to a narrow social elite; by contrast, on the same day there were 12,000 at Hampden for the Scottish Cup Final between Queen's Park and Dumbarton, and similar numbers crowded into regional cup ties in Lancashire and Yorkshire. Big crowds meant substantial gate receipts and Arthur, as FA treasurer, would have been acutely aware of the rumours of money being diverted to attract players, but in the absence of proof there was little the governing body could do to regulate the problem, despite strict rules against payment for players.

He carried on playing regardless, and match reports continued to pay tribute to his speed and strength for the Old Etonians. Their FA Cup campaign of 1881-82 started with a difficult away tie against Clapham Rovers which went to a replay at the Oval, and even that took an own goal to separate the teams. Helped by a bye in the second round, the Etonians' progress in the cup was laboured as they endured a goalless first half against Swifts before coming through, and let slip a three goal lead over

Maidenhead before recovering sufficiently for a 6-3 victory. They benefitted from another bye in the quarter final, which took them into a one-sided semi against Great Marlow, who were thrashed 5-0. Goodhart completed a hat trick, between goals from Macaulay and Dunn, which filled the Etonians with confidence for the final three weeks later.

The FA Cup final, Old Etonians versus Blackburn Rovers, was the first to pitch southern old school against northern new order, leading to a heightened sense of occasion at the Oval on 25 March 1882. There was further recognition of its importance by allowing it to be played centrally, across the cricket crease, making space for over 6,000 spectators around the ropes; previous finals had been pushed to the side of the arena. The Lancashire side was also brimming with confidence, unbeaten that season and having scored heavily against a number of top class sides. They brought a large and raucous support, and such was the interest in the game that the *Blackburn Standard* brought out a Saturday night special edition, with a match report 'specially telegraphed by our reporter'.

Old Etonians
Goal: John Rawlinson
Backs: Thomas French, Percy de Paravicini
Half backs: Arthur Kinnaird (captain), Charles Foley
Forwards: William Anderson, John Chevalier, Reginald Macaulay, Harry Goodhart, Arthur Dunn, Philip Novelli.

Blackburn Rovers
Goal: Roger Howarth
Backs: Hugh McIntyre, Fergus Suter
Half backs: Frederick Hargreaves (captain), Harold Sharples
Forwards: John Duckworth, James Douglas, Geoffrey Avery, James Brown, Thomas Strachan, John Hargreaves.

Referee: Charles Clegg (Sheffield)
Umpires: Charles Crump (Birmingham), Charles Wollaston (Wanderers)

Arthur won the toss, which allowed the Etonians to play with the wind and sun at their backs, and they stormed into attack, quickly creating several good chances in the early minutes: Foley shot just over, a free kick only three yards from the Blackburn goal was blocked (the penalty kick was still several years away), and Dunn had a shot saved by Howarth. It was little surprise that they took the lead after just eight minutes play, although paradoxically it sprung from a Blackburn corner kick which was cleared by Arthur. The ball was picked up by Macaulay, who passed to Dunn, and his cross was volleyed into the goal by Anderson.

The victorious Old Etonians team in 1882, with Arthur in the centre

Play raged from end to end, and Blackburn had chances to equalise, notably when goalkeeper Rawlinson fumbled the ball and conceded a corner. After the break, the Etonian goal was besieged 'but so perfect was the back play of French and Paravicini that no success was met with beyond a corner, which Kinnaird cleverly got rid of.' The result remained in doubt until the final minute, when Paravicini 'literally threw himself in the way' of Douglas's fierce shot. This was Blackburn's last throw of the dice, and Anderson's early goal proved enough to win the cup.

Among those singled out for praise 'the Hon AF Kinnaird played a truly fine game, his speed and tackling being superb'.[13] In fact, Arthur was so delighted with winning the cup again that, famously, he stood on his hands in front of the pavilion. It was to prove a symbolic celebration as this was the last of his five winner's medals.

He concluded the season with a well-attended friendly between Old Etonians and Old Carthusians, played at the Oval to raise money for charity, and the cup winners surprisingly lost to Edward Parry's first half goal.

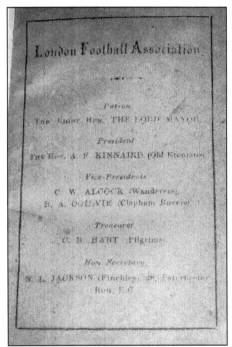

London FA handbook from its inaugural year, 1882, with Arthur Kinnaird as President

The coming 1882-83 season was to mark the end of an era, not just for football, whose power base was moving away from London, but also for Arthur, still possessed by extraordinary energy as he played in all seven ties on his way to a ninth and final appearance in an FA Cup Final.

It is indicative of the metropolitan bias of the Football Association in the early days that it was not until 1882 that a dedicated London FA was formed. The obvious person to lead it was Arthur and he was elected President, despite still being an active player; it was an immediate success, with 52 clubs joining in its first year. It gave him the opportunity to start his season in the newly founded London Challenge Cup, although the venture soon ended for the Etonians with a home defeat to Clapham Rovers.

They had little time to dwell on the reverse as their FA Cup campaign got off to an inauspicious start the following week, with a first round draw against Old Foresters, a match moved to Aldin House in Slough (where 1879 cup winner John Hawtrey was a teacher) as the Oval was not available. Old Etonians came through 3-1 in the replay, and the campaign remained on track as Brentwood and Rochester were also beaten. Next up were Swifts who went down 2-0 at the Oval in the fourth round, in front of a crowd of over a thousand despite it being a Wednesday afternoon.

That Arthur was still considered as a player of the highest order is shown by his selection for London Probables v Possibles, although he did not make the team to face Sheffield; instead, that day he captained 'a weak team' of Old Etonians who lost 5-0 at Cambridge University. There was a glimpse of past glories as Arthur played for a team described as Wanderers at Harrow School, a fixture which kept the old club's name alive once a year.

Hendon were disposed of in the FA Cup quarter final, 4-2, and two weeks later, Notts County came to London for the semi, taking an early lead which they held till the break. However, Old Etonians recovered, equalising through Macaulay and then winning with Goodhart's goal six minutes from the end to set up a monumental final against Blackburn Olympic, who in their own semi had overrun Old Carthusians 4-0 in Manchester.

Olympic, widely considered to be closet professionals, underwent three weeks of special training in Blackpool for their semi-final and final, but the Old Etonians were still considered favourites to lift the trophy. The record cup final crowd of over 8,000, many from Lancashire, who converged on the Oval for this historic event on 31 March 1883 were to witness a tough and uncompromising battle. Years later Arthur joked of the finals against Blackburn Rovers and Blackburn Olympic: 'I carry their marks to this day'[14].

Blackburn Olympic
Goal: Thomas Hacking
Backs: Albert Warburton (captain), James Ward

Half backs: William Astley, John Hunter, Thomas Gibson
Forwards: Thomas Dewhurst, Alfred Matthews, George Wilson, John Yates, James Crossley.

Old Etonians
Goal: John Rawlinson
Backs: Percy de Paravicini, Thomas French
Half backs: Arthur Kinnaird (captain), Charles Foley
Forwards: William Anderson, John Chevalier, Reginald Macaulay, Harry Goodhart, Arthur Dunn, Herbert Bainbridge.

Referee: Charles Crump (Birmingham)
Umpires: Morton Betts (Old Harrovians) and William Peirce Dix (Sheffield)

The first half went to form, with the Etonians making the breakthrough after a fine attacking move on the half hour: Arthur passed to Chevalier, who ran forward with the ball, and although he was tackled by Ward, Macaulay passed the loose ball to Goodhart whose shot found the goal. At the interval, while the Etonians simply stood and took a breather, the London crowd was amused at the novel sight of the Olympic attendant running on with 'a large black bag containing grapes and other fruits, lemonades, etc for their refreshment'.

It all went wrong for the Etonians as they were hit by a series of misfortunes that would cost them the match: Dunn was kicked in the calf by Warburton and had to go off; Macaulay cut his knee in a tackle; Goodhart went down with cramp. This handed the initiative to their opponents, who duly equalised in 65 minutes with a hard shot by Matthews. Arthur then scored what would have been a goal in later years: he took a free kick awarded for handball and his shot went directly into the goal, but the laws at that time specified an indirect free kick. So it remained level after 90 minutes and as Arthur had agreed before the match that extra time would be played in the event of a draw, the teams embarked on an additional half hour.

Injuries continued to cripple the Etonian team, and when Macaulay was hurt again, for the latter stages he 'was of no use to his side'. With the Olympic players 'in the very pink of condition' few were surprised when Crossley got what proved to be the winner

102

in the second period of extra time. Despite valiant efforts by the Etonians to equalise in the last few minutes, there was nothing left in the tank and Blackburn held on for victory. For the first time, the cup and medals were presented at the pavilion by Major Marindin, in view of the cheering spectators.

ASSOCIATION CUP WINNERS
BLACKBURN OLYMPIC. 1883

The victorious Blackburn players

NL Jackson blamed Arthur for being too sporting: 'It was really Kinnaird who lost the Old Etonians the match, for although the extra half-hour was not then obligatory, his good nature prompted him to promise that concession because the visitors explained that a draw would mean their having to come up to London again, which they could ill afford.'[15] He came in for further criticism in the weekly paper *Football*, which said Arthur appeared 'out of it' for the first hour, and only imposed himself on the game when it was too late: 'The long passing of the Lancashire lads appeared to considerably perplex the Etonians, Kinnaird especially showing very poor form against it.' Only in extra time did he show his capabilities: 'Kinnaird played with more dash than he had shown at any other period of the game, and tried hard to stem the tide of fortune which had apparently set against his side.'

The reporter did at least appreciate the significance of the result: 'At last the charm is broken, and a northern club has proved successful in this, the champion competition of the Association game.'[16] The FA Cup would not return to the capital for a generation and, in fact, no southern team would even appear in the final again until the dawn of the new century. The victory of Blackburn Olympic also heralded the era of professionalism, a topic that would exercise the FA for many years to come.

As for Arthur, the cup final brought a close to his top level playing career; but he was not quite ready to hang up his boots just yet.

---

[1] Geoffrey Green, *History of the Football Association*, p66

[2] The Old Etonians Association Football Club celebrated its centenary in 1965, tracing its origins to Quintin Hogg's Old Etonian side in London.

[3] *The Times*, 31 March 1879

[4] *Sheffield and Rotherham Independent*, 31 March 1879

[5] *The Sportsman*, 31 March 1879

[6] *Eton College Chronicle*, 15 May 1879

[7] Vale of Leven were based in the village of Alexandria, Dunbartonshire.

[8] *Aberdeen Weekly Journal*, 29 December 1879

[9] *Leeds Mercury*, 2 January 1880

[10] NL Jackson, *Association Football*, p158

[11] *Sporting Life*, 13 April 1881

[12] *Daily News*, 11 April 1881

[13] *Preston Herald*, 29 March 1882

[14] He made the comment in 1906, in a letter expressing regret that he could not attend a ceremony at Blackburn YMCA; see also Sir Frederick Wall, *Fifty Years of Football*, p26

[15] NL Jackson, *Sporting Days and Sporting Ways*, p70

[16] *Football: a weekly record of the game*, 4 April 1883

CHAPTER 7

Money changes everything
1883-90

THE PAINFUL experience of losing to Blackburn Olympic sent a clear message that it was time to stand aside and let younger men take the strain. Arthur was almost ten years older than any other member of the 1883 cup final team, and was not present when Old Etonians were knocked out in the first round by Hendon, the first time they had ever been beaten by anyone other than the eventual winners. His FA Cup days were over.

To keep him busy, the second great Moody and Sankey mission arrived. It opened in the north of England and toured extensively before finally settling in London in November 1883 for an eight month stint. It was organised like a modern rock band might tour, with two large movable buildings of iron and wood which were erected alternately in strategic centres around the metropolis. This time, the preparations were undertaken by a large committee of volunteers formed from the leading Christian men in London, including Arthur, who hosted Moody and his family. The mission was an uplifting experience for Arthur, who reminisced late in life how he was inspired: 'As I look back over fifty years of evangelistic work I recall that during forty of these years I was constantly in contact with that prince of evangelists, Mr DL Moody. With pleasure and thankfulness I remember his wonderful life-work and I realise more and more what a mighty force he was, and how immensely his labours were used to help thousands in my own country. I have never known anyone whose faith was so real and abounding; no difficulty could daunt him, no perplexity could cloud his faith in God or dim his calm belief that all would be well. His memory still remains and his work lives on.'[1]

Arthur continued to pack in a wide range of philanthropic activities, mainly in support of his parents' charities, although together with Tom Pelham and George Hanbury, he was running a mission for Working Boys and there would eventually be seven Homes for Working Boys in London.[2] He was also appointed treasurer of the Homes for Working Girls, established to provide for 'the almost numberless girl-workers of London, nothing having been done to help these daily bread winners to a better condition of living'.

His family was growing, and he now had an heir, Douglas (born 1879), and two more sons, Kenneth (1880) and Arthur (1885). However, another son, Noel, died as an infant and further tragedy struck in the spring of 1886 with the loss of their first child, nine-year-old Catherine. Her death devastated Alma, who had cared for her through many illnesses, taking her to German spas for the sake of her delicate constitution.

Arthur carried on playing football 'with all the robustness of his younger days'[3] but restricted himself to local cup ties and friendlies, and because few were reported in the newspapers, details of his playing career are sketchy from this point. The only Old Etonian games in which he definitely featured in 1883-84 were in the London Challenge Cup. The next season, in the same competition, he led Old Etonians to a convincing 8-1 victory over Olympians, and in two draws against Dulwich, after which his side withdrew. He also captained Wanderers, now just a ghost of the once great club, in their annual game against Harrow the week before Christmas, scoring the opening goal in a 5-0 victory. Four days later, he stood forlornly on the sidelines in the role of umpire as Old Etonians were thrashed 6-0 by Old Carthusians, and must have wished he had brought his boots.

He had a happier experience as umpire when the Old Etonians beat Middlesbrough 2-0 in the FA Cup, but it is easy to imagine Arthur's delight in October 1885, on turning up at Chiswick to referee a match between a London eleven and the East Midlands Counties, to find the home side a man short. He quickly volunteered to play, and enjoyed it so much that over the next couple of months he featured in several matches, including his competitive debut in the London Challenge Cup for Hanover United, the Polytechnic side formed by Quintin Hogg (who played for them in the FA Cup aged 38). Hogg viewed sport as a catalyst for good health among 'his

106

boys' but surprisingly, given Arthur's lifelong focus on the development of young men, there is little evidence to show that he considered football as a vehicle for personal development. Even as a founding member in 1886 of the National Physical Recreation Society, whose aim was 'the promotion of physical recreation among the working classes', Arthur was content to fulfill the administrative role of treasurer rather than leader.[4]

Despite his veteran status, Arthur still had the power to influence matches: starting in goal for Old Etonians against Old Carthusians at the Oval, when his side went four down he moved into attack and helped to create two late goals, prompting the newspaper comment: 'If the Etonian captain assumed the post of goalkeeper with the idea of graduating his withdrawal from the football field, he may be assured by Saturday's experience that his club are as yet not able to dispense with his services in a more active function.' A few days later, he captained Wanderers to victory over Harrow, possibly the last time he played for the once-famous club[5], and it was also his farewell appearance at the Oval.

Arthur's final matches for Old Etonians came in March 1887, against Old Harrovians and Royal Engineers, just after his 40th birthday. A month later, his father died, and he appears to have withdrawn from playing club football at this point.

Money and football

As FA treasurer, Arthur had an unprecedented amount of committee work as professionalism muscled its way into the game. He was keenly aware of the effect money was having, and the success of the Lancashire teams in the early 1880s, culminating in Blackburn Olympic's cup victory, was tangible proof that the financial growth of football had been far more pronounced in the north of England. Even in the early days, Arthur would have appreciated the contrast between south and north, having played for London against Sheffield in front of up to 8,000 paying spectators at Bramall Lane, while the return at the Oval attracted mere hundreds.

It was not long before this influx of gate money into the game led, inevitably, to professionalism. With cash being paid by thousands of spectators, and without enumerating turnstiles in place, it took little effort to divert some of the piles of sixpences and

107

shillings to a slush fund that would 'motivate' key players, and the gates opened to a flood of Scots who followed the lure of English gold. The amateurs of the south had seen signs of this in 1879 with the heroic performances of Darwen, strengthened by Scots 'professors' who had clearly been persuaded to move south for something more than the opportunity to work in a different kind of mill. While these were not the first veiled professionals, their positive impact on Darwen's fortunes did not go unremarked.

The debate about whether it was acceptable to pay men to play football took years to resolve, and during that time a game of cat-and-mouse developed between the authorities and ambitious clubs, who were almost always one step ahead. Football bodies are not renowned for their quick reaction to new trends, and at the outset the FA did little to respond to reports and rumours of payments to players. However, it was forced to react to the rising number of protests submitted by teams taking part in the FA Cup, and did what governing bodies do best, setting up a sub-committee to investigate the issue. Established in October 1882, it comprised Arthur Kinnaird, Joseph Cofield, Tom Hindle, John Harvey, Morton Betts, Charles Alcock and NL Jackson, and they in turn appointed a commission within themselves to find evidence of paid players.

A full year went by without any proof being uncovered, the commission running round in circles with no prospect of achieving anything, when there was an unexpected breakthrough. In January 1884, Preston North End were accused by their FA Cup opponents Upton Park of paying players. It was not particularly difficult to spot that two prominent Scots, Nick Ross and George Drummond, had joined the club the previous summer. But when Preston club secretary William Sudell appeared before the FA, he astonished those present by openly admitting the charge. Preston were summarily expelled from the competition but Sudell's brazen admission had let the genie out of the bottle.

In some respects it was a relief that the issue was now out in the open and the following month about 200 delegates attended a meeting at the Freemasons' Tavern to debate the way ahead. Arthur and Alcock, treasurer and secretary respectively, formed the pragmatic view that professionalism was here to stay, and that it was better to control it by legislation than to risk a schism in the game (as later happened to rugby football). Paradoxically, they found a fair degree of support in the amateur south, where clubs initially considered it an issue of little concern to the home counties, but there was vociferous opposition from some quarters, particularly clubs in Birmingham and Sheffield who were fearful of their futures if the hidden payments became legitimised.

Alcock's proposal that professionalism be legalised was not only heavily defeated[6], it actually led to a backlash of repression by the FA. Another sub-committee, including Arthur, was delegated to suggest effective ways to suppress the 'abuses' of veiled professionalism and the importation of players. Based on their recommendations, the FA passed a new rule in the summer of 1884 requiring clubs to list any players who were non-native to their own area – the inference being that they were likely to have been paid to move there. This administrative sledgehammer provoked an outright rebellion in Lancashire, and a group of prominent clubs threatened to break away completely unless they were allowed to pay players. Under the chairmanship of William Sudell the 'rebel' movement quickly grew to 70 clubs who attended a conference in Manchester to discuss the formation of their own British Football Association.

Urgent action was required by the FA to prevent such a split and, after a short-term concession to suspend the residency requirement, Alcock drafted a recommendation that it would be 'expedient to legalise professionalism'. When this was put to the vote in January 1885, the wind was clearly changing as the proposal attracted a small majority, but not the two-thirds margin required for a rule change. For the next few months, a stand-off was achieved in which the FA did nothing to discourage professionalism, and even selected players suspected of receiving remuneration for international honours.

When a further proposal to legalise professionalism again fell short of a two-thirds majority, the exasperated FA formed yet another sub-committee with a remit to find a compromise that would achieve a sufficient majority. At last, on 20 July 1885, their resolution, that it would be in the interests of football to legalise the employment of professional players, was voted through at Anderton's Hotel in Fleet Street.[7] The way was now open for clubs to develop along business lines, without recourse to subterfuge and deception.

The acceptance of professionalism brought an uneasy peace to football with the notable exception of Scotland, where the decision was greeted with outrage. The Scottish FA published a list of 68 'outlaw' players who had gone south to take the English shilling, and even threatened to boycott the annual international rather than play against professionals. Not until 1893 did the legislators north of the border finally accept the inevitable.

In the meantime, as a direct consequence of professionalism, the clubs needed to assure a regular source of income. The solution came courtesy of a Manchester journalist, WH Mounsey, who wrote to the *Athletic News*, advocating a league based on the American baseball system. His idea was picked up by Aston Villa director William McGregor (like Arthur, a Scot with Perthshire roots) and the Football League was duly formed in 1888, but without a single southern club among its twelve members.

As more leagues sprung up around the country, the amateurs, who had been prepared to accept the principle of paid players so long as it did not affect them, increasingly found themselves sidelined. They would soon rebel against professional dominance of the game, a bitter argument that would dominate Arthur's forthcoming presidency of the FA.

---

[1] John McDowell, *Dwight L Moody: the Discoverer of Men and The Maker of Movements*, p42

[2] The first was at 30 Spital Square (known as Pelham House) and in 1881 they leased a second property at 14 Fournier Street under the name of Howard House. See W McG Eagar, *Making Men*, p244

[3] Geoffrey Green, *History of the Football Association*, p131.

[4] See *The Times*, 14 June 1886, for a detailed description of the NPRS aims, and members of Council.

[5] In the last ever match, in 1887, the teams are not recorded.

[6] His proposal attracted just three votes at the meeting on 28 February 1884.

[7] For further detail of the struggle for professionalism, see Geoffrey Green's *History of the Football Association*, p95 on; also *History of the Lancashire FA*, p147 on.

CHAPTER 8

The good Lord

1887-1900

ARTHUR SUCCEEDED his father as Lord Kinnaird in April 1887, two months after his fortieth birthday. The title brought new responsibilities, challenges and immense wealth, and he would also soon be elevated to the top position in football. Things would never be the same again.

Less than ten years had passed since two Old Boys teams had contested the final of the FA Cup[1], and the establishment of the Football League was a wake-up call for the FA that the balance of power had swung from the amateur to the professional, from south to north. In an era of rapid expansion, the governing body had to modernise, and an opportunity to revitalise its leadership arose because of Major Marindin's growing disillusionment with the way the game was going. Very much 'old school', he lamented the disappearance of traditional values in football, and after 15 years as President he announced he was stepping down. There was only one man in the frame to succeed him: with impeccable credentials as a 'football man', Arthur had proved himself as a dedicated committee member and treasurer, and was also a nobleman and a respected figure in the city. He was elected unopposed as President of the FA on 1 September 1890.

No-one could have foreseen the challenges which would confront the new President during his time in office: the commercialism of football, six figure crowds, the creation of a world governing body, a bitter split between amateurs and professionals, even a world war. Yet Arthur skilfully negotiated the issues and the entrenched views, with Geoffrey Green, for one, unequivocal about the respect he commanded: 'Kinnaird and his family were a part of the game and will ever remain so. The Council of the Football

Association was proud of its 'football Lord'. His brisk entrance into the Council Chamber had never been allowed to pass without fitting recognition, and whatever the importance of the debate might have been, members would pause to give a hearty greeting to the man who had once led the gallant Old Etonians on the football field and had also represented his native Scotland in the international sphere.'[2]

The game was crying out for fresh ideas and there was no time to waste for the triumvirate of Arthur as President, Charles Clegg as chairman of Council and Charles Alcock as secretary, 'men of sufficient stature and wisdom to adjust themselves to the new meaning and tempo of a widening democracy and to a new outlook.'[3] As if to emphasise that this was a new era, the FA moved from its cramped office in Holborn to 61 Chancery Lane (premises which were conveniently shared with the London FA, of which Arthur remained President). Alcock was delegated to draw up a constitution, which specified an elected Council to take over from the appointed committee men, introduced rigorous financial controls and a range of administrative improvements. It was only three years since the FA had recognised the need to pay a salary to the secretary (a post which Alcock retained[4]) and now it took on a full-time clerk. This was all in marked contrast to the early days, when the organisation had struggled to survive; now, it was a battle to keep the national pastime within disciplined and controlled limits.[5]

As President, Arthur was *ex officio* a member of every committee, and although in practice he was not expected to have a hands-on administrative role, he regularly attended meetings of Council and the Consultative Committee, giving him the opportunity to push through change. The following spring, when he chaired his first annual general meeting of the FA, the members endorsed this new wind blowing through football, agreeing to the introduction of Standing Orders to bring a semblance of order to Council meetings, and new rules governing the registration of professional players. They backed a proposal to replace the role of umpire with that of linesman, and the ground-breaking move to introduce the penalty kick.[6] There was even a healthy profit of £415 on the year for Charles Hart, Arthur's successor as treasurer, to report.[7]

Amongst all this office activity, there was still football to be played, and Arthur concluded his first season by presenting the FA Cup to Blackburn Rovers, who matched Wanderers' record of five victories, and among the players was Jimmy Forrest, who equalled the individual record of five FA Cup wins. It would be almost 120 years before any player did so again.[8]

With ever more leagues and competitions, and unprecedented levels of money in the game, most of the FA's efforts were devoted to administering issues that had not been on the radar a few years before: it had to decide, for example, how to deal with the prevalence of betting, disruptive behaviour by large crowds, transfer fees for players, even suspicions of corruption. To prevent an overspill into the summer, it was also necessary to set a time limit on the season, with no games being permitted from May to August.

One of Arthur's ideas that did not come to fruition was outlined in August 1892 when he performed the official opening of Goodison Park in Liverpool, the new home of Everton FC and one of England's first purpose-built football grounds. While some of his comments were to be expected – his desire for football to be the national sport, and to save the game from 'the taint of rowdyism and betting' – he also had some surprising advice for his hosts. Mindful that the catalyst for Everton's move to Goodison had been a dispute over the ownership of Anfield, Arthur suggested the club buy the freehold of the land, thereby securing the ground for the next generation and avoiding the risk of landowners selling it off for building. What was more, he told them to bring pressure to bear upon the municipal corporation to supply the ground at public expense.[9] The club president, George Mahon, responded that if the Liverpool public gave its backing, in return the club would somehow contribute to the city's public institutions. Everton did buy the freehold of Goodison three years later, and issued shares in the club to supporters, but the continental model of municipal provision of football stadia never took off in Britain.

The FA had stadium problems of its own because of the massive crowds that were flocking to football – Arthur's last final was seen by 8,000, but the cup showpiece now attracted three times as many, and would treble again by the end of the century. The Oval was far too small for such occasions, without sufficient banking and just ropes around the pitch, and it was a blessing in

113

disguise in 1893 when Surrey County Cricket Club withdrew permission for the ground to be used.[10] As a short term solution, the FA chose Fallowfield Sports Ground in Manchester for the FA Cup final, but it proved hopelessly inadequate; the England v Scotland international was taken to Richmond Athletic Ground in south-west London, which at least had a track record of hosting major rugby matches. The 1894 cup final was staged at Goodison Park before the FA resolved that its flagship event belonged in the capital, and settled on the arena within the Crystal Palace grounds from 1895 onwards.

Another link with the past was broken when Charles Alcock retired as secretary in 1896[11] after 25 years in the position – unpaid except for the last ten – but the FA found the ideal replacement in Frederick Wall[12], who outdid Alcock for durability and held the post for almost 40 years.

Although retired from club football, Arthur still enjoyed putting his boots on from time to time and carried on playing for recreation. NL Jackson wrote at the turn of the century that 'down to 1890 he played regularly, and since then he has not missed a season without an occasional game' and added 'it would be rash to assert that his active career in the football field has ended'.[13]

However, on becoming President he gladly ended the tradition that the man at the top should referee the FA Cup Final – Major Marindin had been in charge at the last eight finals. He found it frustrating to be confined to the sidelines, as James Catton recalled: 'The duty of referee did not appeal to him, but I have seen him on the line in important cup-ties, and there he could enjoy the atmosphere of combat.'[14] Among the matches he umpired was the FA Cup final of 1889 between Preston and Wolves when, arriving late at the Oval, he had a severe struggle reaching the pitch because a record crowd had already filled the arena and spectators were being turned away.[15] Once in position, however, he took to the task with gusto: 'Lord Kinnaird was as much on the hop as if he had been in the Alhambra ballet, running here, throwing in the ball, waving that little flag of his, and whistling like the East wind.'[16]

The last organised game Arthur can be confirmed as playing was in December 1896, two months short of his 50th birthday, for a team of Old Internationals[17] against Charterhouse. Played in a ghostly atmosphere, as London was enveloped in 'a rich, thick, yellow and brown fog, deepening almost into black'[18], the press report described him as 'a middle-aged gentleman, whose red beard and white trousers – not curtailed – were so conspicuous when he led the Old Etonians to victory at the Oval in the final for the English Cup.' Arthur was very much the elder statesman as he led his side to a 5-0 victory over the schoolboys, a fitting tribute to his powers of endurance.

A man of means

As well as a place in the House of Lords, Arthur inherited over £250,000 from his father and took possession of Rossie Priory in Perthshire. He was, of course, familiar with the family seat and its surroundings, having visited regularly since a boy, but coming to terms with the ownership of a large estate was a different matter entirely. He took his role as landowner seriously, and would generally spend two or three months a year in Scotland, but first his business instincts prompted him to find out exactly what he had inherited and he inaugurated a full inventory of staff, livestock and possessions.

It took an extensive workforce to run the estate, with four men in the factor's office, four gamekeepers, nine gardeners, ten foresters, seven in the home farm, five tradesmen, a coachman, a man to look after the grass parks and a keeper of the priory house. To this could be added a household staff and 81 tenants, who would all be invited to hear him preach in the chapel; he made a point of inviting the young ploughmen. The inventory[19] of the cellars revealed large quantities of fine wines, including champagne, claret, burgundy, port, whisky, brandy, etc. Despite Arthur's temperance leanings, he was never an advocate of total abstinence, and was also mindful of the need to be a good host, so there was no move to dispose of the alcoholic hoard.

Not everything was to his liking: there was a prize-winning herd of Highland cattle, developed over many years, but his uncle George's enthusiasm had overreached itself. The agricultural show medals, still kept at Rossie Priory, are as impressive in quantity as in the quality of the engraving, but the herd was a severe drain on resources: it cost £40 to rear each head of cattle, three times the prevailing market price. Arthur had had an earlier taste of the inherent difficulties of cattle husbandry on a visit in 1882, when his innocent enquiry as to why the cricket field was not cleared of cattle for the start of the season was answered by an exasperated estate manager: 'I hope to get them out in about a week... We were badly off this time last year for grass for our dairy cows but are a great deal worse this year. The Highland Cattle are now so numerous that all our home parks are as bare as a board.'[20]

Little surprise, then, that the troublesome beasts were among the first to go, with no sentimentality for the prizes won in years gone by. In October 1887 there were bargains to be had at Perth Mart, and although one cow did reach £26, the others fetched half that. Just four calves and three dairy cows were kept, along with the flock of sheep. The prize-winning bull Rossie was granted a stay of execution, and won the gold medal at the Highland and Agricultural Society Show in Glasgow in 1888, but this was his last hurrah before he, too, got the chop.

Arthur kept a private ledger book[21] and his annual summaries give a detailed insight into his healthy financial position. In 1888, his first full year as Lord Kinnaird, Arthur received around £14,000 from the bank, contributing to a total income of around £20,000 (equivalent to around £2 million today). How to spend such a vast income? This is his breakdown of expenditure, which amounted to £10,924: Charity £3,735; Household £1,838; Stables £500; Dress and personal £63; Rent, wages and tax £1,296; Presents and allowances £721; Doctors £237; Travelling £258; Hotel bills £122; Sundries £150; Otto Leyde[22] £200; Insurances £294; Lawyers and surveyors £85; Banks, postage, clubs £255; Plaistow £1,088; Rossie £83.

In 1892, when he drew up proposals for his will for consideration by his solicitors, Markby Wilde and Johnson of Lincoln's Inn, his total net worth was estimated to be at least £238,000, including Plaistow Estate, houses in St James's Square and South Audley Street, capital of £114,000 and personal property worth around £80,000.

He allocated around £6,000 per annum to his chosen charities, and was also known for his habit of giving regular presents to useful contacts such as station masters and church ministers. Money and celebrity attracted a steady stream of invitations to be patron of good causes, many of which he accepted, but being such a well-known philanthropist also made him a target for fraud. One attempt reached the courts in 1893, when Joseph Esser, a 49-year-old German who claimed to be suffering from acute bronchitis and reduced to poverty, was exposed as a serial begging-letter writer to the rich and famous, and his letter was passed to the police.[23] Arthur was obviously an extremely rich man, but if the need ever arose he knew where to turn: he responded to an approach from the fine art dealer Wertheimer of Bond Street, stating that if he were ever short of money, he would consider their offer for the purchase of a Rubens and a Rembrandt.[24]

At the bank, he continued with the strategy of growth by merger and in 1888 Ransom and Bouverie became part of the mouthful of Barclay, Bevan, Tritton, Ransom, Bouverie & Co. This in turn led to Barclays Bank as we know it today being formed in the 'great merger' of 1896, as 15 private banks came together, many of them local institutions in the southern half of England, but stretching as far north as Darlington. The first chairman was Francis Bevan (whose brother had married Arthur's sister), and Arthur had a seat on the board which allowed him to step back from day-to-day management of the bank, while remaining principal director of the local head office at Pall Mall East until his death. He also succeeded his father as chairman of the County Fire Office, one of the oldest insurance companies in Britain, once described as 'a veritable gold-mine to its shareholders'[25].

Politically, his interventions in the House of Lords were sporadic, and although he aligned himself with the Liberal Unionist Party he preferred to focus on direct action through his many charitable ventures. He did, however, understand the value of his position and in his maiden speech he presented a petition from the Dundee Gospel Temperance Union, in favour of the Licensed Premises Earlier Closing (Scotland) Bill.[26]

Arthur was not adept at political debate and met his match when trying to make an obscure religious protest about a joint meeting of the Convocations of York and Canterbury. 'My Lords,' he said, 'I beg to ask Her Majesty's Government whether a joint assembly of members of the two Convocations is not in fact a meeting of the Convocations, and therefore illegal without a licence from the Crown. It may be that the affair is not of much importance in itself, but, in view of recent events in the Church, it is desirable to look rather closely into these matters. I wish to know whether the Government consider that the proceedings were irregular.'

This drew a sarcastic riposte from the Prime Minister, the Marquess of Salisbury: 'My Lords, I am loth to confess that I do not study ecclesiastical literature with the devotion of the noble Earl, and I was utterly ignorant that this awful thing had taken place. It is impossible for this Assembly to recover from the shock it has sustained unless we know the precise nature of the conspiracy against our civil law to which the noble Lord has alluded in his question. I would suggest to the noble Earl for his comfort, if this thing disturbs his sleep, that this confusion has arisen from his not sufficiently dwelling upon the word 'meetings', and the different meanings of it.'[27] End of argument.

Not everyone was as dismissive of Arthur's status as a peer, and he continued to accumulate positions of authority in a range of organisations. He was made Commandant of the Tay Division of the Submarine Miners, a volunteer division of the Royal Engineers, in 1893, with the honorary rank of Lieutenant Colonel; his commission was signed by Prince Edward (the future King George V) and Henry Campbell Bannerman, at that time Secretary of State for War. Another elaborate vellum parchment in the family archive records his appointment as Deputy Lieutenant of Kent; he became a Justice of the Peace, was elected a Fellow of the Royal Geographical Society, and was commissioned in the Royal Company of Archers, the monarch's ceremonial bodyguard in Scotland. He also followed in his father's footsteps as treasurer of the National Rifle Association, giving his name to one of the competitions at Bisley, the Kinnaird, which is for marksmanship over 300 metres.

To keep active he took up cricket again and had a ready-made team, as on inheriting his title he had become patron of Rossie Priory Cricket Club, founded by his uncle in 1828 within view of the house. Arthur had occasionally turned out for the club in his youth, and now that he was approaching middle age, he put on his whites again in 1887 for his first game in almost 20 years.[28] He enjoyed it so much that he continued to turn out for the club whenever he was in Scotland, and even played competitive matches in the Dundee and District Cricket Union past his fiftieth birthday, travelling with Rossie Priory CC as far afield as Montrose and Forfar.

As club patron, he also gave practical help, building two new pavilions (still in use) and contributing 20 shillings a week to the salary of a professional, 26-year-old John Broadley of Yorkshire, on condition that he worked as a gardener in winter.[29] The arrangement was a success and Arthur played alongside Broadley in two memorable wins over the county side, Perthshire, in 1896 and

1897, with his son Douglas also playing in the latter.[30] For his part, Broadley liked it so much that he settled in Inchture for the rest of his life, and was talented enough to be selected for Scotland in 1903.

Cricket at Rossie Priory, a unique setting

While cricket was a good way of keeping active, back in London football was the only sport Arthur had time for. While the game's primary appeal now lay with the working classes, it did attract support from some of the leading figures of the day. Arthur invited the Prince of Wales, the first member of the royal family to attend an association football match[31] to become Patron of the FA in 1892, and he retained the position on becoming King Edward VII, as did his successor, George V. Although the present Queen is not a Patron of the FA[32], the royal links to football have been maintained and the presidency is currently held by Prince William, appointed in 2006, another who – like Arthur – learned his football at Eton.[33]

The establishment came out in force at major matches, and at the 1899 FA Cup Final, which drew a record crowd of 73,000 to Crystal Palace to see Sheffield United defeat Derby County, Arthur entertained two prominent Old Etonians, Lord Rosebery and Arthur Balfour, now Prime Minister, as well as the visiting South African statesman Cecil Rhodes. The following year Lord Rosebery, a renowned racehorse owner, sat next to Arthur at the Scotland v

England international, played at Celtic Park in Glasgow, which Scotland won 4-1 wearing Rosebery's racing colours of primrose and pink hoops.

The game's meteoric growth in his first decade as President was captured in the FA annual accounts for 1899, which showed a profit of over £10,000.[34] Even if that amount still paled into insignificance against Arthur's personal income, it was a clear sign that football had become mass entertainment, and big business.

Philanthropy without boundaries

Arthur remained close to Quintin Hogg, and continued to back his thriving Regent Street Polytechnic, which promoted 'industrial skills, general knowledge, health and wellbeing of young men and women belonging to the poorer classes'.[35] In return, Hogg was a vocal supporter of the Homes for Working Boys, one of Arthur's principal charities.[36]

However, in theological terms their relationship was growing apart. Hogg commented: 'It is very strange how the men who were in our Eton Bible class have become much more strict and narrowly evangelical in their views since they left Eton, whilst I have gone in the opposite direction.'[37] This was made clear in a letter which Hogg wrote to Arthur (marked strictly confidential) as a riposte to some criticism: 'I hate differing from you on such a subject, but still one must preach what in God's sight one believes to be the truth. ... I don't want to lead men to any theology as such, I want to lead them to Christ, and such a Christ as I find in the gospels and by whose grace and in whose strength alone I hope to be made partaker of the divine nature and heavenly state. Honestly, dear Arthur, I do not think I have spoken anything that might not have fallen from your own lips during the past six months.'[38]

In contrast to Hogg's single-minded focus on the Polytechnic, Arthur juggled responsibilities with over fifty charities, and so long as Christian values were at the heart of every mission, Arthur saw no boundaries to his work on the broad theme of providing education, health and opportunity. He was as enthusiastic about raising funds for a rescue mission in Sudan as helping needy Scots who had fallen on hard times. In purely numerical terms, the evangelical part was the most successful, as

Lord Kinnaird was a respected figure in the city in the 1890s

people were 'saved' on an industrial scale, an idea of which can be taken from just one contemporary report: Arthur chaired the annual meeting of the Thames Church Mission, a relatively local charity, which claimed to have made over 100,000 visits to sailors and seamen, held over 150,000 services, and distributed close to one million tracts and bibles.[39]

With the time to travel abroad more regularly, he joined a deputation of politicians and members of the Trades Union Congress who crossed to America in October 1887, to present an address signed by 233 Members of Parliament to President Grover Cleveland, urging him to agree to an Anglo-American arbitration treaty (a measure intended to set an example to other countries who were too quick to go to war).[40] Cleveland was the third President he had met but his primary motivation for undertaking that trip may well have been a visit to Pittsburgh to attend the international conference of the YWCA. Accompanied by his sisters Emily and Gertrude, Arthur was described in the *New York Herald* as 'a handsome, gentle-voiced, pleasing gentleman'.

He took seriously his duties with the YWCA, not least because his mother – who died in 1888 – had founded the organisation, and the family bankrolled a monthly YWCA magazine, *Our Own Gazette*, which reached a circulation of nearly 100,000. Arthur was appointed YWCA President shortly after inheriting the title, although his sisters were the power behind the scenes at a time when it would have been almost unthinkable for a woman to be president of a national organisation. Arthur was also treasurer of the men's equivalent, the YMCA, which he considered 'a valuable agency in the formation of the spiritual, mental and physical well-being of young men ... the greatest and best means that the 19th century possesses for the winning of young men from the service of the devil to that of Jesus Christ.'[41]

The newspapers of the day are peppered liberally with mentions of Arthur fulfilling YMCA and YWCA business, opening new buildings, appealing for funds and presiding over conferences.[42] The speeches he made on these occasions give an insight into his views, such as when he told the Scottish YMCA conference in 1891 of his condemnation of the 'enormous trinity of evil', by which he meant intemperance, impurity and gambling.[43] In 1894, to help celebrate the golden jubilee of the YMCA, he hosted a dinner for delegates who attended the international congress and later that

122

evening, at a packed Albert Hall, Sir George Williams, the organisation's founder, was presented with a bust of himself by Arthur, who said that the association aimed at 'bringing the minds of young men to a perfect state, educating their minds by technical and other classes and, above all, caring for their spiritual welfare.'[44]

Arthur resumed his relationship with DL Moody in the autumn of 1893, sailing across the Atlantic to support the evangelist's World's Fair campaign in Chicago. He spent a month in the States and was becoming a more confident speaker, as observers praised his eloquent contributions: 'The word which the British nobleman speaks is an appeal to the young to keep their record clear and clean, and an assurance to those who have failed that God can, and will, restore and remake that which they have marred, if they will but bring it to Him.'[45] It was his last meeting with Moody before the preacher died in 1899.

On the home front, Arthur was acutely aware of pressing social issues that had to be tackled, having seen at first hand the depths to which some people sank through poverty. He had a particular interest in the welfare of women who, given the lack of opportunities offered by Victorian society, often had no option but to resort to prostitution when they fell below the poverty line. Thus he supported one of the earliest women's all-night refuges, the London Female Preventive and Reformatory Institution, and gave his backing to a range of movements which were trying to clean up the city by monitoring and reporting brothels. These organisations typically had long-winded names, such as the Central Vigilance Society for the Repression of Immorality, and in 1897 Arthur was a founder of the London Council for the Promotion of Public Morality, concerned with making 'some practical effort to purify the condition of the streets of London, and remove obvious temptations to immorality.' These were not, as has been suggested elsewhere, prurient do-gooders who were obsessed with sex, but campaigners against prostitution and the white slave trade. Arthur preferred prevention to cure, and was happy to act as treasurer of bodies which provided women with the means to escape the poverty trap through training, work and shelter. His interest in women's welfare extended in other directions, too: in 1896 he signed a successful petition in favour of admitting women to Cambridge University.[46]

However, perhaps his greatest concern relating to women was further afield, in India. Arthur had succeeded his father as treasurer of the Zenana Bible and Medical Mission, although it was really his mother's project as she had helped to found the organisation in 1852.[47] Zenana are the inner apartments of a house in which women live, inaccessible to men, and the mission encouraged Christian Indian women to study medicine, then funded them to take medical assistance and rudimentary education, as well as religion, into the home; it claimed to have access to 1353 zenanas by the 1880s. Arthur had had first-hand experience of the zenana mission during his travels to India in 1871, and later wrote of 'the utter failure of Hinduism to help, and the glad reception of the True Light,' adding that 'if a country is to be won for Christ, it must be by means of native workers.'[48]

In 1897 he took Alma with him for another six month tour of India, enabling him to assess the changes that had taken place in the intervening years. The country was recovering from a devastating famine the previous year that had seen at least a million people die, and the couple witnessed extraordinary hardship as they travelled around the mission stations of the Punjab and North West Provinces. One of their first stops was in Lucknow to visit the Lady Kinnaird Memorial Hospital, named in honour of his mother (whose other legacy is a school in Lahore, the first women's college in the Punjab, which is now Kinnaird College). At New Year they witnessed a mass baptism at Gorakhpur, and the following day Arthur performed the ceremonial opening of three wells around the new Christian village of Basharatpur; it was announced that if a village ever grew up around one well it would be called Kinnairdpur in his honour (it never happened).

At Calcutta, Arthur and Alma were guests of the Viceroy of India, the Earl of Elgin, and travelled with him by special train to see a solar eclipse at Buxar. A more poignant stop was at the memorial church at Cawnpore, site of the massacre in 1857 that had claimed over 1,000 British lives, among them the parents of William Lindsay, his Scotland teammate in the unofficial football internationals. Throughout the tour, Arthur regularly addressed the students and staff at the mission schools, while Alma was able to enter the zenanas with female missionaries to speak to local women. Back in London, Arthur spoke at a meeting of the Zenana Bible and Medical Mission to describe how educational opportunities for girls had improved since his first visit.[49]

There was one final surprise outcome of the trip to India. His family seemed to have reached its full extent when Margaret was born in 1892, but a full seven years later along came Patrick, in December 1898, by which time Arthur was 51 and Alma 44.

---

[1] Old Carthusians v Old Etonians, FA Cup Final 1881

[2] Geoffrey Green, *History of the Football Association*, p303

[3] Geoffrey Green, *History of the Football Association*, p123

[4] Charles Alcock had been honorary secretary, unpaid, from 1870-1887; for the same job he had earned £200 a year from Surrey Cricket Club since 1871.

[5] See Geoffrey Green, *History of the Football Association*, p146 on, for a detailed analysis of the issues.

[6] The decisions to change the Laws of the Game were formally taken by the International FA Board, which had been formed in 1886.

[7] Geoffrey Green, *History of the Football Association*, p140

[8] Ashley Cole won his fifth FA Cup in 2009, then set a new record the following year.

[9] *Liverpool Mercury*, 25 August 1892

[10] Their excuse was they had decided to returf the cricket pitch.

[11] Alcock remained a vice-President until his death in 1907.

[12] Sir Frederick after he was knighted in 1930

[13] NL Jackson, *Association Football*, p146-7

[14] JAH Catton, *Wickets and Goals*, p246.

[15] Geoffrey Green, *History of the FA Cup*, p47

[16] *Pall Mall Budget*, quoted in Bryon Butler, *Official Illustrated History of the FA Cup*, p25.

[17] His team mates were Harry Swepstone, Arthur Walters, Ralph Squire, Charles Holden-White, Charles Wreford-Brown, John Lambie, William Cobbold, Clement Mitchell, Edward Wynyard and George Brann.

[18] *Glasgow Herald*, 17 December 1896

[19] AK Bell Library, MS100, 21 May 1888

[20] Letters from Duncan Stewart, estate manager, in the Kinnaird family archive.

[21] AK Bell Library, MS100, bundle 1097

[22] Otto Leyde was a German artist based in Edinburgh.

[23] *The Times*, 21 March 1893

[24] AK Bell Library, MS100, bundle 952; the pictures eventually went under the hammer at Sotheby's in 1948, attracting painfully low prices in the post-war depression.

[25] Aubrey Noakes, *County Fire Office*, p103; Arthur had been a director since 1872.

[26] *The Times*, 4 August 1887

[27] *Hansard*, 10 July 1899, vol 74, 294-297

[28] *Dundee Courier*, 5 September 1887; it took place at Glamis Castle and Arthur scored eight runs in a heavy defeat.

[29] Perth & Kinross Library, MS100, bundle 962

[30] *Dundee Courier*, 31 August 1896; 13 September 1897

[31] The Prince has attended his first football match as a 16-year-old in 1857, the Oxford v Cambridge field game at Eton. His first association match was Gentlemen v Players at the Oval in 1886.

[32] The Queen is, however, Patron of the Scottish FA.

[33] Four other FA Presidents were also Old Etonians: the Earl of Athlone, Duke of Gloucester, Earl of Harewood and Duke of Kent.

[34] Geoffrey Green, *History of the Football Association*, p168-9

[35] Following mergers with other colleges, the Polytechnic is now the University of Westminster.

[36] *The Times*, 6 July 1894

[37] Sir Henry Lunn, *Chapters from My Life*, p139

[38] Letter in Kinnaird family archive dated 23 December 1887

[39] *The Times*, 22 May 1891

[40] *The Pall Mall Gazette*, 24 November 1887, has a full account of the meeting.

[41] *The Sheffield & Rotherham Independent*, 26 November 1886

[42] A word search in *The Times* between 1887 and 1923 offers over 1500 mentions of Lord Kinnaird.

[43] *The Scotsman*, 11 September 1891

[44] *The Times*, 7 June 1894

[45] Rev HB Hartzler, *Moody in Chicago*, p191

[46] *The Times*, 17 January 1896

[47] The mission is still going strong today, now known as Interserve.

[48] Introduction to Ada Lee, *The Life of Chundra Lela*, p5

[49] There is a detailed description of the tour in AR Cavalier, *In Northern India*.

CHAPTER 9

Imperturbable and majestic
1900-1914

THE ARRIVAL of the new century gave cause for celebration as Arthur and Alma reached their silver wedding anniversary and, by a happy coincidence, it coincided with 21st birthday of Douglas, the Master of Kinnaird. They were feted at Rossie Priory and the goings-on in August 1900 were recorded in a privately printed book, *A Silver Wedding and a Coming of Age*, which they issued as Christmas presents.

While the slim volume depicts the week through rose-tinted glasses, a genuine sense of contentment shines through: for example, a cricket match was interrupted for Arthur to be presented with a massive silver salver by the Rossie Priory club captain, Robert Constable, who made a speech outlining the duties of a good patron: defraying all expenses, hospitably entertaining the visiting clubs, and paying for the services of highly skilled professionals. Arthur responded, typically, that it was a privilege to assist in the proper cultivation of outdoor sports such as cricket, 'as such manly sports not only develop the physical nature of men, but react in a pure and healthy way on their intellectual and moral characters'. Douglas had a similar presentation from Rossie Curling Club, and the author[1] described events in detail, right down to listing all the guests at a fireworks party, a banquet for the tenantry, a garden party for ladies, an entertainment for children, a concert and finally a benediction by one of the foremost preachers of the day, the Rev John Watson. He also gave a lengthy history of the Kinnaird family, but unfortunately revealed virtually nothing of Arthur's life.

As if to emphasise that the old century had gone, a footballing concept that failed to survive it was hacking; outlawed since 1863, hacking was removed from the Laws of the Game in

127

1899, to be replaced by the more down-to-earth 'kicking'. Arthur was said to be 'imperturbable and majestic in his high position of President'[2] as he led football into the twentieth century, and under his guidance the FA again modernised its structures, becoming a limited company in 1903; two thousand shares were issued, with Share No 1 being in the name of Lord Kinnaird.

The game's influence was spreading, and not only did Tottenham Hotspur become the first southern side to win the FA Cup since Old Etonians, lifting the trophy in 1901, there was also a new international dimension. An FA representative team had gone to Germany in 1899, club teams had also toured abroad (Corinthians reached as far as South Africa in 1897), teams of Canadians had twice visited Britain, and British expatriates had introduced football to every continent. While acknowledging the internationalisation of the game, the FA was less than receptive to proposals for a body to oversee it. This was made perfectly clear in 1903 when Robert Guérin, football secretary of the governing body for sport in France, the Union des Sociétés Françaises de Sports Athlétiques, came to London to offer the FA the lead role in a new federation. To his despair, he encountered prevarication and indifference: first, he spoke to Frederick Wall, but the FA secretary just listened with his head in his hands then abruptly said he would put the matter to the FA Council. Several months passed and Guérin heard nothing, so he requested another meeting and returned to London, this time to see the President. He found Arthur likeable enough but trying to get a meaningful response was, he wrote, like 'cutting water with a sword'[3].

The FA was not so much short-sighted as bound by a hideously slow bureaucratic process: Council referred the matter to the International FA Board, which in turn asked the national associations of Scotland, Wales and Ireland for their opinion. When their responses eventually filtered back, Council simply noted that it 'cannot see the advantages of such a Federation, but on all matters upon which joint action was desirable they would be prepared to confer.'[4] Guérin could wait no longer for the English and in May 1904 he was elected as the inaugural President of FIFA (the Fédération Internationale de Football Association) which had an initial membership of France, Holland, Belgium, Denmark, Spain, Sweden and Switzerland. Ultimately, the FA decided to take a paternal view, joining FIFA in 1905, and at the following year's

128

conference in Berne, Guérin handed over the presidency to Englishman Daniel Woolfall.

Once these contacts had been established, there was soon an appetite for international competition, and although an initial proposal for a FIFA tournament came to naught, the Olympic Games provided the necessary platform. Arthur, as a founding member of the British Olympic Association, was one of the welcoming committee when the International Olympic Committee held its summer conference in London in 1904. In between visits to meet King Edward VII and a cricket match at Lords, he entertained them to lunch at the White Hart in Windsor and arranged a visit to Eton for tea with Edmund Warre, the headmaster.[5] The IOC took a decision at that conference to award the 1908 Olympic Games to Rome, but after a disastrous volcanic eruption of Vesuvius, the honour of hosting was transferred to London. The city had just two years to prepare and Arthur found himself serving on the organising committee, with a remit to stage the inaugural Olympic football tournament (or at least to ensure the FA did so).

This provoked a remarkable change of tune from his initially cool response to the idea of adding a continental dimension to football and Arthur became a strong advocate, insisting that international competition would be a means of raising standards. Speaking after the 1908 FA Cup Final, in which Wolves beat Newcastle, he said that 'struggles between North and South, England and Scotland, were interesting, but in future there existed the possibility of Great Britain's supremacy being challenged by other nations. The international championship might be taken away from these shores, in which event we should go abroad and take it back.'[6] He had obviously come round to Robert Guérin's way of thinking.

That autumn, Arthur took great pride in the Great Britain football team[7] and was photographed with the eleven which won Olympic gold by defeating Denmark 2-0 at the White City Stadium in London. While the football tournament did not fire the public imagination, with just 8,000 spectators at the final, the Games as a whole were judged an outstanding success and Arthur was among 450 people who celebrated a great festival of sport at the closing dinner in the Holborn Restaurant.

Arthur (far left) with the Great Britain team which took the gold medal at the 1908 Olympic Games

Tackling the amateur question

This triumph masked a deep schism in the game. Selecting a Great Britain eleven to take part in the Olympics had not been a simple matter, as some of the best amateur players were intentionally unavailable. The year before had seen a breakaway movement, the climax to a deep-seated problem that had been rumbling on for years, ever since professionalism had been legalised. Although it is hard from a modern perspective to understand such attitudes, the amateurs were deeply set against the principle of men receiving money to play football, and determined to keep resolutely to themselves.

NL Jackson, founder of the Corinthians (who declined to play in the FA Cup as it would mean coming up against professionals) summed it up: 'In the south of England, except at one or two places, the great winter game is still a pleasant means of enjoyment. In the north of England it is nothing but the vastest and the shoddiest of money-making concerns.' He went on to decry the FA Cup itself: 'It was a mistake originally in 1871 to introduce an Association Cup for, while such an inducement is good enough for

130

good sportsmen, upon certain minds it has a very bad effect. The game should be played for its own sake and for no other reason whatever.' He concluded: 'The Association is now absolutely in the hands of the professionals. Many of these men make their living out of the game, and are dead against the South. ... The South were undoubtedly weak and apathetic when the pinch came, and now they suffer for it. ... The evil which has been done no whitewashing can ever undo. ... The amateur and the professional cannot amalgamate and exist together.'[8] It should be noted that Jackson, when he wrote this in 1894, was on the FA Council, and would shortly become a Vice-President.

In the first formal response by the FA in 1897, Arthur (who was a non-playing member of the Corinthians) chaired an inquiry into the position of amateur football and of professional clubs in districts that are governed by amateur associations[9], but it failed to reach a resolution and the situation was allowed to fester. Ten years of increasingly acrimonious debate later, one could still read fatuous opinions such as this, from Bertie Corbett of Corinthians: 'The excellence of professional play generally gives the impression that the many tricks and intricacies of the game are mastered by mechanical activity and laborious training. But the passes of the amateur, though made as often and as accurately, appear to be the result rather of natural instinct.'[10]

Arthur, rather forlornly, expressed his desire that 'professionals and amateurs would continue to play together as at cricket'[11], and when the FA voted to force the county associations – some of which remained exclusively amateur – to accept professional clubs as members it brought matters to a head in 1907. The amateurs protested vehemently, and it was particularly an issue for still-amateur Surrey and Middlesex, where there was a tacit understanding that professional clubs within their area would join the London FA (of which Arthur was still President). The amateurs were so incensed that 900 clubs withdrew from all cup competitions and formed a breakaway Amateur Football Association. The rebels included the major universities and the old boys clubs, although to put it in context the FA retained around 12,000 amateur clubs in membership.

The split caused a personal dilemma for Arthur, as his beloved Old Etonians were among the outcasts, leaving him with no choice but to break off formal contact with the club if he were to remain FA President. He had to find a new member club to represent and, in a clear nod to his Scottish roots, settled on London Caledonians, the London Senior League champions, for the remainder of his time in office.[12]

The FA had to assert its authority, and used its new membership of FIFA to gain agreement from the continental associations that they would not recognise or play against clubs from the Amateur FA. The FA also showed it could fight on behalf of the clubs which remained loyal, and Arthur's voice in the House of Lords was important as he chaired a committee which argued successfully for concessions for football in the Undeveloped Land Tax, part of the Government Finance Bill in 1909[13]; it was a measure which would, ironically, have hit amateur clubs the hardest.

The dispute ran on, and when representatives of the FA and Amateur FA met in 1912, they failed to reach agreement with Arthur pointing out that the Amateur FA's demand to be able to offer membership to unaffiliated clubs would result in an unacceptable overlap of jurisdiction.[14] He was adamant that the FA would not concede any ground, a tough stance that finally forced the Amateur FA to give in, and in February 1914 it consented to affiliate to the FA. The amateurs had to put a brave face on the reconciliation, which meant agreeing to be treated like any other affiliated association, while the existing amateur county associations would cease to exist. They were offered small concessions in return, such as places on the FA Council and the International Selection Committee, but it was a victory for the FA, which was now recognised unequivocally as the governing body for football in England.[15]

Dedicated campaigner for charity

Arthur's public profile became noticeably higher during the first decade of the new century. In a rare personal interview, given in 1903 to the *Sunday Strand*, the extent of his philanthropic commitments was outlined: 'The number of committees on which Lord Kinnaird is engaged it would be difficult, even for him, to say, but from his secretary I learned that more than fifty are regularly entered in his diary, so it will be readily understood that he has to find time on an average for attending three or four every day throughout the year, outside his business hours, while he is President of over thirty institutions, Vice-President of more than forty, and Treasurer to some thirty others. His ordinary working day is from nine in the morning until ten or eleven at night. He has been a worker all his life in many ways, business, politics, philanthropy, and in all ways Christian.'

When his interviewer, Rudolph de Cordova, asked Arthur for his views on charitable giving, his response was: 'The individual's charity is a serious subject because of the tremendous needs which have to be supplied, daily needs which everyone admits are a national necessity. These national needs cannot be met by charity, and in my opinion they will have to be met from the public exchequer. This includes grants for hospitals, and is contemplated for primary and secondary education, and further, nearly the whole of the cost for providing proper dwellings for the poor. Private charity or enterprise is entirely unable to grapple with any of these adequately.'

Having outlined this ideal of a welfare state, Arthur explained that, in his experience, rich people tended to be too selfish to contribute to the common good: 'People seem to be able to spend money on themselves, but not on others. The fact is, I am afraid, that people are getting more selfish, the rich especially so. The greater number always were so, and they remain as they have ever been, useless as far as charity is concerned. The religious man, both rich and a big giver, is a rarity. Practically all the principal, steady, daily giving is done by people of limited income. It is a curious thing that for fancy schemes people can get any amount of money they need. The public will give sentimentally, not systematically, and will give for new objects liberally, but it does not appreciate keeping up institutions which have been already started.'[16]

Clearly, Arthur had spent too many years appealing for funds to have any illusions about the charitable tendencies of his peers, and his increasingly outspoken speeches reflected his frustration that his charities and ventures always lacked money. However, while there is no doubting his sincerity and energy, it is hard to escape the conclusion that he lacked the charisma to make a major impact as a public speaker. This was remarked upon by a *New York Times* reporter, who reported rather less deferentially than the British press would have done when Arthur crossed the Atlantic again to address the 1901 International Jubilee Convention

133

of the YMCA in Boston: 'Lord Kinnaird is a representative of a type of British nobleman seldom seen in this country. His repugnance to notoriety is extreme, evidence of which is found in the fact that his name has hardly been mentioned in connection with the exercises in Boston. In spite of this, he does an immense amount of work in connection with all kinds of benevolent schemes, and he and his sister, the Hon Gertrude Kinnaird, are familiar figures at meetings of philanthropic and religious associations all over the United Kingdom. Lord Kinnaird can seldom be prevailed upon to speak, but when he does so, makes his remarks in a jerky manner, which shows the nervousness under which he labors.'[17]

One only has to read Arthur's speech to appreciate he was not particularly inspiring: 'We hope that what is so near to many of our hearts, namely the world-wide duty of the Young Men's Christian Association not merely to make its organisation perfect in Christian countries, but also to reach out to the young men of non-Christian lands, may be accomplished. Only you and I can evangelize this generation to which we belong. Our sons may evangelize another, but unless you and I wake up in a way we have never done before, many millions of our young men and young women will go into a lost eternity.'[18]

Back home, what was exercising his mind at this time, and that of many other religiously-minded people, was a perceived threat to the Protestant faith of the nation from Catholicism. Early in 1899, Arthur had presided over a meeting which attracted ten thousand people to the Albert Hall in London (and 760 telegrams of support, including the longest telegram ever sent in Britain[19]), to draw attention to the alleged 'great secret conspiracy' to reunite the Church of England with Rome.[20] This conspiracy theory was a recurring theme and in July 1901 Arthur used his position in the House of Lords to table an amendment to the government's Royal Declaration Bill, asking for 'an expression of disbelief in the doctrines of the Pope's supremacy and infallibility, as being contrary to the Protestant religion, and a declaration that neither the Pope nor the Court of Rome has any right to interfere with the temporal Government of British dominions.'[21] In November 1902 he addressed a joint meeting of the Church Association and the National Protestant League, who were working together to put 'Protestantism before politics'.[22]

In the light of these views, it comes as something of a surprise that Arthur sought – and was granted – an audience with the Pope when he visited Rome in March 1902.[23] Pope Leo XIII was then aged 92 and close to death, so the visit was probably more of a sightseeing trip than anything more meaningful, but given the anti-Catholic feeling of the time it is just as well the visit was not reported in the press, as it would likely have caused an uproar if it had been publicised. The explanation for Arthur being willing to associate himself with the Pope can perhaps be gleaned from a letter he wrote several years later, saying 'The weakness of foreign missions has been that we have carried our home divisions into the field where a united foe must be faced. We have deliberately weakened the mission of the church of the living God by our sectarian bias.'[24] He had come to realise that by presenting a united front instead of being split up into many sects, the Christian religion as a whole could be the winner, rather than Protestantism as an uncompromising opponent of Roman Catholicism.

Arthur lost his mentor in January 1903 when Quintin Hogg died suddenly[25], and delivered a touching address at the memorial service, held in the Polytechnic in Regent Street. Tracing Hogg's life, he said that it was impossible to overvalue the results that followed from the Bible class at Eton, and that Hogg had shown what one man could do to move a nation.[26] As a legacy, Arthur led a fundraising campaign to build an athletics ground for the Polytechnic, and in 1910 performed the opening ceremony of the Quintin Hogg Memorial Ground at Chiswick.[27] He added his own personal tribute by presenting the Kinnaird Trophy – initially called Lord Kinnaird's Cup – for the inter-club competition inaugurated by the Polytechnic Harriers and it is still competed for today.

In 1905 he took on the high profile role of President of the British YMCA, on the death of Sir George Williams. Arthur was already President of the YWCA, and led both for a while, but it was too much for one man to manage and two years later he stepped down from the women's organisation. However, he did not sever his connections completely as he remained treasurer of its London division, the biggest in the country with 60 institutes and a membership of 15,000; the south-west London YWCA building was named Rossie House in his honour. The YMCA was a bigger and more vibrant organisation. He attended the world conferences in Denmark and Germany, and presided over the annual British events

135

in Aberdeen (which coincided with the jubilee celebrations of the Aberdeen YMCA), Dundee, Edinburgh, Manchester and Nottingham. There were frequent requests for him to perform opening ceremonies, and in July 1909 he turned the first sod of the new London YMCA in Tottenham Court Road.

There was also public recognition of an entirely different kind, the unexpected accolade of having a town named after him thanks to one of his many investments, a substantial shareholding in the Canadian Pacific Railway. In 1902 the CPR had built a box car station near Castlegar in British Columbia, at an old Waterloo Trail crossing, calling it Kinnaird Station in his honour. Initially servicing a lumber yard and sawmill, its first school was built by volunteer labour in 1916 and, as the area developed, Kinnaird and Castlegar communities grew closer until they formally amalgamated in 1974. Although Kinnaird is now called South Castlegar, there is still a Kinnaird Park Cemetery, Kinnaird Elementary School and, most appropriately, Kinnaird Church of God.

Arthur's distinguished record of public service and a close relationship with the Church brought a prestigious Royal appointment as Lord High Commissioner to the General Assembly of the Church of Scotland. This ancient role dates from the 16th century, as the sovereign's personal representative at the Church of Scotland's annual conference, and confers an almost regal status on the holder. He was first asked to undertake the role in 1906 by Henry Campbell Bannerman, the Prime Minister[28], but on this occasion he replied that he could not accept the position owing to Lady Kinnaird's state of health; she had been advised to go abroad and he said there was 'no chance she would be strong enough to undertake the duties which would devolve upon her.' Arthur and Alma duly went to the south of France and spent most of April in Tours for her convalescence, returning via Paris where he opened a new YWCA building.

A year later, Campbell Bannerman again wrote to ask if he would be available, saying 'I hope that the impediment may be happily now removed, and I venture to ask whether you will allow me to submit your name to the King.'[29] He received a positive response the same day, and the Secretary for Scotland, John Sinclair, immediately wrote 'to say how greatly I rejoice to know from the Prime Minister that he has your permission to submit your name to the King, and that you are to be our Lord High

Commissioner in Scotland this year.' The couple arrived in Edinburgh in May 1907 to stay at the Palace of Holyroodhouse for a week of ceremonial duties, including the opening and closing speeches of the Assembly, hosting several dinners and a garden party. Arthur fulfilled the role again in 1908 and 1909, but this was enough: the following year when the new Secretary for Scotland, Lord Pentland, pleaded with him to resume office, he refused.

In 1908, although busy with the organisation of the Olympic Games, Arthur found time to be outspoken on a number of fronts. He made a speech at a rally in support of the Licensing Bill, which aimed to control the sale of alcohol and limit the number of pubs, and was making its way through Parliament to 'minister for temperance and the well-being of the people'. An estimated 100,000 supporters of temperance, many waving banners with slogans such as 'The Big D Alliance: Drink, Disease and the Devil', marched through London to Hyde Park, where they could listen to a range of speakers including Winston Churchill, newly elected MP for Dundee. Arthur attracted a decent crowd to hear him back the legislation, by which 'the evil of the drink traffic might be stopped'.[30]

Conversely, Arthur was not the most popular of speakers at the Pan Anglican Congress, held in London the same summer, as he returned to the theme of criticising his fellow Christians for not putting their hands in their pockets. Describing the Anglican Church as the richest in Christendom, he said that proportionately to its wealth it gave less than any other, and gave a dire warning: 'Unfortunately, the well-to-do members of our Church do not accept the fact that they are only stewards and trustees of all their wealth and that they will have to give an account on the Judgment Day as to how they spent or misspent their wealth.'[31]

A few months later, he went even further in a prescient speech which closed the Church Congress in Manchester. He berated churchgoers for their parsimony, accused them of being out of touch with the real world, and stridently advocated ethical investments, security of employment and better pay for women – ideas that were well ahead of his time.

He began by asking the delegates to consider giving money as an integral part of worship and suggested that at least a tenth of anyone's income – the Sacred Tenth – should be the yardstick; those in the audience would have known that his own record of philanthropy was beyond reproach. He expressed his frustration that others did not follow his example, as he was weary of always having to appeal for money for good causes: 'I think many of our fellow Church members do not know how harassing it is to carry on the financing of our different organisations.' Despairing that money was spent on 'prettifying churches' rather than on charity, he asked them to consider 'whether we might not for a time refrain from spending large sums in erecting ornate and artistic fabrics. The history of the last fifty years has shown that the more beautiful and artistic the building and the singing, the less appears to be the personal consecration of the members of that church and the amount of their gifts subscribed to home and foreign missions.'

His tirade continued with a plea to the wealthy to consider the source of their wealth: 'We must be careful not to draw our income and profit from investments in business which tend to demoralize our own people or the people of other lands. We must be careful not to allow that the end justifies the means; or that the giving of a tithe from an improper or questionable investment will make that investment a justifiable or righteous one.' He asked them 'whether it is justifiable, in the thoughtless way so often done, to turn off regular employees, simply that larger dividends may be made and paid to the partners and shareholders, even though it may mean starvation to the worker.'

In a plea for women to be treated better in the workplace, he added that 'especially in connection with women workers must the question of a living wage be considered. It cannot be right or just that the wage should be so small that little choice seems left between starving on one hand or leading a vicious or immoral life on the other hand to supplement wages on which it is impossible to live.' He concluded by giving these comments a sound biblical context with quotations from the Old and New Testaments, and implored delegates to 'not see how little, but how much, we can give'.[32]

Ever the realist, Arthur would have appreciated that these pleas would fall mainly on deaf ears, and he continued to seek support for his myriad good causes. The very next month, he wrote to *The Times* to ask for financial backing for the Christian Colportage Association, whose aim was to circulate 'pure, healthy literature' as an antidote to 'the amount of questionable books and literature issued, much of which is full of evil insinuations and

138

suggestions, which many leaders of thought consider dangerous to morality and faith.' As treasurer, he pointed out that it took £50 a year to train and support just one colporteur (a distributor of Christian pamphlets) and there were 124 of them within the organisation.[33]

Arthur concluded the year, perhaps inspired by his experiences of the Olympic Games, by giving an interview to *Sunday at Home* magazine, which described him as 'one of the most daring, strenuous, unstoppable footballers who ever donned a jersey'. Harking back to these youthful endeavours, he took the opportunity to call for clergy and laity to promote sports in boys and girls clubs: 'The presence, support and interest of Christian people in the games and recreations of the young is essential to their betterment and purification,' he said. 'Surely it is a Christian act to assist local authorities to secure open spaces and provide for the healthful recreation of the youth that swarms in our towns and cities.'[34]

He soon returned to the theme of protection for women, joining a delegation of churchmen which met the Home Secretary to press for stronger legislation against procuring and brothel-keeping. Arthur had long fought against the 'white slave traffic' of prostitution, and pointed out that slavery in the dominions had been outlawed before he was born, yet women and children in Britain were still being forced into a life of prostitution, which amounted to the same thing.[35]

Presented with the FA Cup – to keep

The highlight of Arthur's football year was the FA Cup Final each spring, and he attended almost every one from 1873 until 1915[36], playing in nine of them. Indeed cup final day was not the same without him, which perhaps explains the decision, in 1911, to present him with the nation's most iconic sporting trophy as a mark of the esteem in which he was held in the footballing world.

To be precise, it was not the same trophy he had lifted five times as a player. After the famous meeting of 1871 in the offices of The Sportsman, where it was agreed 'That it is desirable that a Challenge Cup should be established in connexion with the Association, for which all clubs belonging to the Association should be invited to compete,' a simple silver cup was commissioned from

Martin Hall & Co. Standing 18 inches high on an ebony plinth, with a footballer figure on top, this original 'tin pot' remained in service until 1895, when it was stolen from a shop window in Birmingham.[37]

THE·FOOTBALL ASSOCIATION DINNER
IN·HONOUR·OF
THE·RIGHT·HON.
LORD·KINNAIRD,
PRESIDENT·OF·THE·ASSOCIATION,
AND
J.C.CLEGG·ESQ,J.P.
CHAIRMAN·OF·THE·COUNCIL
AT
THE·HOLBORN·RESTAURANT.
MONDAY 6TH FEBRUARY 1911.
CHAIRMAN,
CHARLES·CRUMP·ESQ.V.P.

Title page of the menu for the FA Cup presentation dinner

Despite a £10 reward being offered for its safe return, the original FA Cup was never seen again; a deathbed confession many years later suggested it had been melted down to make counterfeit coins. Aston Villa were fined £25 to pay for a replica, made from a cast of the original, and this was presented at the finals until 1910.[38]

Then the FA discovered that the trophy had been copied and, with no recourse to action as the design had never been copyrighted, it resolved: 'That the present Football Association Challenge Cup, having been duplicated without the consent of the Association, be withdrawn from competition and a new cup offered, the design of which should be registered.'[39] Fattorini & Sons of Bradford designed the trophy still competed for today, and ironically the first winners were Bradford City, for the only time in their history.[40]

The FA had to decide what to do with the old cup and agreed that it would make a fine gift for their President to mark his service to the game. Thus on 6 February 1911 a sumptuous dinner was held at the Holborn Restaurant in honour of Lord Kinnaird, and also to acknowledged Charles Clegg's 20 years as Chairman of Council. A dinner committee of FA Council members, comprising Charles Crump (chairman), William Heard, Henry Huband, Herbert Porter, James Buteux Skeggs, and Frederick Wall, commissioned a superb menu as a souvenir of the occasion from Sangorski and Sutcliffe, the outstanding binders of the age; it was bound in dark green crushed levant morocco leather, with the monogrammed initials AFK and JCC picked out in gold above a calf leather inlay of a football, surrounded by an elaborate gilt-tooled design.

Among the 71 guests were three of Arthur's sons (Patrick was too young for such an event) and Douglas's personal copy of the menu is now on display at the Scottish Football Museum along with the table plan, which reveals a top table of 17 overseeing the great and the good of English football. While many of the guests had been at an FA Council meeting that day, Arthur came to the restaurant fresh from the city where he had just been appointed honorary treasurer of an Anglo-German friendship organisation, formally entitled The Associated Councils of Churches in the British and German Empires for Fostering Friendly Relations between the Two Peoples.

The evening was such a lavish gastronomic affair, it is hard to tell where one course ends and another one starts: among the dishes were pot au feu, boiled turbot, devilled whitebait, chicken sauté Windsor, fillets of beef pique Richelieu, roast pheasant and mayonnaise of lobster, all followed by a choice of desserts. The drinks opened with an 1886 Montilla very dry sherry, followed with a choice of Rudesheimer 1906 (white) or Pommard 1904 (red), then an 1898 Irroy Carte d'Or Extra Sec champagne, and finished by a

35-year-old Courvoisier brandy. For entertainment the guests enjoyed actresses Marguerite Herring and Dorothy Varick, the baritone George Baker, and a humorous after-dinner speech by Arthur Helmore.

The dinner over, Charles Crump spoke of Arthur's unrivalled contribution to football, and formally presented him with the cup, which had been specially prepared with two silver shields attached to the plinth, one of which read: *'Presented by The Football Association To The Right Hon Lord Kinnaird in appreciation of long and very valuable services rendered to the game, 6th February 1911'*; the other inscribed *'The Right Hon Lord Kinnaird. International 1873. Final Cup Competition, 1873. 7. 8. 9 & 1882. Member of Council since 1868. President Of The Football Association Since 1890'*.

Charles Clegg, in turn, was presented with an elaborate album of photos of his colleagues, prefaced by an illuminated address which paid tribute to his 'sturdy independence of character, exceptional judgement and knowledge'.

The cup went home with Arthur to go in display in his house at St James's Square, and remained in the family for many years. Latterly it was held in a bank vault, and only resurfaced to the public gaze in 2005 when it was the star lot in an auction of football memorabilia – a bit of a coup for David Convery, then head of sporting memorabilia at Christie's auctioneers, who said before the sale that he thought the buyer would probably be British. 'There isn't much value for English football memorabilia overseas,'

The FA Cup, shown on a cigarette card, was presented to Lord Kinnaird to mark his unique contribution to football

he stated. In the event, interest came all over the world, notably Germany, and after fierce bidding it was acquired by David Gold, at that time chairman of Birmingham City (subsequently owner of West Ham United). He paid £478,400 for Lord Kinnaird's FA Cup, easily a world record for an item of football memorabilia, and explained triumphantly that he was determined that the Cup would not go to an overseas buyer: 'I bought it on behalf of the nation's football fans. I was in a lucky position of being able to preserve a historic piece of British sporting memorabilia.' True to his word, he gave it to the National Football Museum on long term loan, and they made it the centrepiece of a touring exhibition entitled *Saved for the Nation: the story of the FA Cup*, which also featured a life-size statue of Arthur standing on his hands – his celebration after the 1882 victory – ensuring that his legacy was brought to a new generation of football fans.

A sense of perspective

The death of Charles Alcock on 26 February 1907 was a palpable break with football's past, and Arthur was one of many mourners who attended his funeral at Norwood Cemetery. As well as his substantial contribution to the sport's growth and development, it was Alcock who had first proposed that the FA should distribute some of its proceeds to charity, and the organisation had an impressive track record of support for good causes. It is not hard to see Arthur's influence in a donation to the Indian Famine Relief Fund in 1897, and following Alcock's death he backed the proposal to put these ad hoc gifts on a more formal footing, with the creation of the annual Charity Shield matches in 1908, which were played initially between the winners of the Football League and the Southern League.[41]

An attention to charity was one way Arthur could make sure that football kept a sense of perspective in the broader scheme of things. He had commented in the *Sporting Life* that too much importance was being attached to outdoor games and sport in the press and among the public: 'Sport must be kept in its proper place. It must not be allowed to usurp the position that belongs to work or business. The more those who are engaged in factories and workshops spend their time in the open air the better. But the

143

increase of athletics in midweek requires to be carefully watched because much harm might result from this.'[42]

He was perhaps speaking in response to a growing awareness that some people were taking football too seriously. For example, in 1910 Arthur had chaired an FA commission of inquiry into Manchester United, after allegations of illegal payments over several years. Having examined the terms under which the club had changed identity from Newton Heath in 1902, the commission concluded that the club's owner John Davies, chairman of Manchester Breweries, had effectively laundered the club's money to pay extra money to players, including Billy Meredith.[43] Without proof, however, there was little the FA could do, other than instruct the club to improve its management in future.

Arthur made sure the FA responded generously to one of the world's worst maritime disasters, when the RMS *Titanic* sank in the north Atlantic on 14 April 1912 with the loss of 1,513 passengers and crew. As an immediate gesture, on the motion of Arthur, the FA contributed 200 guineas and that was soon doubled by committing the proceeds of the Charity Shield match between Blackburn Rovers and Queen's Park Rangers.[44] The FA also asked its member clubs to support the Titanic Disaster Fund, either by making collections on the ground or by arranging special matches.

Closer to home, his wife's health was a source of concern and it is clear Alma was not an easy patient. The family doctor, Stanley Smith, expressed his frustration in a letter to Arthur: 'With the greatest reluctance I have come to the conclusion that Lady Kinnaird is likely to get on better in health with a doctor to whose religious opinion she is indifferent, or who agrees entirely with her. It is impossible for me to give calm consideration to the needs of her care after being compelled to sit for half an hour or an hour listing to reiterated arguments to which I am unable to reply because to do so would cause excitement of a most detrimental kind.'[45] Smith recommended another doctor, Lanphier Vernon-Jones (Arthur's brother-in-law), but whether his advice was taken is not recorded.

Alma was, at least, able to find plenty of people with whom to trade religious arguments when she and Arthur attended the World Missionary Conference, held in Edinburgh in the summer of 1910. There was plenty more of the same as the couple continued their regular trips to Keswick, an annual gathering in the Lake District whose primary purpose was the deepening of the spiritual

144

life of believers, and to YMCA conferences. For the coronation of King George V in 1911, they were personally invited not just to the ceremony in Westminster Abbey but also to several days of celebrations in Edinburgh, where Arthur took part in the colourful uniform of the Royal Company of Archers.

There was a lasting accolade for Arthur in September 1912, when he was selected by *Vanity Fair* as a *Man of the Day*, a popular series of caricatures of nationally known figures. His father had been portrayed in 1876 as *Piety and Banking*, but Arthur was simply entitled *Soccer*, as he was the first to be selected from the world of association football.[46] The caricature depicted him looking lively in his trademark cricket flannels, but the accompanying script, attributed to Jehu Junior[47], was not the most accurate, asserting that he once kept goal for England. However, it contained a few pertinent comments: 'Arthur Fitzgerald Kinnaird has crowded much into his sixty-five years, during most of which he has been like Dickens's 'three gentlemen rolled into one'. Football, shooting,

Soccer, a 1912 caricature in *Vanity Fair*

145

banking, with a little youth-improving thrown in, are a few of his hobbies. He is as hard-working as he is popular. If you asked him what he thought the most useful work of his life, he would probably tell you that it lay in the founding of the Regent Street Polytechnic with Quintin Hogg.'

Arthur and Alma enjoy a winter break at the pyramids in 1912

Arthur and Alma spent that winter in Egypt, based at the Heliopolis Palace Hotel, and there is a wonderful photo of them sitting on camels at the pyramids. While in Cairo, they met the

146

American financier John Pierpont Morgan, one of the richest men in the world, and Arthur – ever the opportunist – persuaded him to donate £10,000 to the London YMCA appeal.[48]

The jubilee celebrations of the FA in November 1913 provided an opportunity to celebrate and to look back in wonder at the game's growth and achievements since 1863. At the banquet in the Holborn Restaurant there was a guest appearance from the last two survivors of that first meeting, Ebenezer Morley – who gave an account of the early days – and Alfred Mackenzie; they were both presented with silver caskets. Arthur proposed the first toast to the guests, and this was followed by a steady flow of speeches, with Arthur himself lauded by Arthur Conan Doyle, the novelist. The guests covered not just a broad range of sports but also the Football Associations of Argentina, Sweden, Denmark, Norway, Netherlands, Belgium and Austria. During the evening a telegram was sent to King George V, the organisation's Patron, and loud cheers went up when his reply was received.

The King's fondness for football was evident when he attended the FA Cup Final in April 1914, the first time a reigning monarch had attended such a high profile match. Wearing a red rose in his buttonhole to honour the Lancashire finalists, Burnley and Liverpool, he was greeted at the stadium by Arthur who formally presented the King to the FA officers, then escorted him to his seat; he later presented the cup and medals.[49] The royal presence was thought highly significant for football after its emergence from the long amateur dispute, and *The Times* wrote in its match report: 'The fact that the King himself has attended a cup-tie and shown a keen interest in its vicissitudes – he missed none of the humours of a well-conducted contest – will, let us hope, put an end to the old, snobbish notion that true-blue sportsmen ought to ignore games played by those who cannot afford to play without being paid for their services.'[50]

Now 67 years old, Arthur was still closely involved in his insurance business. In 1906 he had negotiated a deal to sell the County Fire Office to the Alliance Assurance Company[51], but the company continued to function independently with Arthur as chairman, a position he held until his death; to mark his contribution, his portrait was painted for the boardroom by John Collier, and still hangs in Rossie Priory. Known as an advocate of greater equality for women, his chairmanship presented Arthur with

147

a moral dilemma when the suffragette movement embarked on a deliberate campaign of destruction, on the premise that the insurance companies were powerful institutions which, if put under pressure, would persuade the government to capitulate and grant votes for women. Public buildings in London were popular targets for arson, and the refreshment pavilion at Kew Gardens – insured by the County Fire Office – was reduced to ashes. The culprits, Lilian Lenton and Olive Wharry, were sent to prison and went on hunger strike, with Wharry setting a record of 31 days without food. Lacking sympathy for their cause, the County Fire Office used legal proceedings to recover its £500 loss from the women. A further case involving the insurance company was the fire-bombing in April 1914 of St Martin-in-the-Fields church, where Arthur had been church warden. Whatever his broader sympathies, he would have deplored the criminal tactics, and there is a hint that he sided with the establishment as he sent a message of support to the National League for Opposing Women's Suffrage.[52]

The suffragette campaign was only brought to an end by a much greater conflict. War clouds were gathering over Europe, and even though Arthur was a member of the Anglo-German Friendship Committee, there was nothing he could do to influence events which would conspire to impact dreadfully on his life, his sport and the nation.

---

[1] Although written anonymously, the author has been identified as John Maclauchlan, the Dundee city librarian.

[2] Geoffrey Green, *History of the Football Association*, p159

[3] Guérin wrote: *'J'eus une entrevue avec cet homme aimable, qui était feu lord Kinnaird, mais ce fut un coup d'épée dans l'eau.'* Quoted in Alfred Wahl, *Les Archives du Football*, p97-98

[4] Geoffrey Green, *History of the Football Association*, p197

[5] *The Times*, 21 & 23 June 1904

[6] *The Times*, 27 April 1908

[7] Actually the England amateur team

[8] 'Creston', *Football*, Fortnightly Review, January 1894, p25-38; (Creston was NL Jackson's pseudonym.)

[9] *The Times*, 26 January 1897

[10] BO Corbett, *Annals of the Corinthian Football Club*, p6

[11] *The Times*, 13 March 1906

[12] He had already been an Honorary President of the club in 1892-93.

[13] Geoffrey Green, *History of the Football Association*, p249

[14] *The Times*, 27 April 1912

[15] Geoffrey Green, *History of the Football Association*, p205

[16] *The Sunday Strand*, February 1903, pp49-52

[17] *New York Times*, 23 June 1901

[18] *The Jubilee of Work for Young Men in North America*, 1901

[19] Sent from supporters in Nottingham, it had 7,327 words and cost £15 5s.

[20] *The Times*, 1 February 1899

[21] *The Times*, 31 July 1901

[22] *The Times*, 4 November 1902

[23] Papal audience ticket, Kinnaird family archive

[24] *The Times*, 18 December 1913

[25] Hogg died in his bath of carbon monoxide poisoning from a faulty heater.

[26] *The Times*, 26 January 1903

[27] *The Times*, 25 July 1910

[28] Letter dated 20 March 1906, Kinnaird family archive: *It would give me great pleasure if you would allow me to submit your name for appointment as Lord High Commissioner to the Church of Scotland. You are no doubt aware of the nature of the office, whose duties involve a week's residence in Edinburgh in May, while representing His Majesty. It is a patriotic historic office, and I imagine would be congenial to you; and I earnestly hope it may have attraction enough to lead you to think favourably of my proposal.*

[29] Letter dated 8 March 1907, Kinnaird family archive

[30] *The Times*, 27 July 1908

[31] *Special Report of the Proceedings of the Pan Anglican Congress*, 1908, p184

[32] *Official Report of the Church Congress, Manchester*, October 1908; paper by Lord Kinnaird

[33] *The Times*, 19 November 1908

[34] Quoted in *Review of Reviews*, December 1908, p538

[35] *The Times,* 25 and 31 March 1909

[36] In 1909 he was 'indisposed'.

[37] It was on display to celebrate Aston Villa's success.

[38] Arthur presented the FA Cup to Newcastle United in 1906, for the third and last time; the previous year, his daughter-in-law Frances did the honours.

[39] FA Minutes, 9 July 1910

[40] Although this design of trophy is still competed for, Fattorini's original cup was retired in 1992 to protect it from further wear.

[41] Geoffrey Green, *History of the Football Association*, p555

[42] Quoted in *Revue Olympique* 62, February 1911, p27

[43] *The Times*, 31 March 1910

[44] Geoffrey Green, *History of the Football Association*, p248

[45] Letter dated 24 April 1910, Kinnaird family archive

[46] Strictly speaking he was not the first footballer, as CB Fry was an earlier selection, but that was for his prowess as an athlete.

[47] Pseudonym of *Vanity Fair's* founder, Thomas Bowles.

[48] *New York Times*, 3 February 1912

[49] Geoffrey Green, *History of the FA Cup*, p99

[50] *The Times*, 27 April 1914

[51] One of the forefathers of the Royal & Sun Alliance insurance company.

[52] *The Times*, 21 January 1913

CHAPTER 10

War, tragedy and succession
1914-1923

THE SUMMER of 1914 began pleasantly enough, as Arthur joined the elite of Scottish chivalry. A letter from 10 Downing Street[1], signed by the Prime Minister, introduced him to the Most Ancient and Most Noble Order of the Thistle, whose members are chosen by the monarch. It was the most prestigious of the many honours granted to Arthur but he was denied the pageantry of an investiture ceremony because of the outbreak of war. The King admitted him to the Order by royal warrant[2], which still cost a £50 joining fee.

When war was declared in August, cricket soon stopped, and rugby fixtures were cancelled, but football decided blithely to embark on its new season with just a half-hearted appeal from the FA to its members: 'Clubs having professional players are urged to give every facility for their temporary release.'[3] The 'temporary' element reflected the widely-held opinion that the war would be over by Christmas, and most clubs were inclined to carry on as scheduled. This caused widespread moral indignation and condemnation that fit young professional footballers were playing sport when they were needed for military duty and Arthur, who was on his summer break at Rossie Priory, was soon drawn into the dilemma facing football.

The evangelical campaigner Frederick Charrington[4], described in the press as 'conducting a crusade against the playing of football during the war' wrote an imploring telegram to the King: 'May it please your Majesty to remember that Lord Roberts recently said it would be disgraceful if football was continued during the war. The Football Association have now decided to continue their matches, despite all protests. Your Majesty has set an example to the nation in sending your two noble sons to the front. Millions of your Majesty's loyal subjects will be anxious to know if your Majesty's name will still be used as patron of the Football Association.'

Lord Stamfordham's response on behalf of the King was a masterpiece of diplomatic nothingness: 'The question raised in your telegram to the King has received the careful consideration and respect which is due to anyone speaking with your great experience and authority ... the doings of the Association will be carefully followed, having regard to the King's position as patron.'

Charrington also telegraphed Arthur, in his role as the sport's figurehead, asking whether he intended to remain President of the FA in the light of its 'unpatriotic decision' to continue football. Arthur was equally evasive and distanced himself from the situation by writing that he had not yet had full details of the action of the FA, but he hardly expected them to do anything unpatriotic: 'Giving up football entirely is not so simple as you think,' he wrote. 'Contracts have been made which can be enforced in a Court of Law, and you could not advocate the breaking of contracts.' And he added in a weary-sounding postscript: 'The reasons for continuing some football are too long for a letter.'[5]

Not everyone was as tolerant of Charrington. The report of this exchange of correspondence in *The Times* was followed immediately by an item headed 'Incident at a Fulham match' which related how Charrington was trying to recruit young men in the crowd 'when he was seized by two men who, without making any request to him to leave, dragged him roughly along the gangway and nearly threw him down the slope'. Charrington duly filed a complaint for assault against the Fulham officials, but lost his case.[6]

He was far from being a lone voice, and many others were equally set against football continuing. CB Fry, the most famous sportsman of the era, called for all professional contracts to be annulled, and for everyone under the age of forty to be forbidden from attending football matches. Arthur Conan Doyle, an erstwhile ally who had toasted Arthur's health at the FA jubilee dinner the year before, also made an impassioned plea: 'There was a time for all things in the world. There was a time for games, there was a time for business, and there was a time for domestic life. There was a time for everything, but there is only time for one thing now, and that thing is war. If the cricketer had a straight eye let him look along the barrel of a rifle. If a footballer had strength of limb let them serve and march in the field of battle.'[7] The players of a few clubs did join up en masse, but most were content to hold off and football continued its scheduled fixture list.

Arthur had returned to London in time for the FA Council meeting of 12 October when the minutes noted, with some bitterness, that football was being unfairly targeted: 'Football, which is essentially the pastime of the masses, is the only sport which is being attacked. It is producing more men for the Army, and money for relief, than all the others. Other sports and the places of entertainment are being carried on as usual without objection. The FA is of the opinion that members should continue to play matches where by so doing they can assist and do not hinder the authorities in recruiting.'[8] It was decided to form a War Sub-Committee.

The reality of war hit home hard for the Kinnairds at the end of October with the death in action of Douglas, Arthur's son and heir (see below), and at its next meeting in December, Council opened with a vote of sympathy for their President.

As it became apparent the war would not be over by Christmas, crowds began falling markedly. The FA was still minded to carry on football as far as possible, and Daniel Woolfall's motion to abandon the FA Cup and Amateur Cup competitions was defeated, countered by a strong argument that if the cups were stopped to satisfy public sentiment, not only would the lack of football remove a recruiting opportunity, many clubs would be ruined. The FA called again for clubs to release professionals from their contracts, but not everyone approved: the *Athletic News'* angry response to this initiative was: 'The whole agitation is nothing less than an attempt by the ruling classes to stop the recreation on one day in the week of the masses ... What do they care for the poor man's sport? The poor are giving their lives for this country in thousands. In many cases they have nothing else. These should, according to a small clique of virulent snobs, be deprived of the one distraction that they have had for over thirty years.'[9]

The FA did at least permit the War Office to recruit at matches, and to form a footballers' battalion, whose members were allowed leave of absence on Saturdays. Arthur sat on the committee responsible for raising it, which was chaired by William Joynson-Hicks MP. Called the 17th (Football) Battalion of the Middlesex Regiment, it had a complement of 1,350 players, friends and supporters. The 1914-15 season staggered on to its end, but after the FA Cup was presented by Lord Derby, in charge of recruiting for Kitchener's Army, he told the Sheffield United and Chelsea players: 'You have played with one another and against one another for the Cup. Play with one another for England now.'[10]

This effectively brought down the curtain on organised football in England for the duration of the war, as shortly afterwards the FA issued its wartime regulations: no internationals, no FA Cup, competitions could only proceed if they did not interfere with war work, and a stark edict that 'no remuneration shall be paid to players'. The FA headquarters in Russell Square was commandeered by the War Office as a store for the Middlesex Regiment. With no home, no matches, and consequently no income, the FA spent almost all of its reserves over the war years. Only when the end of the conflict was in sight did the organisation spring back into life to confront the challenges of getting football started again.

Making the ultimate sacrifice

Arthur was a strong supporter of military service, and had said forcefully in a speech in 1910 that he hoped the nation would see that every man did his duty: 'If men were not prepared to do that, he hoped many national careers would be shut to them, and that the highest honours of the country would only be open to those who had made military training a part of their curriculum.'[11]

It may have been a matter of pride that all four of his sons saw action, but his resolve was severely tested as the conflict took a heavy toll. First to fall was his heir, Douglas, who had joined the Scots Guards straight from university in 1901. As a regular regiment they were readied to fight from the outbreak of war and Captain Kinnaird crossed to Belgium with the 2nd Battalion on 4 October as part of the British Expeditionary Force, which was deployed to protect the Belgian Army in their desperate retreat from Antwerp. Less than three weeks later Douglas was killed near Ypres[12], shot through the heart by a sniper during one of many rearguard actions against ferocious German attacks. He was buried at Zonnebeke, but later reinterred further from the front line at Godezonne Farm Cemetery, a small plot of 79 burials. The news reached his parents on 1 November, a week after he fell, and even the birth of a grandson the next day would have brought little comfort to the family.

A memorial service for Douglas was held at Rossie Chapel, and the impact of his death can be measured by the number of places where his name is recorded: the war memorial tablet on St Marnoch's Church in Fowlis Easter, not far from Rossie Priory; the memorial at Inchture village; the MCC Members' Memorial at Lord's; the Eton College War Memorial; and the Cheam School War Memorial. The tragedy meant that his brother Kenneth became Master of Kinnaird, although it is probable that he would have eventually succeeded to the title in any case, as Douglas never married; in fact, Kenneth was the only one of Arthur's children to become a parent himself.

At a time of national emergency, Arthur had little choice but to bear Douglas's death with fortitude and he led prayers for peace on a national Day of Intercession[13] later that month. With typical dedication, he threw himself into the war effort and ran fundraising campaigns for the YMCA, to create buildings that would house the hastily recruited Kitchener's Army and munitions workers, who in the early months of the conflict regularly found themselves living under canvas in makeshift camps. He explained that 'in closest cooperation with the chaplains we are trying to serve their highest interests'[14], and under his guidance the organisation was a major force on the home front. It offered social and moral welfare for the troops and war workers in more than 500 centres, providing home comforts such as books, magazines, pianos, gramophones and even billiard tables.[15] Latterly, King George V sent a message of thanks to say that the YMCA 'has done everything conducive to the comfort and wellbeing of the Armies'.

Arthur also continued to take a hands-on role at the County Fire Office, most of whose staff signed up to fight, leading to the employment of women for the first time. Strangely, the number of claims for fire damage fell dramatically during the war, and he wrote in its annual report for 1914 that with the 'admitted diminution in serious crime in the country, the number [of claims] in the five months from August to December (war period) was less by 178 than in the corresponding months of 1913, and this diminution is still continuing.' But while the war was good for business in a strictly financial sense, Arthur was careful to point out in the first post-war report that there was no question of profiteering:

'Although companies have borne their full share in the heavy taxation and all other expenses incidental to the business, there has been no advance in rates charged for fire insurance.'[16]

He managed to escape the city to spend long summers at Rossie Priory with Alma, who continued to be in poor health, but further tragedies blighted the family. A favourite nephew[17] died of wounds, then another son, young Arthur was lost. On the outbreak of war he enlisted in the University and Public Schools Brigade, and after serving on the front line as aide-de-camp to Major General Sir William Rycroft, he transferred to the 1st Battalion the Scots Guards. He was awarded the Military Cross 'for gallant and efficient service' just a month before he fell on the opening day of the Battle of Cambrai on 27 November 1917.

The circumstances are recorded in detail as one of his men, Sergeant John McAulay, was awarded the Victoria Cross for his courageous efforts to save him, the only serving Scottish police officer to win the decoration. Lieutenant Kinnaird led his company in a morning raid on German troops in Fontaine-Notre-Dame and nearby Bourlon Wood, both of which were pounded by heavy artillery before the attack began. As the Scots Guards advanced cautiously along the road the banking at the side dropped away, exposing them to machine gun fire, and he was one of the first to fall: a bullet struck him in his leg, spinning him round, only for him to be hit in the back by another. Sergeant McAulay raced to the aid of his stricken officer, lifted him onto his shoulders and headed for cover. Twice knocked down by bursting shells, he reached safety and left his fatally wounded company commander with a doctor. Now the senior NCO, he set up his men and successfully repelled a counter-attack, with more than fifty enemy killed. After the war, the Kinnaird family thanked McAulay by presenting him with an engraved brass clock.[18] Young Arthur was buried in the nearby military cemetery at Ruyaulcourt, a village that changed hands several times in the course of the war; his headstone has a date of 30 November, although he died three days earlier.

The remaining two sons also saw active service. Kenneth was a Captain in the Scottish Horse Yeomanry, a territorial regiment incorporated into the Black Watch for the conflict, and fought at Gallipoli and in Egypt. Patrick enlisted straight from school in 1916 and served with the Scots Guards in France and Belgium, winning the Military Cross. On account of being wounded in October 1918 he was put on half pay and appointed aide-de-camp to the Duke of Devonshire, Governor General of Canada; he finally retired from the army in 1925.

Arthur spent his 70th birthday in bed, suffering from a severe chill, the first indication that his health was starting to fail. From the window of his London home there were daily reminders of the war as the normally private gardens in St James's Square were opened to wounded servicemen. With the arrival of the American forces, the YMCA had constructed a 'Washington Inn' in the gardens, providing much-needed accommodation for American officers posted to London, and latterly for demobbed British officers looking for work. However, it overstayed its welcome and was closed down at the end of 1920 at the insistence of the square's trustees, of whom Arthur was one.

It was evident long before the armistice that returning soldiers would find it hard to adapt to civilian life. Arthur foresaw some of these difficulties, and in November 1917 he and Alma helped to launch a new organisation, Comrades of the Great War[19], which aimed to promote the welfare of discharged soldiers and sailors; in 1921, it merged with three similar organisations to form the British Legion.

Football also had a role to play, and in February 1918, Arthur was appointed President of the National Football War Fund, which aimed to assist soldier footballers and their dependents, in the knowledge that thousands of players would come back maimed, or not at all.[20] For those who did make it back in one piece, Arthur was behind the formation of the Chevrons Football Club, open to warrant officers, petty officers and non-commissioned officers interested in football; the club never really got off the ground.

The day after the armistice was signed, he chaired a meeting of the FA Council[21] to discuss the way ahead for football. Some saw this as an opportunity to turn the clock back and reshape the game without its commercial focus. According to a report in *The Field*, Charles Clegg proposed that players be required to have paid employment outside football: 'The professional must be prevented from getting back to the old habit of loafing. It cannot be necessary to devote the whole week to preparation for an hour and a half on the football field.' There was also a move to ban player transfers during the course of the season, and a suggestion that leagues should be reorganised on district lines, as 'the increase of local interest would prove beneficial for all concerned.' This backlash against professionalism revealed a yearning for a more innocent age of football, but these reactionary ideas found little support and when the FA wrote to its members after the meeting it made just this watered-down appeal: 'It is desirable that players, in addition to playing the game, should continue their trade, and those in the Services should resume their work after the war, and that clubs should give facilities for their so doing.'[22]

After addressing the practicalities of resuming competitive football in the 1919-20 season, and an interim set of Victory Internationals, among the issues facing the FA in the post-war years were women's football, football pools, Sunday football, and the construction of a new national stadium at Wembley.[23] There was also a growing appreciation of the worldwide dimension of football, so when a request came from Japan (via Arthur's old friend AJ Balfour, now foreign secretary) for a national trophy, on the model of the FA Cup, the FA was quick to respond positively.[24]

Arthur remained busy in many charitable activities, and was re-elected President of the YMCA, hosting its 75th anniversary celebrations[25], and remained in post until December 1922 when failing health finally forced him to stand down. He was also appointed President of the Old Etonian Association, with a committee that included Percy de Paravicini, who had partnered him in the FA Cup-winning side of 1882. However, his strength and influence were starting to fade, and he was an increasingly distant figure for the FA. There is no record of the President attending meetings in the last two years of his life, and at the AGM in May 1921 it was agreed to send a message of support: 'The members of the FA in General Meeting assembled deeply regret the absence of their President and desire to express sincere sympathy with him in his illness.'

One of the last mentions of Arthur in the national press was a curious one. In January 1922 he attended Bow Street Police Court to testify to the good reputation and character of a country vicar, the Rev Alfred Freeman of Gloucestershire, who was prosecuted for drunkenly exposing himself to some women late at night in Trafalgar Square. Arthur said he had known the accused for about 30 years, and stood surety of £25 for his future good behaviour.

158

In his daily diary for 1922 (the only one which has survived) important dates in the football calendar were written in, including FA Cup rounds, international matches and Council meetings, and there are numerous meetings with friends and business associates. However, he was again too weak to attend the AGM and the members expressed 'their deep regret at the continued indisposition of Lord Kinnaird, and their earnest hope that he will make a speedy and complete recovery'. In July he found the strength to head north with Alma, attending the Keswick Convention on their way to Rossie Priory for what turned out to be the last time. They stayed until the end of October, but he was clearly in poor health: a diary note on 20 September says 'first day downstairs since July'. On returning to London, he continued to receive visitors at home, and on 2 December recorded 'I went out first time', but then the diary entries dried up.

The end

Arthur's last weeks were the subject of brief reports in *The Times* Court Circular: 'Lord Kinnaird is seriously ill'[26], then 'a little better' for a couple of days, and on 13 January he was 'a little weaker'. Alma was also in terminal decline and died on 19 January. As Arthur had been carried to her room every day to talk to her, the bad news had to be broken to him, but he was too ill to attend her memorial service at St James's in Piccadilly. The newspaper bulletins on Arthur resumed: 'weaker', 'no improvement' and finally 'It was learned yesterday afternoon that the condition of Lord Kinnaird was one of grave anxiety. On enquiry later in the evening, it was stated that he was a little weaker.' On Tuesday 30 January 1923, he faded away.

His family was clearly prepared for the worst: death notices appeared the next day – as did a detailed obituary – stating that a memorial service would be held at St Martin-in-the-Fields Church on Thursday afternoon, and the funeral at Rossie Priory 24 hours later. The church was packed with representatives from many spheres of Arthur's life: football, banks, charities and religious concerns. Several family members, including his children Kenneth, Patrick and Margaret, then took the night train to Scotland to attend his funeral service, which was conducted at Rossie Priory by Rev James Davidson, brother-in-law of Alma. The coffin was drawn

Arthur's grave, shared with Alma, in the family burial ground at Rossie Priory

on a hand carriage by eight of the oldest estate workers to his final resting place, the ancient Rossie chapel graveyard. There were nearly 100 wreaths.

Further tributes were paid at a memorial service on the Sunday in King George's Hall, the YMCA headquarters in London. Among them, the Solicitor General, Sir Thomas Inskip, said that Arthur and his co-workers 'took off their coats and went down into the world to help the men and women whom they found there.' Dr Robert Gillie also delivered an appreciation, asking 'Was Lord Kinnaird really great?' In his affirmative answer he spoke of Arthur's mental power, personality and more than anything his greatness of heart: 'a piquant blend of the unfailing courtesy of the aristocrat with remarkable democratic tendencies.'[27]

The next day, FA recorded its own tribute: 'The FA in Council assembled place upon record their esteem and affection for their late President, the Rt Hon Lord Kinnaird, and express their appreciation of his valuable services to the game.' Those sentiments were echoed around the country, and players wore black armbands the following weekend as a mark of respect.

Arthur's lifelong devotion to association football had encompassed an extraordinary journey, as player, administrator and national leader. While football continued its great progress and the name of Kinnaird faded from memory, there remains ample testimony to his unequalled impact on the game. Two short memorials, from the men who knew him best, summarise what he meant to football.

Sir Frederick Wall, one of Arthur's closest allies as secretary of the FA, wrote: 'The FA was fortunate to have such a man on their side when the spectacular Association game was always being denounced. Kinnaird recognised that life is an education in ever-changing values, and that views and opinions of 1860 were as entirely different from those of 1900 as are those of 1914 for 1934.'[28]

William Pickford, who rivalled Arthur's longevity in the game[29], also summed up his contribution in glowing terms: 'Kinnaird was a remarkably popular figure everywhere, and if not a great legislator in the game, he was a staunch supporter of the Association. Through all the controversies that seemed likely to split the national body, he stood by it and never wavered in his allegiance. When so much criticism was hurled at the Association for its recognition of professionalism, the fact that its head was a nobleman was in itself an asset. That a man in his eminent position, both at Court and in the City, sponsored the organisation had a great influence in many quarters.'[30]

Legacies

The FA elected Charles Clegg as President in Arthur's place, and one of his first acts was to approve Council's decision to endow a bed in Arthur's memory, at a cost of £1,000, in the children's ward at the London Lock Hospital in Harrow Road. This less-than-fashionable institution specialised in the treatment of the 'dire scourge'[31] of sexually transmitted diseases, including the newly-born children of infected women, a cause Arthur had supported passionately (he succeeded his father as its chairman and treasurer). Clegg was nominated a life president of the hospital to oversee the endowment.

For its part, the London FA, now under the presidency of Henry Huband, set up a Lord Kinnaird Memorial Fund, with an annual match between London Professionals and London Amateurs, and again the proceeds went towards the Lock Hospital. This match started out as a prestigious event to conclude the season, the players being presented with a gold medal to mark the occasion, but it was short-lived and the last match in 1927 attracted just 2,000 spectators on a miserable day at Millwall.[32]

161

When Arthur's will was published, his estate was valued at £250,000. His family was well provided for and there were numerous personal bequests to staff, including annuities to his gardener, gamekeeper, housekeeper and coachman. Although he specified many donations to good causes, Arthur had penned a note to express his frustration at his inability to do more: 'I regret that the depreciation of securities and the increase of the death duties make it impossible for me to do more for the cause of charity than I have done in my lifetime. I have had to omit from this will several deserving charities in which I am interested.'[33]

His philanthropic concerns were continued by his three spinster sisters. Louisa, who had worked alongside her mother in the London Bible and Domestic Mission, headed up the YWCA branch in Plaistow. Gertrude worked for the YWCA and the Zenana Bible and Medical Mission, both in London and in India. The most energetic of the three was Emily, secretary of the London YWCA, finance secretary of the British organisation as a whole, and Vice-President of its Scottish council. During the First World War she established more than 300 YWCA centres for nurses and war workers, for which in 1920 she was made a CBE. A lively and tough-minded person, she wrote two volumes of memoirs and died in 1947, the last of her generation.

Only three of Arthur's eight children were still alive – three had died young and two were killed in the war – and he was succeeded by Kenneth. Educated at Eton and Trinity College, Cambridge, Kenneth was a pillar of society like his father: he went into banking with Barclays, served as Lord High Commissioner to the General Assembly of the Church of Scotland, was a member of the Royal Company of Archers, and a Knight of the Thistle. He was also Chairman of the Scottish Branch of the British Red Cross Society, Lord Lieutenant of Perthshire, and a county councillor for 35 years. He inherited his father's sporting prowess and was an outstanding fives player, in 1924 donating the Kinnaird Cup which is still Britain's primary fives competition. Of Arthur's other surviving children, Margaret never married and lived a quiet life in London until her death in 1954, while Patrick, a director of Barclays Bank, married twice but had no children and died in 1948.

On Kenneth's death in 1972, the title passed to his elder son Graham. Born in 1912, educated at Eton, he served in the Second World War with the RAF Volunteer Reserve and in the Black

Watch (TA). After a career in London as a stockbroker, he retired to Rossie Priory to run the estate, although he made regular visits to speak in the House of Lords.[34] Graham married twice: briefly to the teenage daughter of an American film magnate, and more successfully in 1940 to Diana Copeman, with whom he had five children. However, tragedy intervened with a stunning finality as their only son, Nicholas, died of an illness in 1951 before reaching his fifth birthday. As their other children were girls, and Graham's younger brother George had no children, there were now no surviving male branches of the family.

On 27 February 1997, with the death of Graham, 13th Lord Kinnaird, the ancient title became extinct.

---

[1] *My Lord, I have the pleasure, with the King's approval, of proposing that you should receive the honour of a Knighthood of the Order of the Thistle on His Majesty's approaching birthday.* Letter from HH Asquith, in Kinnaird family archive.

[2] King George V signed the warrant, dated 21 August 1914 (Kinnaird family archive).

[3] FA Consultative Committee minutes, 31 August 1914

[4] Frederick Charrington (1850-1936), from the great brewing family, gave up his inheritance to be an evangelical temperance worker; despite some shared causes with Arthur, Charrington's uncompromising and humourless approach meant they had little in common.

[5] *The Times*, 8 September 1914

[6] The officials were WG Allen and Phil Kelso, Fulham chairman and secretary. Not only did Charrington lose his court case, he was ordered to pay two guineas costs.

[7] Speech made on 6 September 1914

[8] FA minutes, 12 October 1914

[9] *Athletic News*, 7 December 1914

[10] Geoffrey Green, *History of the FA Cup*, p101

[11] He was opening a school hall in Ramsgate; *The Times*, 14 February 1910.

[12] It is recorded on his gravestone as 24 October, but his father wrote in his notebook that it was actually the day before.

[13] On 20 November 1914

[14] *The Times*, 9 October 1914

[15] *The Times*, 9 December 1914

[16] Aubrey Noakes, *History of the County Fire Office*, p154

[17] Arthur Jones, son of his sister Frieda, died in November 1916.

[18] His nephew, Ian Wells, gave it to Glasgow Police Museum in 2007.

[19] *The Times*, 14 November 1917

[20] Geoffrey Green, *History of the Football Association*, p292

[21] The meeting on 12 November 1918 was described by the FA as 'an informal conference of members'.

[22] Circular letter from the FA to member clubs, 13 November 1918

[23] Geoffrey Green, *History of the Football Association*, p298

[24] *The Times*, 3 and 19 January 1919

[25] In June 1919 he entertained the YMCA National Council to lunch in the Holborn Restaurant.

[26] *The Times*, 28 December 1922

[27] *The Times*, 5 February 1923

[28] Sir Frederick Wall, *Fifty Years of Football*, p29

[29] He became a member of FA Council in 1888 and was elected President in 1937 just before his death.

[30] William Pickford, *A Few Recollections of Sport*, p44

[31] Letter from Lord Kinnaird to *The Times*, 3 January 1914

[32] Lord Kinnaird Memorial Fund matches: 5 May 1924, Professionals 3, Amateurs 1, at Highbury; 4 May 1925, Professionals 9, Amateurs 0, at White Hart Lane; 3 May 1926, Professionals v Amateurs at Stamford Bridge; 9 May 1927, Professionals 1, Amateurs 1, at Upton Park; 21 November 1927, Professionals 6, Amateurs 3, at The Den.

[33] *The Times*, 1 March 1923

[34] Obituary, *The Times*, 6 March 1997

APPENDIX 1

Arthur Kinnaird's football playing record

Over 300 matches have been found but records are incomplete and it is likely that Arthur played in many more, particularly for Old Etonians and Hanover United in later seasons.

Clubs: Old Etonians (92), Wanderers (88), other Etonian teams (Eton FC, Eton and Harrow, Cambridge Etonians, London Etonians, 22), Gitanos (15), University teams (Cambridge University, Trinity College, 10), West Kent (8), Hanover United (2), Flying Dutchmen (2), others (Civil Service, Old Harrovians, Avengers, Crusaders, 4), scratch elevens (33).

Representative teams: Scotland (4 inc 3 unofficial internationals), London (15 inc one each for London Probables and London Seconds), Middlesex (5), Kent (2), North (1).

THE FA CUP FINALS

1873	**Wanderers 2**, Oxford University 0
1875	Royal Engineers 2, **Old Etonians 0** (after a 1-1 draw)
1876	Wanderers 3, **Old Etonians 0** (after a 1-1 draw)
1877	**Wanderers 2**, Oxford University 1
1878	**Wanderers 3**, Royal Engineers 1
1879	**Old Etonians 1**, Clapham Rovers 0
1881	Old Carthusians 3, **Old Etonians 0**
1882	**Old Etonians 1**, Blackburn Rovers 0
1883	Blackburn Olympic 2, **Old Etonians 1**

1865-66 (11 matches)

16 Nov 1865	Eton College 2g 1r, **Hon F Pelham's XI 0** (Eton, Field)
30 Nov 1865	**Cambridge Univ 1g 1r**, Oxford University 0 (Eton, Field)
14 Dec 1865	Eton College 2r, **Hon F Pelham's XI 0** (Eton, Field)
27 Dec 1865	Westminster 0, **Old Etonians 4** (Vincent Square)
30 Dec 1865	SD Headlam's XI 1, **AF Kinnaird's XI 1** (Tunbridge Wells)
3 Jan 1866	**Old Etonians 0**, Wanderers 0 (London)
5 Jan 1866	**Old Etonians 0**, Civil Service 0 (Battersea Park)

165

27 Jan 1866	Charterhouse 1, **Old Etonians 2** (Charterhouse)
21 Feb 1866	Charterhouse 3, **Old Etonians 1** (Charterhouse)
23 Mar 1866	**Old Etonians 0**, Harrow Chequers 0 (Battersea Park)
31 Mar 1866	**London 2**, Sheffield 0 (Battersea Park)

1866-67 (27 matches)

15 Oct 1866	Eton College 1s, **Mr Kinnaird's XI 1s** (Eton, Wall)
16 Oct 1866	Eton College 1g 1r, **Mr Kinnaird's XI 1r** (Eton, Field)
20 Oct 1866	**Trinity College 2**, St John's College 1 (Cambridge)
1 Nov 1866	St John's College 0, **Eton Football Club 3** (St John's)
3 Nov 1866	Eton College 1g, **A Cambridge XI 2r** (Eton, Field)
15 Nov 1866	**Eton Football Club 0**, The University 0 (Cambridge)
17 Nov 1866	**Eton Football Club 4**, Emmanuel College 0 (Trinity)
20 Nov 1866	**Eton Football Club 0**, Harrow (Cambridge) 0 (Cambridge)
22 Nov 1866	**Eton Football Club 2**, St John's College 0 (Trinity)
28 Nov 1866	Westminster 1, **Third Trinity College 2** (Vincent Square)
1 Dec 1866	**Cambridge Univ 1g**, Oxford Univ 1r (Trinity, Field)
10 Dec 1866	**Eton Football Club 1**, Harrow (Cambridge) 0 (Cambridge)
13 Dec 1866	Eton College 1g 2r, **Cambridge University 0** (Eton, Field)
17 Dec 1866	Forest School 2, **Mr Kinnaird's XI 2** (Walthamstow)
20 Dec 1866	Wanderers 0, **Old Etonians 1** (Battersea Park)
22 Dec 1866	**Wanderers 1**, Harrow Chequers 1 (Battersea Park)
8 Jan 1867	**Eton and Harrow 2**, The World 2 (Vincent Square)
10 Jan 1867	Westminster Holiday Team 1, **Wanderers 2** (Vincent Sq)
22 Jan 1867	**Eton and Harrow 0**, The World 2 (Vincent Square)
26 Jan 1867	Charterhouse 0, **Mr AF Kinnaird's XI 0** (Charterhouse)
29 Jan 1867	Eton College 1r, **Mr AF Kinnaird's XI 0** (Eton, Field)
30 Jan 1867	Charterhouse 3, **Civil Service 0** (Charterhouse)
9 Feb 1867	Hitchin 0, **Eton Football Club 1** (Hitchin)
16 Feb 1867	Oxford University 0, **Wanderers 1** (Oxford)
19 Feb 1867	**Trinity College 1**, St John's College 1 (Trinity)
27 Feb 1867	Charterhouse 0, **Eton Football Club 0** (Charterhouse)
9 Mar 1867	Hitchin 0, **Old Harrovians 3** (Hitchin)

1867-68 (26 matches)

12 Oct 1867	Eton College 1r, **Mr Kinnaird's XI 0** (Eton, Field)
16 Oct 1867	Charterhouse School 6, **Avengers 0** (Charterhouse)
17 Oct 1867	Eton College 10s, **Lord Fitzmaurice's XI 0** (Eton, Wall)
18 Oct 1867	Eton College 1g 1r, **Lord Fitzmaurice's XI 1r** (Eton, Field)
28 Oct 1867	**Eton Football Club 0**, Wanderers 0 (Cambridge)
29 Oct 1867	Harrow Club 1, **Wanderers 0** (Cambridge)
30 Oct 1867	St John's College 1, **Wanderers 2** (St John's)
31 Oct 1867	King's College 1, **Wanderers 0** (Trinity)
1 Nov 1867	**Cambridge University 3**, Wanderers 0 (Parker's Piece)

2 Nov 1867	Eton College 2r, **Mr Ferguson's XI 1r** (Eton, Field)
5 Nov 1867	**Eton Football Club 2**, Christ's College 0 (Cambridge)
7 Nov 1867	St John's College 0, **Eton Football Club 1** (St John's)
16 Nov 1867	**Cambridge Etonians 1**, Jesus College 0 (Cambridge)
23 Nov 1867	Westminster 0, **Cambridge Etonians 2** (Vincent Square)
6 Dec 1867	**Cambridge Etonians** v Harrovians, a draw (Cambridge)
7 Dec 1867	Eton College 1g 1r, **Hon FG Pelham's XI 0** (Eton, Field)
13 Dec 1867	Wanderers 0, **An Eton Eleven 0** (Battersea Park)
17 Dec 1867	Forest School 2, **Mr Kinnaird's XI 1** (Walthamstow)
21 Dec 1867	Old Westminsters 1, **Old Etonians 1** (Vincent Square)
31 Dec 1867	**Eton and Harrow 0**, The World 1 (Vincent Square)
16 Jan 1868	**Eton and Harrow 0**, The World 0 (Vincent Square)
25 Jan 1868	Surrey 0, **Kent 0** (Brompton)
29 Jan 1868	**Flying Dutchmen 4**, Mr HR Dupre's XI 1 (Vincent Square)
30 Jan 1868	Eton College 2r, **Lord E Fitzmaurice's XI 2r** (Eton, Field)
20 Feb 1868	Hitchin 0, **Wanderers 2** (Hitchin)
29 Feb 1868	Charterhouse 1, **Cambridge University 2** (Islington)

1868-69 (16 matches)

16 Oct 1868	Eton College 1r, **Hon FG Pelham's XI 2r** (Eton, Field)
7 Nov 1868	Westminster Scholars 5, **Flying Dutchmen 0** (Vincent Sq)
16 Nov 1868	**Eton Football Club 3**, Wanderers 0 (Cambridge)
28 Nov 1868	**Cambridge University 1r,** Oxford Univ. 1g (Eton, Field)
12 Dec 1868	Eton College 1r, **Lord E Fitzmaurice's XI 2r** (Eton, Field)
19 Dec 1868	Bedouins 0, **Gitanos 2** (Blackheath)
16 Jan 1869	Wanderers 1, **Old Etonians 1** (Islington)
30 Jan 1869	CCC 1, **Gitanos 0** (Clapham)
13 Feb 1869	**Eton Football Club 1**, St John's College 0 (Cambridge)
20 Feb 1869	Wanderers 1, **West Kent 0** (Islington)
27 Feb 1869	**Kent 2**, Surrey 0 (Barnes)
6 Mar 1869	Westminster 0, **West Kent 1** (Vincent Square)
10 Mar 1869	Westminster 1, **Wanderers 3** (Vincent Square)
13 Mar 1869	Upton Park 0, **Wanderers 8** (Upton Park)
15 Mar 1869	Charterhouse 4, **Mr E Tayloe's XI 0** (Charterhouse)
24 Mar 1869	Charterhouse 2, **Wanderers 3** (Charterhouse)

1869-70 (27 matches)

8 Oct 1869	Eton College 0, **CR Alexander's XI 1g 3r** (Eton, Field)
9 Oct 1869	Eton College 0, **CR Alexander's XI 0** (Eton, Wall)
15 Oct 1869	Eton College 1g, **AC Thompson's XI 2g** (Eton, Field)
23 Oct 1869	Wanderers 0, **Old Etonians 2** (Kennington Oval)
30 Oct 1869	Forest Club 0, **Wanderers 5** (Woodford)
13 Nov 1869	Civil Service 0, **West Kent 1** (Kennington Oval)
17 Nov 1869	Westminster 0, **Wanderers 1** (Vincent Square)

20 Nov 1869	Wanderers 0, **Gitanos 0** (Kennington Oval)	
1 Dec 1869	**Wanderers 4**, Civil Service 2 (Kennington Oval)	
4 Dec 1869	Crystal Palace 1, **West Kent 1** (Crystal Palace)	
14 Dec 1869	**Wanderers 1**, Desperadoes 2 (Kennington Oval)	
5 Jan 1870	Crystal Palace 0, **Wanderers 1** (Crystal Palace)	
8 Jan 1870	**Crusaders 4**, Civil Service 2 (Kennington Oval)	
15 Jan 1870	**Wanderers 1**, Gitanos 1 (Kennington Oval)	
19 Jan 1870	**Wanderers 1**, Harrow Pilgrims 0 (Kennington Oval)	
22 Jan 1870	**Wanderers 3**, Civil Service 0 (Kennington Oval)	
27 Jan 1870	Harrow 3, **Mr PM Thornton's XI 0** (Harrow)	
29 Jan 1870	**West Kent 2**, Civil Service 0 (venue not known)	
5 Feb 1870	Harrow 1, **Wanderers 0** (Harrow)	
9 Feb 1870	**Wanderers 0**, Crystal Palace 2 (Kennington Oval)	
26 Feb 1870	Westminster 4, **West Kent 2** (Vincent Square)	
5 Mar 1870	England 1, **Scotland 1** (Kennington Oval)	
9 Mar 1870	Westminster 0, **Old Etonians 1** (Vincent Square)	
12 Mar 1870	Upton Park 0, **Wanderers 3** (Upton Park)	
19 Mar 1870	Charterhouse 1, **Wanderers 1** (Charterhouse)	
19 Mar 1870	**Wanderers 2**, Hampstead Heathens 1 (Kennington Oval)	
23 Mar 1870	Charterhouse 2, **Mr CF Reid's XI 1** (Charterhouse)	

1870-71 (26 matches)

8 Oct 1870	**Wanderers 1**, CCC 0 (Kennington Oval)
14 Oct 1870	Eton College 1g 2r, **Mr C Tait's XI 1g 1r** (Eton, Field)
2 Nov 1870	Charterhouse 3, **Wanderers 1** (Charterhouse)
5 Nov 1870	Harrow 1, **Wanderers 2** (Harrow)
9 Nov 1870	**Wanderers 5**, Brixton Club 1 (Kennington Oval)
12 Nov 1870	Oxford Association Club 0, **Wanderers 2** (Parks, Oxford)
16 Nov 1870	Westminster 0, **Wanderers 0** (Vincent Square)
19 Nov 1870	England 1, **Scotland 0** (Kennington Oval)
26 Nov 1870	**London Etonians 2r**, Oxford Etonians 0 (Eton, Field)
26 Nov 1870	Eton College 1g, **Mr AF Kinnaird's XI 1g** (Eton, Field)
30 Nov 1870	Westminster 1, **West Kent 0** (Vincent Square)
3 Dec 1870	Eton College 1g 2r, **Gitanos 0** (Eton, Field)
13 Dec 1870	**Wanderers 4**, Harrow Rovers 0 (Kennington Oval)
16 Dec 1870	**Wanderers 0**, Etonian Rovers 0 (Kennington Oval)
17 Dec 1870	South 1, **North 0** (Kennington Oval)
18 Jan 1871	**Wanderers 3**, Crystal Palace 0 (Kennington Oval)
21 Jan 1871	Wanderers 0, **West Kent 0** (Kennington Oval)
25 Jan 1871	Charterhouse 1, **Eton Club, Cambridge 2** (Charterhouse)
1 Feb 1871	Westminster 1, **Mr AJ Baker's XI 2** (Vincent Square)
4 Feb 1871	Harrow 0, **Wanderers 0** (Harrow)
11 Feb 1871	Wanderers 2, **Gitanos 0** (Kennington Oval)
18 Feb 1871	**Wanderers 2**, Hampstead Heathens 0 (Kennington Oval)

23 Feb 1871	Westminster 1, **Wanderers 2** (Vincent Square)
25 Feb 1871	England 1, **Scotland 1** (Kennington Oval)
18 Mar 1871	**Wanderers 2**, Forest Club 0 (Kennington Oval)
25 Mar 1871	**Wanderers 1**, The World 1 (Kennington Oval)

1871-72
No matches.

1872-73 (24 matches)

26 Oct 1872	Westminster 3, **Gitanos 0** (Vincent Square)
29 Oct 1872	**Wanderers 4**, Forest School 1 (Kennington Oval)
2 Nov 1872	Sheffield 4, **London 1** (Bramall Lane)
9 Nov 1872	**Wanderers 1**, Gitanos 1 (Kennington Oval)
12 Nov 1872	Eton College 0, **Wanderers 0** (Eton)
16 Nov 1872	**Old Etonians 2**, Old Harrovians 1 (Kennington Oval)
23 Nov 1872	Eton College 0, **Gitanos 0** (Eton)
30 Nov 1872	**Wanderers 0**, Royal Engineers 2 (Kennington Oval)
13 Dec 1872	Eton College 2, **AF Kinnaird's XI 1** (Eton)
14 Dec 1872	Surrey 4, **Middlesex 2** (Kennington Oval)
23 Dec 1872	**Wanderers 3**, Old Reptonians 1 (Kennington Oval)
4 Jan 1873	**London 1**, Sheffield 0 (Kennington Oval)
29 Jan 1873	**Wanderers 2**, Uxbridge 1 (Kennington Oval)
1 Feb 1873	Surrey 1, **Middlesex 3** (Kennington Oval)
20 Feb 1873	**Wanderers 3**, England Candidates 1 (Kennington Oval)
22 Feb 1873	**Old Etonians 1**, Old Harrovians 0 (Kennington Oval)
1 Mar 1873	Royal Engineers 4, **Wanderers 0** (Chatham)
5 Mar 1873	Charterhouse 4, **Wanderers 2** (Charterhouse)
8 Mar 1873	England 4, **Scotland 2** (Kennington Oval)
12 Mar 1873	**Wanderers 2**, Gitanos 2 (Lillie Bridge)
15 Mar 1873	Sheffield 2, **London 1** (Bramall Lane)
17 Mar 1873	Notts Club 0, **London 0** (Trent Bridge)
27 Mar 1873	Royal Engineers 1, **Gitanos 0** (Chatham)
29 Mar 1873	**Wanderers 2**, Oxford University 0 (FACF, Lillie Bridge)

1873-74 (2 matches)

| 10 Jan 1874 | **Wanderers 5**, Harrow Chequers 1 (Kennington Oval) |
| 31 Jan 1874 | Oxford University 1, **Wanderers 0** (FAC3R, Oxford) |

1874-75 (16 matches)

17 Oct 1874	Surrey 1, **Middlesex 1** (Kennington Oval)
5 Nov 1874	Swifts 0, **Old Etonians 0** (FAC1, Slough)
7 Nov 1874	Sheffield 2, **London 0** (Bramall Lane)
14 Nov 1874	**Old Etonians 1**, Swifts 1 (FAC1R, Kennington Oval)
21 Nov 1874	Eton College 2r, **Gitanos 0** (Eton (Field)

26 Nov 1874 Swifts 0, **Old Etonians 3** (FAC1R, Slough)
28 Nov 1874 Royal Engineers 1, **Gitanos 0** (Prince's Club)
5 Dec 1874 1st Surrey Rifles 0, **Gitanos 0** (Camberwell)
9 Jan 1875 **Wanderers 9**, Harrow Chequers 1 (Kennington Oval)
16 Jan 1875 **London 3**, Sheffield 1 (Kennington Oval)
19 Jan 1875 **Gitanos 1**, Wanderers 1 (Kennington Oval)
23 Jan 1875 **Old Etonians 1**, Maidenhead 0 (FAC3, Kennington Oval)
27 Feb 1875 **Old Etonians 1**, Shropshire Wands. 0 (FACSF, K Oval)
13 Mar 1875 Royal Engineers 1, **Old Etonians 1** (FACF, K Oval)
16 Mar 1875 Royal Engineers 2, **Old Etonians 0** (FACFR, K Oval)
27 Mar 1875 Sheffield 0, **London 2** (Bramall Lane)

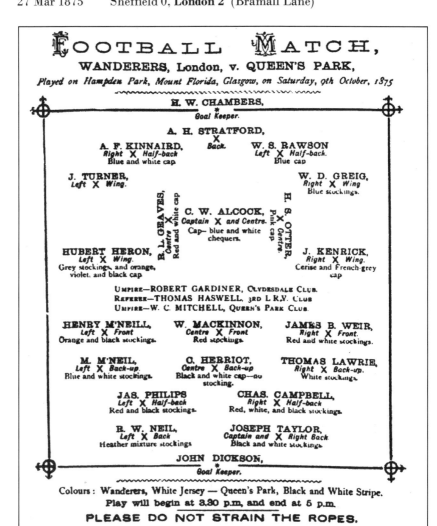

1875-76 (16 matches)

9 Oct 1875	Queen's Park 5, **Wanderers 0** (Hampden Park)
23 Oct 1875	Eton College 1r, **REH Murray's XI 1g** (Eton, Field)
30 Oct 1875	Surrey 5, **Middlesex 1** (Kennington Oval)
3 Nov 1875	Westminster 2, **Wanderers 3** (Vincent Square)
9 Nov 1875	**Old Etonians 4**, Pilgrims 1 (FAC1, Kennington Oval)
11 Dec 1875	**Old Etonians 8**, Maidenhead 0 (FAC2, Kennington Oval)
14 Dec 1875	Eton College 1g 1r, **GM Reade's XI 1r** (Eton, Field)
17 Dec 1875	Eton College 0, **Old Etonians 1r** (Prince's Club)
1 Jan 1876	**London 4**, Sheffield 0 (Kennington Oval)
26 Jan 1876	**Gitanos 3**, Civil Service 0 (Kennington Oval)
29 Jan 1876	**Old Etonians 1**, Clapham Rovers 0 (FAC3, K Oval)
19 Feb 1876	**Old Etonians 1**, Oxford University 0 (FACSF, K Oval)
29 Feb 1876	Westminster 1, **Wanderers 0** (Vincent Square)
11 Mar 1876	Wanderers 1, **Old Etonians 1** (FACF, Kennington Oval)
18 Mar 1876	Wanderers 3, **Old Etonians 0** (FACFR, Kennington Oval)
25 Mar 1876	Sheffield 6, **London 0** (Bramall Lane)

1876-77 (15 matches)

25 Oct 1876	Westminster 0, **Wanderers 2** (Vincent Square)
1 Nov 1876	Eton College 2r, **GM Reade's XI 1r** (Eton, Field)
11 Nov 1876	Sheffield 5, **London 1** (Bramall Lane)
25 Nov 1876	Harrow School 3, **Wanderers 2** (Harrow)
9 Dec 1876	1st Surrey Rifles 0, **Wanderers 4** (Camberwell)
13 Dec 1876	**Wanderers 0**, Oxford University 1 (Kennington Oval)
16 Dec 1876	Southall Park 0, **Wanderers 6** (FAC2, Southall)
19 Dec 1876	**Wanderers 5**, Harrow School 0 (Kennington Oval)
20 Jan 1877	**Wanderers 3**, Pilgrims 0 (FAC3, Kennington Oval)
3 Feb 1877	Clapham Rovers 1, **Wanderers 3** (Streatham)
8 Feb 1877	Upton Park 1, **Wanderers 0** (Camberwell)
10 Feb 1877	Royal Engineers 1, **Wanderers 0** (Chatham)
21 Feb 1877	Westminster 0, **Wanderers 1** (Vincent Square)
20 Mar 1877	**Wanderers 1**, Cambridge University 0 (FACSF, K Oval)
24 Mar 1877	**Wanderers 2**, Oxford University 1 (FACF, K Oval)

1877-78 (16 matches)

3 Nov 1877	**Wanderers 4**, Royal Engineers 0 (Kennington Oval)
7 Nov 1877	Panthers 1, **Wanderers 9** (FAC1, Sandhurst)
17 Nov 1877	Sheffield 0, **London 6** (Bramall Lane)
21 Nov 1877	Westminster 0, **Wanderers 1** (Vincent Square)
11 Dec 1877	**Wanderers 2**, Oxford University 1 (Kennington Oval)
15 Dec 1877	High Wycombe 0, **Wanderers 9** (FAC2, Wycombe)
18 Dec 1877	**Wanderers 4**, Harrow 1 (Kennington Oval)

171

22 Dec 1877	Herts Rangers 2, **Wanderers 4** (Watford)
5 Jan 1878	Old Foresters 0, **Wanderers 0** (Snaresbrook)
26 Jan 1878	**Wanderers 4**, Barnes 1 (FAC3R, Kennington Oval)
13 Feb 1878	Westminster 2, **Wanderers 5** (Vincent Square)
16 Feb 1878	**Wanderers 3**, Sheffield 0 (FAC4, Kennington Oval)
7 Mar 1878	Westminster 4, **Civil Service 1** (Vincent Square)
9 Mar 1878	1st Surrey Rifles 1, **Wanderers 9** (Camberwell)
23 Mar 1878	**Wanderers 3**, Royal Engineers 1 (FACF, K Oval)
13 Apr 1878	**Wanderers 1**, Vale of Leven 3 (Kennington Oval)

1878-79 (13 matches)

5 Oct 1878	**Wanderers 2**, Old Harrovians 3 (Kennington Oval)
9 Nov 1878	Wanderers 2, **Old Etonians 7** (FAC1, Kennington Oval)
16 Nov 1878	Oxford University 2, **Old Etonians 0** (Parks, Oxford)
20 Nov 1878	Westminster 1, **Wanderers 1** (Vincent Square)
7 Dec 1878	Eton College 1, **Gitanos 0** (Eton)
18 Dec 1878	Reading 0, **Old Etonians 1** (FAC2, Reading)
11 Jan 1879	**Old Etonians 5**, Minerva 2 (FAC3, Kennington Oval)
8 Feb 1879	Westminster 3, **Gitanos 1** (Vincent Square)
13 Feb 1879	**Old Etonians 5**, Darwen 5 (FAC4, Kennington Oval)
8 Mar 1879	**Old Etonians 2**, Darwen 2 (FAC4R, Kennington Oval)
15 Mar 1879	**Old Etonians 6**, Darwen 2 (FAC4R, Kennington Oval)
22 Mar 1879	**Old Etonians 2**, Nottingham Forest 1 (FACSF, K Oval)
29 Mar 1879	**Old Etonians 1**, Clapham Rovers 0 (FACF, K Oval)

1879-80 (8 matches)

22 Nov 1879	Cambridge University 0, **Old Etonians 1** (Parker's Piece)
27 Dec 1879	Vale of Leven 5, **Old Etonians 2** (Hampden Park)
30 Dec 1879	Edinburgh 3, **Old Etonians 4** (Edinburgh)
1 Jan 1880	Darwen 3, **Old Etonians 1** (Darwen)
24 Jan 1880	**Old Etonians 3**, Wanderers 1 (FAC3, Kennington Oval)
7 Feb 1880	**Old Etonians 5**, West End 1 (FAC4, Kennington Oval)
21 Feb 1880	Clapham Rovers 1, **Old Etonians 0** (FAC5, K Oval)
20 Mar 1880	**Old Etonians 1**, Vale of Leven 3 (Kennington Oval)

1880-81 (11 matches)

23 Oct 1880	Royal Engineers 0, **Old Etonians 5** (Chatham)
30 Oct 1880	**Old Etonians 1**, Old Foresters 1 (Kennington Oval)
6 Nov 1880	Brentwood 0, **Old Etonians 10** (FAC1, Brentwood)
13 Nov 1880	Oxford University 4, **Old Etonians 0** (Oxford)
20 Nov 1880	Eton College 2, **Old Etonians 3** (Eton)
4 Dec 1880	**Old Etonians 2**, Hendon 0 (FAC2, Kennington Oval)
31 Dec 1880	Sheffield FC 2, **Old Etonians 6** (Bramall Lane)
5 Feb 1881	**Old Etonians 3**, Herts Rangers 0 (FAC3, K Oval)

19 Feb 1881	**Old Etonians 4**, Greyfriars 0 (FAC4, Kennington Oval)
19 Mar 1881	Stafford Road 1, **Old Etonians 2** (FAC5, Wolverhampton)
9 Apr 1881	Old Carthusians 3, **Old Etonians 0** (FACF, K Oval)

1881-82 (11 matches)
22 Oct 1881	Eton College 1g 1r, **Old Etonians 1g 1r** (Eton, Field)
29 Oct 1881	Cambridge University 2, **Old Etonians 2** (Parker's Piece)
5 Nov 1881	**Old Etonians 2**, Clapham Rovers 2 (FAC1, K Oval)
19 Nov 1881	**Old Etonians 1**, Clapham Rovers 0 (FAC1R, K Oval)
17 Dec 1881	**Old Etonians 3**, Swifts 0 (FAC3, Kennington Oval)
7 Jan 1882	Berks and Bucks 5, **Middlesex 0** (Maidenhead)
14 Jan 1882	**Old Etonians 6**, Maidenhead 3 (FAC4, Kennington Oval)
4 Mar 1882	**Old Etonians 5**, Great Marlow 0 (FACSF, K Oval)
18 Mar 1882	**London 1**, Oxford and Cambridge 1 (Kennington Oval)
25 Mar 1882	**Old Etonians 1**, Blackburn Rovers 0 (FACF, K Oval)
1 Apr 1882	**Old Etonians 0**, Old Carthusians 1 (Kennington Oval)

1882-83 (14 matches)
28 Oct 1882	**Old Etonians 1**, Clapham Rovers 3 (LCC1, K Oval)
4 Nov 1882	**Old Etonians 1**, Old Foresters 1 (FAC1, Slough)
9 Nov 1882	**London Probables 1**, London Possibles 3 (K Oval)
18 Nov 1882	Old Foresters 1, **Old Etonians 3** (FAC1R, Walthamstow)
25 Nov 1882	Cambridge University 5, **Old Etonians 0** (Parker's Piece)
2 Dec 1882	Brentwood 1, **Old Etonians 2** (FAC2, Brentwood)
16 Dec 1882	Rochester 0, **Old Etonians 7** (FAC3, Chatham)
19 Dec 1882	Harrow School 1, **Wanderers 1** (Harrow)
24 Jan 1883	**Old Etonians 2**, Swifts 0 (FAC4, Kennington Oval)
14 Feb 1883	Westminster 1, **Old Etonians 6** (Vincent Square)
28 Feb 1883	Charterhouse 2, **Old Etonians 1** (Godalming)
3 Mar 1883	Hendon 2, **Old Etonians 4** (FAC5, Hendon)
17 Mar 1883	**Old Etonians 2**, Notts County 1 (FACSF, K Oval)
31 Mar 1883	Blackburn Olympic 2, **Old Etonians 1** (FACF, K Oval)

1883-84 onwards (24 matches)
17 Nov 1883	Hermits 0, **Old Etonians 1** (LCC1, West Ham)
8 Dec 1883	West End 1, **Old Etonians 8** (LCC2, Shepherd's Bush)
18 Dec 1883	**Wanderers 6**, Harrow School 1 (Kennington Oval)
5 Jan 1884	Bart's Hospital 0, **Old Etonians 1** (LCC3, Bart's)
23 Feb 1884	**Old Etonians 1**, Old Foresters 1 (LCCSF, K Oval)
22 Mar 1884	**Old Etonians 0**, Old Foresters 1 (LCCSFR, K Oval)
25 Oct 1884	**Old Etonians 8**, Olympians 1 (LCC1, Kennington Oval)
29 Oct 1884	Westminster 3, **Old Etonians 0** (Vincent Square)
12 Dec 1884	**Old Etonians 2**, Dulwich 2 (LCC3, Kennington Oval)
16 Dec 1884	**Wanderers 5**, Harrow School 0 (Kennington Oval)

31 Dec 1884	Dulwich 3, **Old Etonians 3** (LCC3R, Dulwich)
31 Oct 1885	**London Seconds 2,** East Midlands 5 (Chiswick)
2 Nov 1885	Eton College 1g 3r, **Old Etonians 0** (Eton, Field)
18 Nov 1885	London Scottish 2, **Hanover Utd 1** (LCC1R, Wimbledon)
21 Nov 1885	Eton College 0, **Old Etonians 0** (Eton, Field)
28 Nov 1885	Oxford University 4, **Old Etonians 0** (Oxford)
19 Dec 1885	**Old Etonians 2**, Old Carthusians 4 (Kennington Oval)
22 Dec 1885	**Wanderers 3**, Harrow School 1 (Kennington Oval)
26 Dec 1885	Windsor 0, **Hanover United 2** (Windsor)
6 Feb 1886	Charterhouse 3, **Old Etonians 1** (Godalming)
5 Mar 1887	Old Harrovians 3, **Old Etonians 3** (Harrow)
19 Mar 1887	Royal Engineers 2, **Old Etonians 0** (Chatham)
15 Nov 1890	Eton College 3g 1r, **Lord Kinnaird's XI 1g 1r** (Eton, Field)
16 Dec 1896	**Old Internationals 5**, Charterhouse 0 (Queen's Club)

Key:

FAC – FA Cup

LCC – London Challenge Cup

Cup rounds are indicated by number, SF or F, with R indicating a replay

Eton: g – goal; r – rouge; s – shy.

174

APPENDIX 2

A register of philanthropy

ARTHUR KINNAIRD gave his name to an extraordinary number of charities and philanthropic organisations, acting as president or treasurer to many, a committee member of others. Some occupied much more of his time than others, and his favourites would feature strongly throughout his life: they included the Ragged School Union, Evangelical Alliance, Homes for Working Boys, Christian Colportage Association, and of course the YWCA and YMCA.

Most can loosely be categorized into broad headings of education (ragged schools, refuges and youth); religion (including bible propagation and Sunday observance); and rescue work (poverty relief, health and international aid). There are also organisations with political and financial aims, with some of whom he held a directorship, but surprisingly few with sporting connotations.

Education (ragged schools, refuges and youth)
Aged Pilgrims' Friend Society
Boys' Brigade
Camberwell Mission and Ragged Schools (treasurer)
College of Teachers of the Blind
Cripples' Home and Industrial School for Girls
Destitute Children's Dinners Society (treasurer)
Dr Barnardo's Homes for Orphan and Destitute Children
East End of London Juvenile Mission (Vice-President)
Factory Helpers' Union
Farningham and Swanley Homes for Little Boys
Field Lane Refuges and Ragged Schools Institution
Homes for Working Boys in London
Homes for Working Girls (treasurer)
London City Mission, Cowcross District (treasurer)
London College of Divinity (treasurer)
London Diocesan Home Mission (treasurer)
London Female Preventive and Reformatory Institution
London Schools Dinner Association (hon treasurer)

London Society for the Prevention of Cruelty to Children
Metropolitan Association for Befriending Young Servants
National Association of Grocers' Assistants
Nelson Street Ragged School and Mission (treasurer)
Orphan Working School
Polytechnic Institute
Pastors' College
Queen's Jubilee Institute for Nurses
Ragged School Union
Reformatory and Refuge Union
Royal Association in Aid of the Deaf and Dumb
St Martin-in-the-Fields Church Board of Works, Free Library
St Giles Mission for the Aid of Discharged Prisoners
Sailors Orphan Girls' School and Home
Young Helpers' League
YMCA (President 1907-1923)
YWCA (President 1887-1909)

Religion (including bible propagation and Sunday observance)
Admiral de Coligny Memorial Fund
The Biblewomen and Nurses Mission
The Bible League
British and Foreign Bible Society
Church Missionary Society
Christian Colportage Association
Evangelical Alliance
Imperial Sunday Alliance
National Protestant Church Union
Railway Mission
Religious Tract Society
Soldiers' Christian Association
Sunday School Union
Thames Church Mission
Tower Hamlets Mission
Working Men's Lord's Day Rest Association

Rescue work (poverty relief, health and international aid)
Anglo-Indian Temperance Association
Anglo-Indian Evangelization Society
Armenian Massacre Relief Special Fund
Bechuana Relief Fund
Bible Lands Missions Aid Society
British Syrian Mission
Cabmen's Shelters Fund

176

Central Vigilance Society for the Repression of Immorality
Charing Cross Hospital

PROMINENT FOOTBALLERS.

THE RIGHT HON.
LORD KINNAIRD.
PRESIDENT
FOOTBALL ASSOCIATION.

Being treasurer of the National Society for the Suppression of Juvenile Smoking did not stop Arthur being featured on this cigarette card

Congo Balolo Mission
Congo Reform Association
Dental Hospital of London
Emin Bey Relief Fund Committee
Field Lane Institution
Football Charity Fund
Flying Services Fund
Great Ormond Street Hospital (vice president)
Indian Famine Relief Fund
International Congress against Alcoholism
Japan Society
The Liberator Relief Fund
London Council for the Promotion of Public Morality
London Lock Hospital and Asylum
London Playing Fields Society
National Physical Recreation Society (treasurer)
National Society for the Suppression of Juvenile Smoking (treasurer)
National Vigilance Association
Royal Scottish Corporation
Surgical Aid Society
Turkish Missions Aid Society
Veterans Relief Fund
Zenana Bible and Medical Mission

Political, financial and recreational
Aero Club of Great Britain (treasurer)
American Freehold Land Mortgage Company of London (director)
Anglo-American Club
Anglo-German Friendship Committee
Betterment of London Association
British and Foreign Arbitration Association
British Committee for the Study of Foreign Municipal Institutions
British-American Peace Centenary Committee
British Empire League
Central Association of Bankers
Central Temperance Legislation Board
Canadian Pacific Railroad

Football Association (1868-1923; President from 1890)
Further Strand Improvement Committee
Hull and Barnsley Railway and Dock Company
Imperial British East Africa Company
International Arbitration League
Liberal Union Club
Merchants' Trust Company Ltd (director)
National Aeronautical Defence Association
National Rifle Association (treasurer)
North British and Mercantile Insurance Company
Railway Passengers' Assurance Company
Royal Agricultural Society of England
Royal Geographical Society (Fellow)
Savings Bank of the Country and City of Perth
Southern Coal Company of New South Wales
Trust and Agency Company of Australasia (director)
Trust Houses, Limited (director)
Trafalgar Square Petition Committee
Westminster Electricity Supply Corporation Ltd

APPENDIX 3

A thousand years of the Kinnaird family

THE KINNAIRD name is literally as old as the hills, deriving from the Gaelic *ceann ard* loosely meaning 'head of the hill'. That describes the domain of Radulphus de Kinnaird, also known as Radulphus Ruffus (ie the red-haired) who was granted a charter around 1172 by King William I (the Lion) for lands overlooking the River Tay, at the heart of the province of Gowrie.

The origins of this first recorded Kinnaird are lost in time but a likely theory is that he came to Scotland as part of an influx of Flemish and Norman families who were given land by William to consolidate his power base in what is now Perthshire, while he attempted to subdue the northern reaches of his kingdom.[1] Radulphus had good hunting grounds in the forests, as well as the potential to farm the carse - the low-lying expanse between the hills and the river – which at that time was largely a swamp with islands of elevated dry land.[2] There was the added bonus of being within easy reach of Scotland's then capital, Scone. His descendants laid down roots by marrying into other great Scottish families, creating alliances both locally and further afield. As the wars of independence unfolded the Kinnairds adapted to circumstance, first swearing fealty to King Edward I of England, then jumping sides to help King Robert the Bruce win back Scotland's crown at Bannockburn in 1314.

Towards the end of the 14th century Thomas Kinnaird of Kinnaird married an heiress to land at Culbin in Moray; the Kinnaird and Culbin estates were then split between their children. Meanwhile, Thomas's younger brother Reginald married Marjory, only child of Sir John Kirkcaldy of Inchture; when Sir John died, Reginald became the first Kinnaird of Inchture, and built a castle which stood almost exactly where Inchture Inn is now. Of the three branches, Kinnaird, Culbin and Inchture, in time only the last survived. The senior branch got into financial difficulty, forcing the sale of Kinnaird Castle and its lands in 1618. The Kinnairds of

Culbin were doubly unfortunate: the estate was ruined by coastal erosion, forcing landowner Alexander Kinnaird to sell at a low price; then, in an effort to clear his debts, he joined the disastrous Darien expedition to Panama in 1698, dying there along with two sons.

That left the Kinnairds of Inchture, who had added the nearby estates of Moncur and Baledgarno through marriage, and moved into Moncur Castle, whose ruins still stand in the grounds of Rossie Priory. Their step up to a family of national importance can be pinpointed to George, a staunch royalist who represented Perthshire in the Scottish Parliament. Following the death of Oliver Cromwell in 1658, he allowed General Monck's royalist army to camp on his estates, and provisioned the troops for their march to London. After King Charles II regained the throne, he recognised this service to the crown's cause with a knighthood, and then in 1682 elevated him to Lord Kinnaird of Inchture. It was not a universally popular gesture as George had upset a few people along the way and was described as profligate and vicious. One contemporary remarked: 'None are willingly lords now since Kinnaird was made one,' but the Scottish aristocracy only had to put up with him for a short time as George died in 1689.

Within a decade, everything he had gained was nearly lost. First, Moncur Castle burned to the ground in 1691, so Patrick (2nd Lord) was obliged to move into Drimmie House, a hunting lodge that would be a 'temporary' home for over a hundred years. To cap that, he lost heavily in the Darien scheme, which effectively bankrupted the Scottish nation and was one of the principal factors that forced Scotland into the Act of Union with England in 1707. His son Patrick (3rd Lord), a fervent patriot, was an opponent of the Act of Union but his arguments in the Scottish Parliament failed to prevent it going ahead.

When his son, also Patrick (4th Lord), died unmarried in 1727 the title reverted to the third Lord's younger brother Charles (5th Lord), who provided one of the more farcical episodes in the family history. After 18 years of marriage he and his wife Magdalen had no children and therefore no heirs, then in September 1747 suddenly announced the surprise 'birth' of twin sons. These were immediately denounced as a fraud by the heir-presumptive, his third cousin Charles, who submitted a convincing argument to court: Lady Kinnaird was past child-bearing age, had never announced her pregnancy and had often been heard to say injurious things of the father of the pursuer. Lord Kinnaird was ordered to pay Charles £600 for failing to defend the action, and shortly afterwards announced the 'deaths' of the twins.

So the succession did, after all, fall to Charles (6ᵗʰ Lord) in 1758, but his tenure was brief and he died in 1767. His intellectual and charming son George (7ᵗʰ Lord) was appointed manager of the London banking house of Ransom, Morland and Hammersley and by the simple expedient of marrying Elizabeth, daughter and sole heir of Griffin Ransom, one of the partners, he restored the family fortunes. After Ransom's death in 1784, the remaining partners refused to give him a share of the business, but George proved an astute manager and the bank, in its various manifestations, was often referred to as 'Kinnaird & Co'. By employing French-speaking staff the bank developed a good reputation with aristocrats fleeing the French Revolution, although it was not necessarily deserved: Madame du Barry deposited her treasures in its vaults, but after she returned to France and was sent to the guillotine, her jewels 'mysteriously disappeared'[3]. From the same source, George began a magnificent art collection with a purchase in 1792 of works by Flemish, Dutch and German masters from the Duke of Orleans; later, he sold some at a healthy profit to the National Gallery.

His wife's inheritance provided the wherewithal to modernise his Scottish estate[4], but just as he was on the verge of realising his dream, the end came suddenly. One October morning in 1805 he travelled to Perth races on a foul day and caught a severe chill; it developed into a fever and he died without seeing his home again. Lady Kinnaird was so affected that she died just ten days later.

Their son Charles (8ᵗʰ Lord) was in Venice, on the Grand Tour, when he heard of his father's death. A graduate of three universities and an MP[5], he was notoriously dour and single-minded. The diarist Joseph Farington wrote of his 'avaricious disposition' and quoted a satirical ditty:

Here's a park without deer,
A cellar without beer,
A kitchen without cheer,
Lord Kinnaird lives here.[6]

The subdued atmosphere of the House of Lords did not appeal to him so he returned to Perthshire where he took over the running of Dundee Bank, and threw himself into the construction of Rossie Priory. Meanwhile, his younger brother Douglas remained in London, where he was appointed managing partner of Ransom & Co's Bank, became an MP, and was literary agent for the poet Lord Byron.

Charles was a close friend of Arthur Wellesley, Duke of Wellington, but they fell out in the aftermath of Britain's victory over France, as Charles supported the (republican) Jacobins while Wellington, in charge of the army of occupation, was in favour of restoring the French monarchy. Another factor may have been rumours that Lady Kinnaird was romantically involved with the Duke.[7] Then, in 1818, Charles got wind of a Jacobin plot to assassinate the Duke, who dismissed the idea as a fantasy. After the attempt was actually made, Charles travelled to Paris to see the Duke with the source of his information, Louis-Joseph Marinet, but was arrested by the French authorities on suspicion of complicity. Although soon released, Charles vented his anger in an open letter criticising the Duke.[8] Byron immortalised the argument in his epic *Don Juan*, with this dig at Wellington:

I don't think that you used Kinnaird quite well
In Marinet's affair – in fact 'twas shabby –
And, like some other things, won't do to tell
Upon your tomb in Westminster's old Abbey.[9]

Never in the best of health, Charles sought a sunshine cure and spent much of his later life in Italy, investing in fine art. One of his more adventurous purchases was a mosaic pavement from the Hadrianic period; he had great difficulty getting it out of the country, with the curator of the Vatican Museum granting permission only on the stipulation that it be shipped from Civita Vecchia without anyone seeing it.[10] He died in 1826, aged 46.

His son George (9th Lord) was a social reformer and champion of the working class, and was appointed chairman of a Royal Commission into dangerous working conditions, which covered occupations from coalminers to child chimney sweeps. He set about improving Rossie Priory, whose start he had witnessed as an infant, adding a west wing, a picture gallery, dining room and conservatory. He installed running water, built estate roads, nurtured a prize-winning herd of Highland cattle, and later restored the ancient parish church of Rossie as a family memorial chapel. He took his responsibilities as a landowner seriously, improving the lot of the workers in and around his estate by draining the land, introducing threshing machines and steam ploughs, erecting houses for the staff, and bore the costs of evening classes for the ploughmen.[11]

Towards the end of his life an economic downturn saw the price of land plummet to a quarter of its value. He reduced the rents of his tenants, so his own income fell sharply, and he had to shut up a large part of the house. However, he took consolation in the collections of art and antiquities, which were described with awe by the American diarist Richard Henry Dana, a distant relative, who visited Rossie Priory in 1875 and listed the outstanding works by Rembrandt, Titian, Leonardo da Vinci, Raphael and Gainsborough.[12]

An active sportsman, George established Rossie Priory Cricket Club in 1828, one of the first in Scotland, laying out a pitch in view of the house and encouraging membership from the estate staff and local community. As captain of the Perth Golfing Society, he was instrumental in it being granted royal patronage in 1833, the first golf club to have this honour. In 1844 he laid out curling ponds on the estate for the Rossie Curling Club, and was later elected President of the Royal Caledonian Curling Club, the game's governing body. However, his love of sport and social welfare did not always mix, and the teetotal lord felt a media backlash in 1864 when he refused permission for a cricket match between the Rossie and Inchmartine clubs, objecting to the visitors' 'too free use of spiritual liquors'. He compounded the insult by blaming the Inchmartine patron, Mrs Ferguson Blair, who hit back indignantly with what the *Glasgow Herald* described as a 'moral horse-whipping'. The resulting storm in a teacup reached the London papers, with one satirical magazine publishing a lengthy lampoon, part of which read:

It's very good of Lord Kinnaird
To entertain the sweep
To dabble in philanthropy
And do it on the cheap.

But 'twas not handsome, Lord Kinnaird,
To charge intoxication
Upon a club of gentlemen
Who sought your grounds for cricket. [13]

He was raised to the rank of a Peer of the United Kingdom with the title of Baron Rossie of Rossie, but this title was exchanged in 1860 for that of Baron Kinnaird of Rossie due to the failure of the male line. George and his wife Frances were victims of a series of tragedies. First, his younger brother Graham, a Naval Lieutenant, drowned when the ship he commanded, HM Brig *Rapid*, was driven onto rocks and wrecked in a storm at Bona (now Annaba, in eastern Algeria) in 1838. Although his valiant efforts saved the lives of his crew, he went down with his ship.[14] To enable him to be buried on British soil, his body was taken to Malta on the Brig *Giuseppina* and laid to rest there in the Lazaretto.

A male heir, Victor, was born in 1840 but the boy was never in the best of health and died aged 11. Their second son, Charles set off in 1860 to undertake the Grand Tour but two months later, a telegram arrived at Rossie Priory with the news that he was seriously ill in Naples, having contracted malaria. His parents set off to be with him but had only reached London when another telegram informed them of Charles' death. He was just 17.

This succession of unfortunate events brought George's youngest brother into line for the succession. Born in 1814 in the newly-completed Rossie Priory, he was christened Arthur Wellesley Kinnaird in honour of his godfather, the Duke of Wellington, but his middle name was changed to Fitzgerald (his mother's maiden name) following his father's arguments with the Iron Duke.

As a third son with no obvious prospect of a title, he had been lined up for a career in banking, although first he was taken on as an unpaid attaché to the Earl of Durham, Ambassador to the Russian Court in St Petersburg. Setting out in July 1835, he had a leisurely journey via Greece and the Crimea before arriving in Russia, where he stayed for a year. Late in 1836 he returned to London to join Ransom & Co, where 'being of a polite and sociable disposition he was able to draw many depositors to the little bank.'[15] Arthur also went into politics and in 1837 was elected to represent Perth as a Liberal. He became close friends with William Gladstone, the future Prime Minister, and even accompanied him to Italy in 1838 when Gladstone proposed to Catherine Glynne. However, after

Arthur Kinnaird senior

two years in parliament, Arthur's youthful idealism prompted him to support a bill in favour of religious education, against the wishes of his local party. He was obliged to resign his seat.

Already leaning towards evangelical Christianity, he was introduced to his future wife at a Bible study reception in the Duchess of Beaufort's drawing room. Mary Jane Hoare, from another banking family, was daughter of William and Louisa Hoare, but the birth killed her mother and her father died when she was just three. Brought up by various relatives, Mary became private secretary to her uncle, the evangelical preacher Reverend Baptist Noel (it was his real first name, not an allusion to his Christian credentials), and in 1841 she set up the St John's Training School for Domestic Servants. In time she became one of the Victorian era's great social reformers for women and girls.

Arthur and Mary found much in common, although he was personable and full of energy while she was said to be quiet and single minded. They married in Hornsey Church on 28 June 1843 and set up home in Southwick Terrace, near Paddington, where their first daughter Mary was born in the spring of 1844. A year later they moved into Hyde Park Gardens, where their son Arthur was born in 1847.

Arthur senior returned to Parliament in 1852, and would represent Perth until his elevation to the House of Lords. A radical who stridently promoted Christian values — he considered Protestantism as 'essential to the maintenance of civil and religious liberty' — *Hansard* records over 700 contributions he made in the House of Commons. He gave vocal support to Lord Shaftesbury and William Gladstone's social reforms and was particularly outspoken against slavery; even after it was outlawed in Britain and the United States, Arthur led campaigns against the enduring Arab slave trade on the east coast of Africa. He also engineered an expansion of his bank in 1855[16] and as senior partner of the newly-created Ransom, Bouverie & Co, successfully negotiated the financial crisis of 1866 when many small banks collapsed.[17]

Mary was undoubtedly the power behind the scenes, writing her husband's speeches and driving forward their social improvement projects, drawing upon powerful family and banking connections for support. She is best remembered for her role in establishing the Young Women's Christian Association (YWCA), which went on to become a worldwide movement. It began in 1855 when she opened a home for Florence Nightingale's nurses on their return from the Crimea; this grew into the North London Home, for girls coming to work in the city. Her organisation, initially called the United Association for the Christian and Domestic Improvement of Young Women, aimed 'to care for their souls, and to desire earnestly to remove the pressure of over-work, by which their bodily and mental health is so often impaired.'[18] She worked closely with Emma Robarts, who had formed a successful women's prayer union called the YWCA and in 1877, just before Robarts' death, the women agreed to merge the two bodies. It is a measure of Mary's impact that, unlike her husband, she was deemed worthy of a biography after her death.[19]

Arthur was 64 when he succeeded his elder brother as 10th Lord Kinnaird in 1878. Although he took up his seat in the House of Lords, he was too set in his ways to give up the banking business and remained senior partner until his death, a stance that brought criticism for continuing 'in trade' while a peer.[20] He also took on the management of Rossie Priory estate in Scotland, but was in declining health.

His successor in 1887 was his only son, Arthur Fitzgerald Kinnaird, a 40-year-old footballer, banker, philanthropist and evangelical, described in the press as 'the busiest man in London'.[21] Fully twenty-five generations had passed since Radulphus de Kinnaird arrived in Scotland.

Arthur Kinnaird's family

Arthur [Wellesley] Fitzgerald, 10th Lord Kinnaird (1814-1887)
m 1843 Mary Jane Hoare (1816-1888)
   ARTHUR FITZGERALD, 11th LORD KINNAIRD (1847-1923)
    m 1875 Mary Alma Victoria Agnew (1854-1923)
       Catherine Mary Kinnaird (1876-1886)
       Harry Kinnaird (1877)
       Douglas Arthur Kinnaird (1879-1914)
       Kenneth Fitzgerald, 12th Lord Kinnaird (1880-1972)
       m 1903 Frances Victoria Clifton (1876-1960)
          Anne Barbara Teresa Kinnaird (1904-1962)
          Madeleine Kinnaird (1906)
          Madeline Elizabeth Kinnaird (1908-2001)
          Graham Charles, 13th Lord Kinnaird (1912-1997)
          m1 1938 Nadia Alexandra Jardine Fortington (1919-2010)
          m2 1940 Diana Margaret Elizabeth Copeman (1918-2009)
             Nicholas Charles Kinnaird (1946-1951)
             Caroline Kinnaird (1949-)
             m1 1970 Christopher Wigan (1947-)
                Leila Willow Wigan (1974-)
                George Rowen Wigan (1977-1998)
             m2 1986 James Douglas Best (1948-)
                Samuel Douglas Best (1987-)
                Arthur Jack Best (1989-)
             Anna Kinnaird (1952-)
             m 1988 Edward Henry Liddell (1953-)
                Patrick Edward Charles Liddell (1991-)
             Susan Kinnaird (1956 -)
             m 1987 Francis Rupert Chad Lea (1957-)
             Mary Clare Kinnaird (1960-)
             m 1988 John Christian Staib (1954-)
                James Alexander Christian Staib (1990-)
                Annabel Mary Staib (1992-)
         Kenneth George Kinnaird (1914-1973)
      Noel Andrew Kinnaird (1883)
      Arthur Middleton Kinnaird (1885-1917)
      Margaret Alma Kinnaird (1892-1954)
      Patrick Charles Kinnaird (1898-1948)

A more extensive family tree is available on www.lordkinnaird.com

[1] Another account suggests he was a Celtic noble who considered support for the King as the best way forward.

[2] Inchture, the village next to Rossie estate, owes its name to having once been an 'inch', ie an island.

[3] *New York Times*, 19 July 1908

[4] It was long overdue, as Drimmie was not fit for purpose, being little more than an extended lodge; it had even had to be completely re-roofed in 1795 (although as an astute businessman George used this opportunity to cut his window tax by reducing the number of garret windows).

[5] He had entered the House of Commons in 1802 as Whig member for Leominster

[6] *Diary of Joseph Farington*, 8 April 1807.

[7] Elizabeth Longford, *Wellington*, p35.

[8] Lord Kinnaird, *Letter to the Duke of Wellington on the Arrest of M. Marinet*, 1818.

[9] *Don Juan*, Canto IX, verse II.

[10] George, 9th Lord Kinnaird, *Notes and Reminiscences*

[11] Perth & Kinross Library, MS100, bundle 791.

[12] RH Dana, *Hospitable England in the Seventies*, p99

[13] *Fun,* 8 October 1864.

[14] *The Examiner*, 20 May 1838.

[15] Emily Kinnaird, *My Adopted Country*, p5

[16] *We take leave to inform you that Mr Williams and Mr Squire, two of the partners in this House, having for some time contemplated retiring altogether from business, an arrangement has been made by Mr Kinnaird to form a junction between himself, as representing the firm of Ransom & Co, and the highly respectable banking firm of Messrs Bouverie & Co of the Haymarket.* Letter to bank customers, December 1855, held in Kinnaird family archive

[17] Overend & Gurney, one of London's leading banks, went into liquidation and brought down many other small banks with it The next time there was a run on a major bank was Northern Rock in 2007.

[18] United Association for the Christian and Domestic Improvement of Young Women, *First Annual Report*, 1862.

[19] *Mary Jane Kinnaird*, by Donald Fraser, 1890

[20] Emily Kinnaird, *My Adopted Country*, p4

[21] Rudolph de Cordova, *The Sunday Strand*, February 1903, p49

APPENDIX 4

The Kinnairds at home

Arthur and his family on the steps of Rossie Priory

'THERE ARE few views which can match that on a summer evening from the terrace of Rossie Priory, with its gentle slope down through the parks beneath, over the road leading from Perth to Dundee and down from that to the broad waters of the Tay with the Fife hills beyond.'[1]

Rossie Priory, in its day, was one of the finest homes in Scotland. It was built by Charles, 8th Lord Kinnaird, who in 1805 commissioned the architect William Atkinson to design the house in Regency Gothic style, on such a vast scale that it took five years to complete. His valuable art collection was displayed in the cloisters, and there was a china room with rare Chelsea, Worcester, Dresden and Sevres. After the Perth-Dundee railway opened in 1847 his son George built a branch line from Inchture Station to the gates of the estate.[2]

In Arthur's time, it was described as 'a superb monastic-looking pile, spacious and elegant within, and of imposing aspect without; contains a valuable collection of antiquities, chiefly Roman; and has pleasure grounds, gardens and policies of great extent and singular beauty.'[3] However, he was not a natural country type and Rossie was effectively reduced to the status of a holiday home, although he did enjoy the shooting season.[4] The house was enormously expensive to maintain and after Arthur's death it fell into disrepair. In 1948, two thirds of the building was pulled down and the contents, including much of the art collection, were sold at auction. Only the west wing was spared (the steps to the old entrance are still there), a handsome red stone building, listed Grade B, which remains in the family. The estate pays its way with crops, sheep and – as a throwback to the halcyon era – Highland cattle.

Arthur's birthplace in London, at 35 Hyde Park Gardens, is in an exclusive terrace of white stucco-fronted houses with

Arthur Kinnaird's birthplace at Hyde Park Gardens

columned porch entrances, overlooking a small private garden. Built around 1840, the street is divided into two, and Arthur was born in the short cul-de-sac off Brook Street. The houses were converted

190

into flats in 1953 and renumbered, so Arthur was born in part of what is now number 30.

Kinnaird House stands on the site of the family home in Pall Mall East

Early in 1856 the family moved to live at 2 Pall Mall East, which had been built in 1823 by Douglas Kinnaird as upstairs living apartments for Ransom's Bank. Arthur's father remained in Pall Mall East until his death in 1887, after which Arthur kept some of the rooms for private entertaining, while the rest were let out to businesses including the London office of the *New York Times*.[5] The entire block was demolished in 1916 and rebuilt as Kinnaird House, which has 60,000 square feet of office space over eight floors.

The newlywed Arthur and Alma settled in 1875 just off Grosvenor Square at 50 South Audley Street, which no longer exists and is now a Majestic Wine Warehouse with flats above. In 1892 they moved to 10 St James's Square, built in 1736 and home to three Prime Ministers, the last of whom was WE Gladstone. They remained at St James's Square until their deaths, when it was purchased by the Royal Institute of International Affairs and renamed Chatham House.

The family also had properties within reach of London, and Emily Kinnaird wrote that they spent half the year in the country. The first was West Farm, Barnet, then in 1862 they bought Pickhurst Manor, a medieval farmhouse in Hayes, and in 1870 acquired Plaistow Lodge, a palatial mansion built in 1777, which came with an estate to the north of Bromley. The family were regular weekend visitors until 1889 when burglars forced a window and ransacked the sitting room before disappearing in the direction of Lewisham with a haul of jewellery.[6] Not surprisingly, the isolated house was put on the market but it did not sell and Arthur struck a deal with developers to found the Kinnaird Park Estate Company, which covered the 135 acres of woodland with housing (including a street named Kinnaird Avenue). The house was sold in 1895 for £12,000 (which bought 12 bedrooms, four reception rooms, five dressing rooms, two bathrooms, a billiard room, servants' accommodation and stabling for four horses). It still stands, having been for many years the Quernmore School, and is now Bromley Parish Church of England Primary School. The ornamental gates were donated to the town of Bromley and can be seen in Queen's Garden.

---

[1] Emily Kinnaird, *Reminiscences*, p5

[2] This horse-drawn tramway remained in place until 1916; Inchture Station closed in 1964.

[3] *Ordnance Survey Gazetteer of Scotland*, 1885

[4] For a typical year's game shooting in 1911/12 the estate accounted for over 5,000 rabbits and hares, 698 partridges, 1215 pheasants and small numbers of woodcock, wild duck, grouse, snipe, capercailzie and six roe deer – with a total value of £507, 11 shillings and two pence.

[5] See the *New York Times'* history of the site, 14 October 1912

[6] *The Times*, 28 October 1889

Bibliography

Manuscript and archival sources
AK Bell Library, Perth: MS100, Baron Kinnaird of Rossie
muniments 1172-1960
Kinnaird family archive, personal papers and scrapbooks
Eton College archive, record books of the Eton Society and Sports
Eton College Chronicle, 1863-74
The Football Association, minute books, 1895-1923

Historical and biographical
Alex Alexander FRGS, *A Wayfarer's Log* (John Murray, 1919)
AJ Balfour, *Chapters of Autobiography* (Cassell & Co, 1930)
Prof David W Bebbington, *Evangelicalism in Modern Britain*
(Unwin Hyman, 1989)
Geoffrey Best, *Mid-Victorian Britain 1851-75* (Weidenfeld &
Nicolson, 1971)
Clyde Binfield, *George Williams and the YMCA* (Heinemann, 1973)
James Brinsley-Richards, *Seven Years at Eton* (Richard Bentley &
Son, 1883)
Lord Byron, *Don Juan, Canto IX* (John Hunt, 1823)
Tim Card, *Eton Renewed, a history from 1860 to the present* day (John
Murray, 1994)
AR Cavalier; introduction by Lord Kinnaird, *In Northern India, a
story of Mission Work in Zenanas, Hospitals, Schools and Villages*
(SW Partridge & Co, 1899)
George Cawthorne, *Royal Ascot, its history and its associations*
(Treherne & Co, 1902)
Lord Clarendon, *Report of Her Majesty's Commissioners appointed to
inquire in the Revenues and Managements of certain college and
schools, and the studies pursued and instruction given therein* (HM
Government, 1864)
John Coffey, *Democracy and popular religion: Moody and Sankey's
mission to Britain, 1873-1875*; in Eugenio Biagini (ed), *Citizenship
and community* (Cambridge University Press, 1996)
Hon Gilbert Coleridge, *Eton in the Seventies* (Smith, Elder & Co,
1912)
Hon ECF Collier, *A Victorian Diarist* (John Murray, 1944)

Richard Henry Dana, *Hospitable England in the Seventies; the Diary of a Young American 1875-1876* (John Murray, 1921)

Blanche EC Dugdale, *Arthur James Balfour, First Earl of Balfour, Vol 1* (Hutchinson, 1936)

Rev C Dunkley, *The Official Report of the Church Congress held at Manchester* (Bemrose and Sons, 1908)

Walter Durnford, *Memoir of the Right Hon William Kenyon-Slaney MP* (John Murray, 1909)

W McG Eagar, *Making Men, The History of Boys Clubs and Related Movements in Great Britain* (University of London Press, 1953)

CL Ferguson, *A History of the Magpie and Stump Debating Society 1866-1926* (W Heffer & Sons Ltd, 1931)

Donald Fraser, *Mary Jane Kinnaird* (James Nisbet & Co, 1890)

Stephen Halliday, *The Great Stink of London* (Sutton Publishing, 1999)

Rev HB Hartzler, *Moody in Chicago* (Fleming H Revell Company, 1894)

Edwin Hodder, *John MacGregor ("Rob Roy")* (Hodder Brothers, 1894)

Ethel M Hogg, *Quintin Hogg, a biography* (Constable, 1904)

Emily Kinnaird, *Reminiscences* (John Murray, 1925)

Emily Kinnaird, *My Adopted Country 1889 to 1944* (privately published, 1944)

Charles, Baron Kinnaird, *A letter to the Duke of Wellington, on the arrest of M. Marinet* (J Ridgway, 1818)

Ada Lee; introduction by Lord Kinnaird, *An Indian Priestess, The Life of Chundra Lela* (Fleming H Revell Company, 1903)

'An Old Boy' [Thomas Hughes], *Tom Brown's School Days* (Macmillan, 1857)

Elizabeth Longford, *Wellington, Pillar of State* (Weidenfeld and Nicolson, 1972)

Alfred Lubbock, *Memories of Eton and Etonians* (John Murray, 1899)

Sir Henry Lunn, *Chapters from My Life* (Cassell & Co, 1918)

HCG Matthew (ed), *The Gladstone Diaries, Vol IX 1875-1880* (Oxford University Press, 1986)

John McDowell, *Dwight L. Moody: the Discoverer of Men and the Maker of Movements* (Fleming H Revell Company, 1915)

John MacGregor, *The Voyage Alone in the Yawl "Rob Roy"* (Sampson Low, 1880)

J.M.L. [John Maclauchlan], *A Silver Wedding and a Coming of Age: the Silver Wedding of Lord and Lady Kinnaird and the Coming of Age of the Master of Kinnaird, August 1900, with a Sketch of the History of the Barons of Kinnaird.* (privately published, 1900)

Rev RC MacLeod of MacLeod, *The MacLeods: a short sketch of their Clan, history, folk-lore, tales and biographical sketches of some eminent clansmen* (Clan MacLeod Society, 1906)

George E Morgan; introduction by Lord Kinnaird, *A Veteran in Revival: RC Morgan, His Life and Times* (Morgan and Scott, 1909)

William R Moody, *DL Moody* (Macmillan, New York, 1930)

Aubrey Noakes, *The County Fire Office 1807-1957* (HF&G Witherby Ltd, 1957)

Old Etonian Association (comp), *Eton School Register, Part III 1862-1868* (Spottiswoode & Co, 1906)

Pan Anglican Congress, *General Report of the Proceedings, Vol 1* (Society for Promoting Christian Knowledge, 1908)

FHW Sheppard (ed), *Survey of London, Vol 27: Spitalfields and Mile End New Town* (English Heritage, 1957)

HEC Stapylton, *Eton School Lists 1853-1892* (R Ingalton Drake, 1900)

Eugene Stock, *The History of the Church Missionary Society* (CMS London, 1899)

R de Courtenay Welch, *Register of Harrow School 1801-1893* (Harrow, 1894)

AN Wilson, *The Victorians* (Hutchinson, 2002)

Sport

CW Alcock, *Football: our Winter Game* (Field, 1874)

CW Alcock, *Football, the Association Game* (George Bell, 1890)

CW Alcock (ed), *The Football Annual*, 1871-1883

CW Alcock (ed), *Football, A Weekly Record of the Game*, 1882-1883

J Keith Angus (ed), *The Sportsman's Year Book for 1880* (Cassell, Petter, Galpin & Co, 1880)

John Blythe-Smart, *The Wow Factor*, second edition (Blythe-Smart Publications, 2005)

The Book of Football (Amalgamated Press, 1906)

Keith Booth, *The Father of Modern Sport* (Parrs Wood Press, 2002)

Bryon Butler, *The Official Illustrated History of the FA Cup* (Headline, 1996)

'Tityrus' [JAH Catton], *The Rise of the Leaguers* (Sporting Chronicle, 1897)

JAH Catton, *The Real Football* (Sands & Co, 1900)

JAH Catton, *Wickets and Goals* (Chapman and Hall, 1926)

Rob Cavallini, *The Wanderers FC, five times FA Cup winners* (Dog n Duck Publications, 2005)

Theodore Andrea Cook (ed), *The Fourth Olympiad, being the Official Report of the Olympic Games of 1908* (British Olympic Association, 1909)

Lord Desborough (arr), *Fifty Years of Sport at Oxford, Cambridge and the Great Public Schools*, 3 vols (Walter Southwood & Co, 1916-1922)

Morley Farror and Douglas Lamming, *A Century of English International Football 1872-1972* (Robert Hale & Co, 1972)

James Ferguson and JG Temple, *The Old Vale and Its Memories* (privately published, 1927)

Roddy Forsyth, *The Only Game* (Mainstream, 1990)

CB Fry, *Life Worth Living* (Eyre and Spottiswoode, 1939)

Alfred Gibson and William Pickford, *Association Football & The Men Who Made It* (Caxton, 1906)

Geoffrey Green, *The History of the Football Association* (Naldrett Press, 1953)

Geoffrey Green, *The History of the FA Cup* (Naldrett Press, 1949)

Adrian Harvey, *Football: the first hundred years* (Routledge, 2005)

NL Jackson, *Association Football*, second edition (George Newnes Ltd, 1900)

NL Jackson, *Sporting Days and Sporting Ways* (Hurst & Blackett 1932).

Charles JB Marriott & CW Alcock, *Football*, second edition (George Routledge, 1903)

Maurice Marples, *A History of Football* (Secker and Warburg, 1954)

Tony Mason, *Association Football and English Society 1863-1915* (Harvester Press, 1980)

A Wallis Myers (ed), *The Sportsman's Year Book 1905* (George Newnes Ltd, 1905)

A New Book of Sports, Reprinted from the Saturday Review (Richard Bentley & Son, 1885)

Philip Norman, *Scores and Annals of the West Kent Cricket Club* (Oxford University Press, 1897)

John J Pawson, *The Field Game* (Spottiswoode, Ballantyne & Co, 1935)

196

William Pickford, *A Few Recollections of Sport* (Bournemouth Guardian, 1938)
Richard Robinson, *History of Queen's Park Football Club 1867-1917* (Hay Nisbet & Co, 1920)
Routledge's Football (George Routledge, 1867)
Richard Sanders, *Beastly Fury, the strange birth of British football* (Bantam Press, 2009)
Montague **Shearman**, *Athletics and Football* (Badminton Library, 1889)
RJ Spiller (ed), *The Early Years 1863-1878* (Association of Football Statisticians, 1983)
'Old International' [Alexander Steel], *25 Years Football* (John Menzies, 1890)
CE Sutcliffe and F Hargreaves, *History of the Lancashire Football Association 1878-1928* (Geo. Toulmin & Sons Ltd, 1928)
JCT [John Charles Thring], *Rules of Football: the Winter Game* (Uppingham, 1863)
Martin Tyler, *Cup Final Extra!* (Hamlyn Publishing, 1981)
Alfred Wahl, *Les Archives du Football* (Gallimard Julliard, 1989)
Sir Frederick Wall, *Fifty Years of Football* (Cassell, 1934)
Keith Warsop, *The Early FA Cup Finals and the Southern Amateurs* (Soccer Data, 2004)
Frederick Wood, *Beeton's Football* (Frederick Warne & Co, 1866)
Percy M Young, *A History of British Football* (Stanley Paul, 1968)
Percy M Young, *Football in Sheffield* (Stanley Paul, 1962)

Selected articles in magazines and periodicals
CW Alcock, *Association Football* (English Illustrated Magazine 88, January 1891, p282-288)
Anon., *Arthur Fitzgerald, 11th Baron Kinnaird KT* (Spread Eagle, house magazine of Barclays Bank, Vol 37, 1962, p4-6)
Anon., *Football* (The London Review, 23 January 1864, p84-85)
Rudolph de Cordova, *The Gospel of Wealth* (Sunday Strand, February 1903, pp49-52)
JDC [John D Cartwright], *Football at Rugby, Eton and Harrow* (London Society 5:28, March 1864, p246-255)
Graham Curry, *Forgotten man: The contribution of John Dyer Cartwright to the football rules debate* (Soccer & Society 4:1, p71-86, 2003)

Graham Curry, *The Trinity Connection: An Analysis of the Role of Members of Cambridge University in the Development of Football in the Mid-Nineteenth Century* (Sport in History, 22:2, p46-73, 2002)
CB Fry, *Teams that have won the Football Association Cup* (Strand Magazine, 23:136, April 1902, p455)
RG Graham, *The Early History of the Football Association* (Badminton Magazine, January 1899, p75-87)
'Creston' [NL Jackson], *Football* (Fortnightly Review 55:235, January 1894, p25-38).
Lord Kinnaird, *Work in which I am interested, the Young Women's Christian Association* (Quiver 32:543, January 1897, p387-394)
Harold Macfarlane, *Football of Yesterday and to-day, A Comparison* (Monthly Review 25, October 1906, p129-138)
A Veteran, *Football* (The Boy's Own Magazine, March 1864, p249-256)
DL Woolmer, *YWCA, the World's Great Sisterhood* (Quiver, 45:4, February 1910, p342-348).

Selected online resources
British Library: British Newspapers 1800-1900: http://newspapers.bl.uk/blcs/
British Periodicals: http://britishperiodicals.chadwyck.co.uk/marketing.do
Hansard: http://hansard.millbanksystems.com/
Kinnaird Worldwide: http://www.kinnaird.net/
New York Times Article Archive: http://www.nytimes.com/ref/membercenter/nytarchive.html
Sir Basil Spence Archive Project: http://www.basilspence.org.uk/
The Times, Digital Archive 1785-1985: http://archive.timesonline.co.uk/tol/archive/

Index

201

Made in the USA
Charleston, SC
15 August 2011